Tang Soo Tao
The Living Buddha
in Martial Virtue

Robert Caputo

Tang Soo Tao: The Living Buddha In Martial Virtue

Robert Caputo

First published in 1981
Revised edition March 2023

Published by WM (UK)

ISBN 978-1-914265-55-6 Hbk

The rights of Robert Caputo to be identified as author of this work and Dieter Spielkamp to be identified as Editor have been asserted in accordance with Sections 77 and 78 of the Copyright Designs and Patents Act, 1988.

A CIP catalogue record for this book is available from the British Library.

Disclaimer: *Tang Soo Tao: The Living Buddha In Martial Virtue* is intended for information and education purposes only. This book does not constitute specific advice unique to your situation.

The views and opinions expressed in this book are those of the authors and do not reflect those of the Publisher and Resellers, who accept no responsibility for loss, damage or injury to persons or their belongings as a direct or indirect result of reading this book.

All people mentioned in case studies have been used with permission.

Note: Registered titles of Tang Soo Tao™

The Tang Soo Tao Emblem

The Tang Soo Tao black belt emblem is the combination of the symbols common to all forms of martial art and esoteric philosophy. (Please refer to the full colour emblem on the front cover of the book.)

The broken circle in the centre is the symbol of Tai Chi or the Grand Ultimate. This signifies the universal harmony of all things through the working of Yin Yang.

Yin is represented by the colour blue; yang by the colour red. Yin represents female energy, night and recessive. Yang symbolises male energy, the sun and dominance. These are the complimentary forces of nature which rule our daily life. Man cannot survive without woman; woman cannot survive without man. This is represented by the uneven halves of the circle. The dot in each of the separate circles inside the main circle, signifies the creative energies of male and female; i.e. the blood and sperm. The existence of either of the energies in the other sphere defines the absolute inseparability of the internal energies of positive and negative and all existent phenomena.

The Five Colours

The five colours represent the Hsing-I or the five elements of the physical world used in divine alchemy. It relates the five internal organs with five ruling planets of our solar system, relating the microcosmic universe of the individual with the macrocosmic external universe.

The five colours also represent the five Dyhana Buddhas of esoteric Buddhism. The five Buddhas symbolise the five levels of wisdom necessary to gain enlightenment. Tantric Buddhism stresses purification of the five senses (aggregates) which control the five basic delusions of hate, lust, anger, greed and jealousy.

The Dorjes

The Dorjes are a ritual instrument of Tantric Buddhism symbolic of the most direct method of overcoming desire and attachment to attain enlightenment through one-ness with universal wisdom.

The Dorje on top of the circle signifies male energy and method. The circle inside the Dorje is the female energy: wisdom; again in Buddhism as in Tai Chi, the universal theme of the inseparability of male and female energies.

Pa-Kua

The eight triagrams of the inside ball make up the eight palms of the defense art of circle walking.

There are eight varieties multiplied by the eight palm changes which create sixty-four movements in circle walking of Pa-Kua Kung Fu. The sixty-four palms relate to the sixty-four hexigrams of the I-Ching.

I-Ching

Nucleus of Chinese culture comprised of sixty-four triagrams which expound the philosophy, astrology and all phenomena of past, present and future of Chinese culture.

The Laurels

Green symbolises growth and progress. Laurel leaves symbolise peace. Ideologically peace and progress sustain our world and combat evil and destruction, which creates decay and unrest in the world.

Contents

'If I have a clear conscience I dare face an army of 10,000 men.'

Confucius

Foreword Dieter Spielkamp

I can't believe that over forty two years ago, in February 1981, Master Robert Caputo published *Tang Soo Tao: The Living Buddha In Martial Virtue.* Divided into three sections, it included a comprehensive guide to the history and practice of martial arts philosophy and training; a pictorial guide from white to black belt in our Tang Soo Tao training syllabus; and Master Caputo's autobiography. Incredibly, it captured Master Caputo's commitment to martial virtue and is an invaluable reference book for Tang Soo Tao students and martial arts practitioners worldwide.

There can often be pitfalls in simply reprinting a book forty years after it was first written. Time alters our perceptions and changes our way of seeing the world. In reading this book, some of the ideas may now seem as though they lack subtlety. Some may not sit easily with today's sensibilities.

It is a book of its time.

It covers many essential and deeply important subjects that are part of our common human heritage that Master Caputo highlights and draws on that are timeless and indispensable and especially relevant in this day and age. They speak to the incredible synthesis and vast gathering of knowledge that was Master Caputo's great talent and legacy.

In writing this book he pointed straight to the heart of the spirit in martial arts. His thirst for knowledge and real lived experience of all forms of this art was unquenchable and led him to one of the highest, most advanced and eminently practical and effective spiritual disciplines on earth.

After careful consideration the choice was made that rather than changing the book to fit with the current times, it was deemed better to let Master Caputo's voice reach us through time and touch our love and practice of the martial arts with his original words and sensibilities.

Master Caputo didn't have the good fortune of living a long life, but the strength of his dedication in developing a Martial Art which can be used by all people as a tool for personal development has stood the test of time.

This book captures the spirit and virtue of martial arts and is an invaluable resource that stands on its merits.

Our Martial Art of Tang Soo Tao has prospered and grown, with many schools across Australia thriving and evolving in accordance with the underpinning philosophy of being a living art form.

Inspired by the author of this book, Instructors and students have continued to develop the art form, ensuring that Tang Soo Tao remains true to Master Caputo's desire to provide a methodology which remains relevant to modern times.

It is with this background that we present this book.

Tang Soo!

Dieter Spielkamp

Sa Bom Nim

Dedication

The author spent fifteen years researching and developing the ideas outlined in this book. It was a long complicated search which led him around the world three times and exhausted his entire financial resources. Driven by the desire to link esoteric spirituality with martial arts training; so often talked about by martial artists but rarely taught or experienced, he studied in every oriental country historically linked with martial arts. He has personally met most of the world's leading masters, visited dozens of Buddhist centres, lived in monasteries and has discussed at great length with martial arts masters and spiritual leaders alike, the fundamental aim of discipline and spirituality.

This book is dedicated to his teacher who was the invaluable vital link to a life time search for the key linking Buddhism, Taoism and all forms of truth to martial art; His Holiness the Dalai Lama of Tibet.

It is also dedicated to his kind Holy Gurus, His Holiness Trijang Rinpoche and Ratto Rinpoche, who provided detailed instruction in the esoteric teachings of the Dharma. Most of all this book is dedicated to his kind and most precious Root Guru, His Holiness Ling Rinpoche, (Senior Tutor to the Dalai Lama).

Preface

This book was written because there wasn't one.

It started as a training manual at the request of students and instructors of the Tang Soo Tao Martial Arts Institute in Darwin, Australia, who expressed the desire for a comprehensive literary guide, covering all aspects of their martial arts training.

In these times a most precious heritage of spirit and tradition, thousands of years old, is endangered by politics, exploitation, commercialism and improper motivation. Few of the truly great pioneers of martial art are left today. The loss of the direct lineage linking oriental arts with the training methods, philosophy and spirit, to their ancestors and proper origins, has greatly weakened the world of Bushido. Poor standards and lack of qualified masters who understand the nature of their arts from beginning to end have created great confusion in the hearts of many sincere persons aspiring to locate the secret that lies at the core of every true martial art.

The author has had the opportunity to travel the world extensively and to research at length with some of the greatest martial arts and spiritual masters still alive today. The extent of that research ranges from the grand masters of the Korean, Chinese and Japanese art systems, to the high Lamas of Tibet and India.

It is hoped that this series will answer for the sincere martial artist, many of the obscure questions difficult to find the answers for. Also it is hoped that this book will encourage all serious martial artists to examine thoroughly the primary objectives of themselves and their arts.

The basic theme of the book is that mind and body are one and inseparable. It suggests that ultimate martial arts training begins with the first basic technique and does not end until the seeker has gained true wisdom by transcending the downfalls of worldly existence. It is hoped that the information supplied will encourage all martial artists to share the common experience of love, friendship and harmony.

Although the book is written about the specific style of Tang Soo Tao, the author has endeavoured to display the relationship between the fundamental principles uniting all martial arts.

Any martial artist who has suffered the problems mentioned above will find this book to be a true oasis in a desert of illusive mirages. To the beginner student it will serve as an introduction to the living spirit that comes to life the first time he walks in the door of a true martial arts institute.

The authors would like to extend an open invitation for anyone who reads this book, to extend their comments, criticisms and feelings concerning the subject matter.

Introduction

Since I was a boy I always wanted to be a martial artist. I never wanted to do anything else.

Anyone who has ever become involved in martial arts of any kind has heard legendary stories of great masters with extraordinary powers and mental control. Martial artists all over the world grow up venerating these masters as the pinnacle of martial art status and achievement. Along with the stories of these Masters there have always been secrets and mystique centering around Buddhism, from which martial arts took its origin. I never cared about Buddhism per se or any religious trip, I just wanted to be a martial artist. I wanted to know everything about anything that had something to do with perfection of martial arts. This desire to know everything from beginning to end, so that I could practice without questions in my mind, initially motivated me to travel the world.

I began my travelling in the East and met many martial artists of all varieties and sorts. I met some with good spirit, some who were fantastic technicians and some who had successfully combined both to a relatively high level of quality. I also met many martial artists who hid their ignorance and lack of experience under the guise of special secrets that only could be taught to a perfect disciple. I have also met and fought with fierce men who were not afraid of death and had treated killing as something mundane and trivial.

Most of the people I have met, regardless of their level of ability in defense or killing, were not of a high level of spirit in martial virtue. The high masters whom I have referred to in this book, from Korea and Japan, etc., were undoubtedly on the highest spectrum of physical adeptness, mental awareness and true spirit of martial virtue.

The problem was that there was so few masters and though I trained to the utmost of my ability at all times I intuitively knew that physical technique is limited and that for perfect martial art we must rely on something else as well. I then learned internal yoga, but found that though one could gain extraordinary powers, which did not rely merely on the physical, many people who did this were incredibly powerful but insincere. On the other hand I have met only mediocre external martial artists who knew nothing about internal yoga or spirituality in any sense, but had great devotion to their arts and instructors. They tried their best and were genuinely sincere and honest. I have met martial artists who were honestly willing to share the spirit of martial art as best they could.

This spirit I am talking about, although it contained no super powers, contained some of the essence of martial harmony. But from intuition and experience, I knew there had to be a perfect way to combine internal and external movements with pure spirituality. Every martial arts master I have either met personally or read about is famous for meditating. All high practitioners of any art meditate. I heard time and time again about meditation and learned many various methods but never met anyone who could tell me the end result or that he'd experienced the ultimate realization of meditation. Although I would have liked to have found it purely in martial arts, I found that to enter the source I had to break the spiritual path and physical path into two sections.

The physical aspect is easy to explain. I simply went to every type of martial arts institute I could find and studied the techniques and characters of students and masters of the schools. Although there was some spirituality involved in this it could still be included in the physical planes of the art.

I found as much variety in spirituality as I did in martial art systems. I found semi-sincere masters, I found highly developed masters and I found people who prayed to external Gods as though they were real. I studied Christianity and I studied Buddhism. The absolute teaching of both of these great doctrines was loving compassion for all creatures. Though this was obviously noble it was too broad to bring me to the deepest understanding of martial arts. I needed something more detailed and methodological. I met two kinds of people in all religions; people who believe and pray to external deities and people who meditate as a deity within themselves.

The first of these was too shallow for me because it didn't pertain to martial arts. The second of these made a lot of sense. I knew that masters such as Jesus Christ or the great Buddha, had to have been common men just like me. No great man ever came to this earth as a god. If the leaders of our world's spirituality were essentially different from common man, then it would be useless to practice what they taught. If they were different from us then what worked for them would not work for us. What made them different was the transcendent level of their own mind, which many people title God and then separate themselves from it. If you separate yourself from the great teacher, then you can never be like him. Even in martial arts a person strives to become like his instructor. If he does not believe he can gain these qualities then what is the use of starting in the first place?

So whether we are on the plane of martial art or spirituality we have the same situation. Our religions have grown out of man's need for a tangible method to gain insight and wisdom to the absolute. Any methods, practices and beliefs, which cause a man to develop himself or seek higher wisdom, can be called religion. Any method, regardless of trivial names we tack onto the method, is just a tool and useful only to those who know how to use it. There can only be one truth. If there were more than one truth nothing would make any sense. If there was more than one truth, then truth would become dual and relative and absolute could not exist. If absolute truth did not exist then there would be no incentive to strive for anything at all. This would make us nihilistic.

I searched for that truth in martial arts and through that search inevitably became involved with Buddhism. Studying Buddhism alone explained all the goals of mind and esoteric sciences. It gave many spiritual methods to practice but it left the body which was attached to myself, empty of method to practice. This emptiness was filled with martial arts training. The spiritual people often neglect their health and physical development. Often the martial artist places too much emphasis on the body. I didn't want one without the other.

When I first began my travels I was looking for a link for something I had not yet found in my martial arts training, but was absolutely sure was there. I didn't care for religion, culture or lifestyle and I didn't care if the instructor was black, white, or green.

From my inner experience I knew what I was looking for and that I would easily recognize it once I found it.

PART ONE
TANG SOO TAO

1.1 The Spirit of Man

On first consideration, physical self-defense or hand-to-hand combat is a subject that does not register to people as being vitally important in our modern complex society. Those that do think about such things usually become involved for all the wrong reasons.

Man's destructive nature has invented a labyrinth of sophisticated weapons on every scale imaginable. From the atom bomb to chemical warfare, man has devised incredible ways to annihilate any and all forms of perceivable existence.

What use then is an old fashioned self-defense art in a world that can be totally destroyed by the push of a button? The most competent martial arts master would find great difficulty matching the speed of an assassin's bullet. Even in the remote case of being attacked, should we succeed in defending ourselves, what would we really accomplish? We could succeed in living a bit longer in our appropriately named 'rat race' society, or we could finish our life off on a holiday cruise or in a rest home somewhere. Regardless of how long we live and for what reasons, we are sure to die sooner or later.

So what is this all about any way?

All things must pass. Even the great Christ with all his super powers demonstrated this to the world. *'What gaineth a man if he profit the whole world, yet suffers the loss of his soul.'*

The key to this question can only lie in the spirit of man, the spirit that lies in the human body. Because it lies in this body we must use the body as a vehicle to work with the spirit. This is the progressive development of the mind and the body through the martial arts experience.

1.2 The History of Tang Soo Tao

Forms of self-defense are older than man himself. From beginningless time all creatures from birth, regardless of origin, are faced with the task of survival. From birth all creatures must survive the danger from lack of food, adverse weather conditions and attack from enemies. As all animals have some means of self-defense such as tooth, claw, poison glands, etc., so too did man have to learn to use his natural resources to protect himself.

Before our ancestors had weapons they fought their enemies using only bare hands, teeth and their bodies. From this beginning of initial contact for defense the present martial arts were developed.

Because the exact age of man-kind is uncertain, it is difficult to trace the true beginnings of the original defense art. For all practical purposes there are four basic eras we can refer to in relation to this subject.

These are:

- **Instinctive Action Age** – The Dawn of Man. Approximately one million years ago when no conscious action was involved in defense.

- **Conscious Action Age** – This covers from the Stone Age, approximately 500,000 years ago to the primitive era. During this time man consciously developed methods to protect his body and to gather daily necessities. Anthropologically, mankind at this time migrated from the central Asian plateau into Asia and Europe.

- **Early Age of Systemization** – The Iron Age. This period covers from 10,000 to 2,600 years ago, at which time self-defense arts were consciously developed and systemized by man.

- **Cultivation of the Arts** – This period stems from 2,600 years ago until now. The art is said to have flourished in its finest capacity during the 12th Century. It is this period which is of most importance to us.

Of all of the forms of fighting and self-defense, the oriental arts have proved to be the most effective. Because of their secret methods and obscured training techniques it is difficult to trace the pure history of many of these arts. Many historical facts are entangled with legends, folklore and histories learned by word of mouth only. The initial origins of martial arts began with legends but materialized with well recorded history. Regardless of origin, martial arts in Asia flourished extensively during the cultivation era and played a formidable role in shaping the history and culture of the then known Asian world.

Oddly enough the origin of the self-defense arts have their roots in the walls of Buddhist monasteries (a religion which completely condemns violence or killing in any way, shape or form what-so-ever.) Although to practise the art it is not necessary to practise Buddhism, it is sometimes interesting and helpful to understand a little bit about Buddhism in relation to the philosophy and historical background of these arts. This is especially true because it is sometimes difficult and confusing for the average person to see the relation between a seemingly aggressive art and the pacificity expounded in the non-violent Buddhist philosophy.

1.3 Buddha

Siddhartha Gautama was a prince born in India in 500 BC. At the age of twenty-eight he forsook his wealthy kingdom and took the life of a renunciate in search of truth. It is said that although he had all the luxuries of life he was unable to bear seeing the poverty and suffering of all those beneath him. He also made the observation that regardless of caste or creed all men were subject to birth, sickness, old age and death. His heart was sickened by this dilemma and with firm conviction he left his kingly estate and lived for many years as a poor ascetic in the jungle.

Shakyamuni Buddha

Following the ways of the yogis of the time, he spent harsh years in self-denial and abstained from all physical activities, even to the extent of denying himself food and shelter. After a long period of time, understandably enough, he almost died. Although not afraid of death, he realized that should he die, he would not have solved the problems of suffering for himself or anybody else. Much to the dismay of his fellow comrades he left his austere way of life and settled on a new path which he called the *Middle Way*.

Convinced that extremes of either life, hard or soft, were not only unnatural but undesirable towards spiritual growth of any kind, he entered upon another six years of moderate, simple life style, based on meditation, compassion and dedication of his actions towards helping others.

Following this period of life he was said to have received a divine inspiration whereupon he entered a deep state of meditation like trance and remained so for a long time. During this time he was said to have achieved enlightenment and divine wisdom. After this occurrence, he lived and taught for forty more years. His teachings were simple and they were based on what he termed the *Four Noble Truths*.

- Life is suffering
- There is a reason for suffering
- There is an end to suffering
- There is a correct path leading to the end of suffering

He taught that without cause there is no effect. Subsequently, man's suffering, mental and physical, stems from a cause; the suffering being the effect. The Buddha taught that the cause was the individual himself. The individual's cause in turn was created by the ego, which is driven by desire.

In order to control the ego and cut the root of desire he preached an eightfold path of *Correct Thought, Correct View, Correct Speech, Correct Conduct, Correct Livelihood, Correct Devotion, Correct Mindfulness* and *Correct Meditation*.

This philosophy taught a life of simplicity based on morality, devoid of racial prejudice and greed, which ran rampant during those times. The way of life based on harmony and compassion urged the warring people of the time to put down their weapons and live a life of peace through respect and love for one another.

It was a philosophy unlike any other taught by great saints and wise men of any country or time. The power of his realization influenced and spread rapidly throughout Asia.

To advise the common man he set rules for a way of life. To advise the spiritually minded he taught methods of meditation to relax troubled minds and to encourage concentration. Because of the intense austerity suffered in his earlier years, he recognized the need to protect and preserve health. For this he taught yogic methods of exercise and diet. This philosophy was not restricted to man alone. The fundamental principals of birth, sickness, old age and death, suffering and fear, were observed in all creatures. The Buddha urged all people to examine this point and be aware that all living beings really desired the same things and deserved the right to live. Because of this he condemned killing of any kind and encouraged a life of living in harmony with the environment.

This philosophy spread and flourished for centuries after the death of the Buddha through India, Thailand, Korea, Asia, Japan, Tibet and the entire Eastern World.

The Mahabohi Temple in Bodhgaya. The site of Buddha's enlightenment

1.4 Bodhidharma

An age of Buddha-Dharma flourished throughout India until the invasion of the Muslims a thousand years later. From this invasion the entire culture, which was now based on Buddhism, was almost completely destroyed. It was during this period in the 11th Century that one of the most famous of all Buddhist monks made his epic journey from India to China.

His name was Bodhidharma (Daruma Daesa). His mission was to preserve the devastated Dharma (the word Dharma being synonymous with Buddhist philosophy) by spreading it to other lands where it had not previously been and to reconstruct it in places where it had spread, flourished and already degenerated in the past thousand years. Bodhidharma is said to have journeyed from India, travelling the entire Chinese continent on foot performing his mission.

Bodhidharma. Legendary Buddhist monk of the 11th Century,

One of the most prolific and historical tales in the history of Chinese Buddhism and martial arts was Daruma's epic journey to the Shaolin monastery of Northern China.

Upon his arrival at the monastery he found a poor nucleus of sick, degenerated monks who lived in fear, misery and ill health. Because of the conditions they could hardly maintain themselves, much less pursue the arduous task of meditation. The basic principals of monastic life had suffered a sad demise. To make matters worse, the feudal system of the times and the anarchy that prevailed, threatened the lives of the monks if they dared venture out of the monastery. Due to Buddhist vows, which forbade monks from killing much less bearing weapons or arms of any sort, the monks of the time suffered severe consequences whenever they had to travel between the monasteries or when they had to perform social duties outside the premises. With fear, violence and ill health prevailing, Daruma had a difficult task to produce a proper environment conducive to the practice of the Dharma. He prayed and meditated for a solution to the dilemma. According to the legend, after much meditation and prayer, he fell asleep and had a dream. In the dream he was shown a method of exercise which incorporated the mental and physical yogas of Buddhist meditation in the pattern of sitting and standing movements. These exercises he taught to the monks who diligently practiced them and in a very short time received health, concentration and the ability to practice the essence of the Dharma properly.

From this point he began to teach a text called the *I-Ching Sutra*, which was a text outlining discipline to free the mind from all conscious control in order to attain the goal of Buddhism; enlightenment. In order to create incentive and to relieve boredom during practice, Daruma modified the exercises into a pattern of movements which not only produced good health and concentration, but could also inadvertently be used as a means of self-defence. This was a very wise move on his part because it not only accomplished his primary goal but it also produced confidence in the fear stricken monks. With this new discipline they could successfully defend themselves, live in harmony without fear and still maintain their Buddhist vows of not carrying weapons or harming others.

This training method also produced something tangible for the human mind. It is important to note here that this martial art or method as it came into existence, was purely passive, based on harmony, compassion and non-aggression. Just as a man endangered by a falling tree, does not confront the tree but merely steps aside, so too could the monks confront the dangers of everyday life with confidence and awareness. With their new abilities they could learn to step aside and evade conflicting situations without causing harm to themselves or others.

1.5 The Spread of Martial Art

This new discipline was an incredible success and spread rapidly throughout China and further on to Korea, Japan and the rest of the Orient. By the 12th Century, these arts had been so well developed and adapted that they began to be popular even outside the monastic circle. Tales leaked out of strong, robust, fearless fighters who sometimes were known to accomplish super physical feats. The exercises were by no means ordinary and it was said practitioners of this now well developed art could produce semi miraculous actions by controlling certain body energies. Quite naturally, in time more and more people became interested in what the monks were doing.

Although incredible secrecy was maintained, lest these arts fall into the hands of evil doers, slowly some of the secrets eventually leaked out from the religious spheres. The first privileged few in most of the countries were usually the nobility and servants of the feudal lords. Quite naturally the military began to be interested in any form of advanced defense. Because gun powder had not been developed, hand-to-hand combat was the mode of the day. It was at this time that the Tang Soo Tao, as we know it, came to flourish in its purest aspects. By this time, the science of body, study of nerves, control of vital pressure points combined with extensive physical discipline, created the most advanced human machine of discipline and self-defence ever known till now. The arts which spread far and wide varied greatly in style and tactics as well as in training methods. To date, there are literally hundreds of different styles and offshoots from the main schools.

Many of the styles which developed came out of abbreviated adaptations from artists who did not have the time, patience or insight to persevere with the long rigorous years of dedication and meditational practices. In addition to this, the war lords and military experts saw ways to adapt useful defence means which could be taught more quickly to common soldiers. Many times the internal practices were given up all together or in part, in an attempt to extract a quicker way of teaching basic fighting arts in the shortest time possible. Because of this, many of the arts taught did not contain the full scope of internal as well as external training methods. Often the artist placed more emphasis on the defense aspect of the arts and neglected the primary objective of spiritual advancement.

Of all the arts, there are four basic schools of thought from which all the internal and external schools can be traced. They are the oldest most traditional and purest arts of the *Shaolin, Hsing-I, Pa-Kua* and *Tai Chi Chuan.*

1.6 Shaolin

The first of these, the Shaolin School, made much emphasis on external physical disciplines and external strength. Innumerable methods of weight training, muscle development and physical austerities were devised. The art was based on forms modelled after careful observation of the self-defence movements of animals. The essence of the art dealt with the perfection of certain dance patterns or forms, which contained all the movements of the animals.

Internally the school taught concentration methods and yogic techniques of breath control, sublimation and internal body energies and control of the secretion glands.

1.7 Hsing-I

The second school, Hsing-I, taught a series of linear movements based on the Wu-Shing (O-Heng) or the five elements; metal, water, wood, fire and earth.

Although they used dance patterns formed after animals, the Hsing-I placed more emphasis on the elements than the animals and placed a great deal more emphasis on gaining strength by internal breathing methods which went along with the external defense actions. This differed with the Shaolin in that the former emphasised more external development in the defense aspects of the art.

1.8 Pa-Kua

The third of these schools is Pa-Kua, or the sixty four palms.

The Pa-Kua was a school of circular walking, with eight changes of eight different palms, for a total of sixty four. The Pa-Kua was also entirely internal and based its practice primarily on walking a circle for long periods of time, stopping only to change the position of the palms.

The sixty four different palms were directly related to the *I-Ching Sutra*, which in Chinese philosophy was said to hold all the scientific knowledge and the key to life. Because the I-Ching also governs the science of astrology, the expert in Pa-Kua was respected as a wise learned sage.

1.9 Tai Chi Chuan

The last of these was Tai Chi Chuan or the Grand Ultimate. The form consists of a series of thirty-seven moves which follow the flow of the natural body forces.

Unlike the other arts, the Tai Chi had only one form which contained all the movements, and yogas in one *one hundred and eight movement* form. Also this particular art was practiced in very slow motions, placing great emphasis on one point concentration, total relaxation and regulation of exceptionally slow breathing. The breathing played an integral part of harmonizing the flow of body movements with the internal flow of blood, sperm and body fluids. This differed from the other forms in that they were exercised at regular speeds and emphasized development of speed.

Yang style movements of Tai Chi Chuan

1.10 Philosophies

The description of these forms is hardly adequate to describe the incredible differences separating the various arts, the scope of which is too deep to deal with here in this short history. The basic importance in relating these art forms is in their primary objective in relation to Chinese philosophy and their methods as scientifically related to health and meditation.

All the schools share two common patterns: *external training methods*; and *internal Chi development* (energy).

In relating to philosophy all martial arts are structured as a basic discipline for training the mind, with a secondary function of learning self-defense. Because the intrinsic nature of mind is illusive, confusing and invisible, we need some tangible method to work with an unseeable object. The martial artist uses certain motions which correspond to the movements of internal body energies. The goal is to gain wisdom by perfecting the character and by purifying man's basic elements.

1.11 Five Elements

In order to do this, all the aforementioned arts, though differing in personality, rely on the theory of the Wu Shing. This philosophy teaches that in the beginning of time there was a void. From the void there was an explosion, out of which came the four basic elements – *air, fire, earth and water.*

As time passed, from the earth came wood and out of water came metal. The five elements of the metal, water, wood, fire and earth created our solar system and the known universe. The Chinese term this *the macrocosm.*

Likewise in the body the five elements were also maintained in the primary organs. This was called the *microcosm.*

This basic idea is the foundation of all oriental philosophy. The five basic planets in our solar system, Jupiter, Mars, Saturn, Venus and Mercury, correspond directly with the elements wood, fire, earth, metal and water. These planets and elements in the microcosmic aspect correspond to the liver, heart, spleen, lung and kidney. These organs in turn control our five fluid secretions, tears, sweat, saliva, mucous and urine.

The Wu-Shing not only acknowledges the five elements but also a set of opposites which rule our relative as well as absolute life. This is the positive and negative or *Yin and Yang*, the harmonious balance of male and female energy as contained in all opposites which create our world. i.e. *left/right, up/down, good/bad, black/white, cold/hot,* etc.

Element	Wood	Fire	Earth	Metal	Water
Yin organ	Liver	Heart	Spleen	Lungs	Kidney
Yang organ	Gall bladder	Small intestine	Stomach	Large intestine	Bladder
Sense commanded	Sight	Words	Taste	Smell	Hearing
Nourishes the	Muscles	Blood vessels	Fat	Skin	Bones
Expands into the	Nails	Colour	Lips	Body hair	Hair on head
Liquid emitted	Tears	Sweat	Saliva	Mucus	Urine
Bodily smell	Rancid	Scorched	Fragrant	Fleshy	Putrid
Associated temperament	Depressed	Emotions up & down	Obsession	Anguish	Fear
	Anger	Joy	Sympathy	Grief	
Flavour	Sour	Bitter	Sweet	Hot	Salt
Sound	Shout	Laugh	Sing	Weep	Groan
Weather	Wind	Heat	Humidity	Dryness	Cold
Season	Spring	Summer	Mid Summer	Autumn	Winter
Colour	Green	Red	Yellow	White	Black
Direction	East	South	Centre	West	North
Beneficial cereal	Wheat	Millet	Rye	Rice	Beans
Beneficial meat	Chicken	Mutton	Beef	Horse	Pork
Musical Note	chio	chih	kung	shang	yu

Table 1:The elements and their effects within the Microcosm and Macrocosm.

In dealing with the five elements of the body, we not only have the female organs, but also the male organs. We call this the principal of the five hollow and five solid organs. The Yin organs of the wood, fire, earth, metal and water correspond to the liver, heart, spleen, lung and kidney. The Yang organs correspond to the gall bladder, small intestine, stomach, large intestine and bladder.

Altogether, the governing organs are ten in number. These organs control the physical and mental well-being of the human animal. The balance, control and purification of the secretions and the energies contained in these organs is the primary objective in the practice of a true martial art. Also, corresponding to the five elements: wood, fire, earth, metal and water, are the sounds shout, laugh, weep, sing and groan. The tastes: sour, bitter, sweet, pungent, salty; the seasons: spring, summer, change of seasons, autumn and winter. Seasonal manifestations of these elements are wind, heat, humidity, dryness and cold. Corresponding colours are green, red, yellow, white and black. Corresponding emotions are anger, joy, sympathy, grief and fear. Excess emotions are anger harms liver, joy harms heart, thought harms spleen, grief harms lung, fear harms kidney. Corresponding directions are East, South, Centre, West and North. Corresponding polarity, Minor Yang, Major Yang, Neutral, Minor Yin, Major Yin. Corresponding orifices: eyes, ears, mouth, nose and lower orifices of the anus and urethra. The psychic value of each element is: spirit, conscience, ideas, animal spirits, will and with will, resolutions.

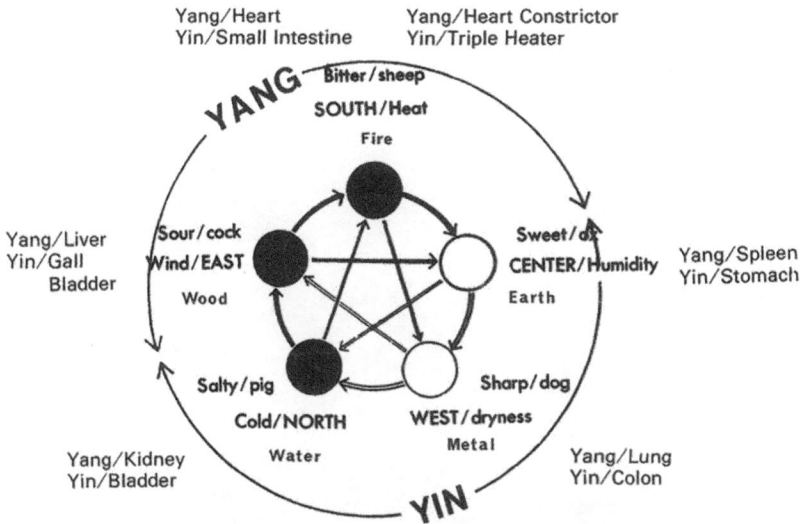

Course followed by Yang and Yin energy and related organs.

The list of these groups of five can go on, but the purpose here is to show the general relationship between the Macrocosmic universe and the Microcosmic man. This entire subject can be explained with the understanding of the theory of the five elements connected with the complimentary theory of the Yin Yang. In relation to the working of martial arts, this is necessary in order to maintain the theme of this brief history in relating historical Buddhism, yoga and oriental philosophy to Tang Soo Tao. As we can see, there is an incredible interlocking of cosmic energies, philosophies and sciences, too many and too numerous to be coincidental. This brings us to our primary subject.

What is Tang Soo Tao?

1.12 Tang Soo Tao

Tang Soo Tao is a Chinese name for an art which reached its summit during the most cultural years of the Tang Dynasty in Mainland China. Roughly translated *Tang* refers to the name of the emperor at the time; *Soo* refers to the *hand*; and *Tao* means the *Way*. So all together we have *The Way of the Chinese Hand*. This translation however, loses much of its meaning in English. What it really signifies is the name for a philosophy and way of life based on harmony of self and nature.

As it spread to other parts of the world, the name of the art changed slightly, sometimes called Tang Soo Do, sometimes changed to Kong Soo Do; Tang Soo Do being Korean; Kong Soo Do referring to the Japanese version.

The art went through various adaptations of techniques as it spread to other countries. Although the art defined in this book refers to all three, the author has had his most extensive research and experience in both the Chinese and Korean facets of the art. Although the words Tao and Do mean exactly the same, the author has chosen to use the term Tao because it refers to the mother art of China which can incorporate the art of Korea, rather than Do which at the time of this writing, refers only to the Korean art form. The choice of Tao also is to avoid confusion with other schools, using the name Tang Soo Do.

(At the time of this writing, many schools seem to have emerged suddenly, all using the name Tang Soo Do. This has caused great confusion in many areas because though they use the same name the basic philosophies, training methods and ideals differ so greatly as to make the schools entirely unrelated. This of course has raised questions of standards and authenticity. The true purpose of this book is not to become involved with politics, names, or sporting aspects, but to expound the essence and philosophy of the true art.)

Tang Soo Tao is a methodical science which man can use to explain the existence of himself and all perceivable phenomena. In order to do this, it uses the vehicle of self-defence as a tool to combine the gross physical levels of the human, with the finer planes of esoteric mind.

1.13 Instinctive Survival

The first level of training begins with man's most gross animal instinct: the will to survive.

All animals, man included, are born with physical defense mechanisms to protect themselves. The senses keep animals aware of apparent dangers and the hands, feet, teeth, limbs, etc., enable him to protect himself. Although man is regarded as the most superior animal on our planet, he has actually become inferior to most of the lower animals. Abnormal living conditions have dulled most of his natural instincts. Electricity, with its air-conditioning, refrigeration, stoves and hot water heaters, etc., have dulled man's ability to cope with natural climatic conditions, food and natural situations.

The advent of the automobile has stripped man of vital strength and use of his legs. Modern chairs have weakened his back, automatic appliances have lessened the use of his upper limbs and the all pervasive television has stripped most of mankind of his desire to do anything physical for himself at all, even to the point of having to think. Modern social culture has encouraged the use of tobacco to destroy our breathing, alcohol to destroy our kidneys and liver and to dull our brain, and exotic foods which throw man's life cycle entirely out of tune with natural seasonal changes of foods and weather. Media, competition and social pressure create excessive stimulation to man's senses and promote unnatural desires. Consequently, as a result of our seemingly advanced technology and culture, man has all but lost one of his most important attributes; the ability to be natural.

We find in modern man infinite varieties of diseases and ailments entirely unrelated to any other of the animal kingdoms.

These problems range from backache, migraines and obesity, to heart conditions, blood disorders, neurosis and sexual malfunctions. That diseases of this nature are found only in the modernised man is proof that man has indeed lost something. Even the so called primitive man of uncivilized countries does not suffer the types of problems outlined here. Obviously, the more removed from nature we become, the more problems we create for ourselves.

When man relies on inventions or external tools for his sustenance, he disregards one very important point. It is impossible to use a tool or instrument to solve basic problems of self support. Any other utensil alien from the natural human ability has an unknown quality which cannot be relied upon. The human being is a complete and separate entity in himself. A tool or device is not. The only usefulness of a tool or device is when it is behind the touch of a human being. Without the human being, any instrument is completely useless. It can be good or bad, depending on who is using it. Though certain tools and instruments are convenient to use they are only temporarily useful at a given time or place and should not be relied upon as an ultimate means of sustenance. Because the individual is a complete entity in himself, the basic nature of body and mind is of utmost importance to his survival. This principal exists on the mundane as well as esoteric planes. It is a primary truth which applies to all living beings regardless of age, culture or geographical location. It is our only duty to follow the supreme laws of nature and to maintain and develop the natural balance of body and mind.

1.14 Development Of The Art

Although their culture had not degenerated to the level of ours, our ancestors of the Tang Soo Tao realized the necessity to develop a science which would enable man to live socially without losing his natural instincts and to advance spiritually. By careful observation, over many years the original Tang Soo Tao men observed basic living habits and personality traits common to all animals. They noticed the changes of the seasons and their effects on all living beings, the changes of various crops at different times of the year and the changes of human attitudes at different times. They observed the rhythmic cycle of the nocturnal and daytime animals. They also observed the eating, stretching and fighting habits of the animals of the wild. From all these observations came the original Tang Soo Tao.

Tang Soo Tao is a form of self-defense based on animal movements of defense as adapted to the human being. The art is divided into three parts: defense practices, yogic practices and meditational practices. All these are inseparably related.

The yogic exercises are styled after the observation of the movements of human babies and animals such as lions, tigers, bears and monkeys etc. They promote toning of the muscle tissue, regularity of the body functions, increased blood flow and produce a general feeling of well being in the individual.

Yogic breathing is designed to strengthen the internal organs of the body, (i.e. the five elements and ten organs, hollow and solid, as previously mentioned) and to develop increased stamina through rhythmic breathing during physical activity. This cuts down wasted expenditure of energy which occurs with sporadic breathing during times of agitation and tension. When a person becomes excited, his blood usually reddens his face, breath becomes short and heart beat increases. Hence, yogic breath control aids greatly in controlling damaging conditions of anger, hate and fear which drain a person of energy causing him to act in an unwise manner, leaving him totally exhausted. In turn, breath control enables him to act in a calm rational way befitting any situation and not to make costly and foolish mistakes. This pertains whether or not we are talking about defense situations or in just coping with problems of everyday life.

1.15 Defence

The defence movements are a form of physical discipline which incorporates kicks, strikes, blocks, stances and evasive actions, used in defense situations.

There are five basic movements in all defence actions. They are *down, up, centre, left* and *right.*

All defence movements move in two directions, these are *linear* and *circular.*

Movements can be done individually; or in a stylized series of patterns.

The five basic elements, as previously mentioned of metal, water, wood, fire and earth, correspond directly to the five organs of the body: lungs, kidney, liver, heart and stomach. Movements done individually effect one organ, while movements done in a series or in patterns effect several or all of the organs at the same time.

The dance patterns also correspond with the five element theory by moving North, South, East, West and Centre. Thusly, we have all the external movements constantly effecting all the organs of the body in relation to the five element theory.

1.16 Yoga

As in the yogic exercises, breathing plays an integral part in performing these movements. Without proper breathing the movements not only lose their health aspect, but lose much of their power for effect and defense. Done correctly, metal makes water, water makes wood, wood makes fire, from fire comes earth. Adversely, wood covers earth, fire melts metal, earth retains water, metal smashes wood, water quenches fire.

Physiologically speaking, lungs replenish kidneys, kidney energy replenishes liver, liver replenishes stomach. Conversely, liver controls the stomach, heart controls lungs, stomach controls kidneys, lungs control liver and kidneys control heart.

When applied to defense movements, the same principles always apply. For example, all downward movements are related to metal, all straight or linear movements are regarded as wood. Therefore, if a man punches straight and a man blocks down on top, the metal smashes the wood. So, whether in health or defense, the organs, the principles and the elements always relate.

1.17 Meditation

Meditation is the final of the three areas of Tang Soo Tao training. It is such a vast area, it is difficult to know where to begin or where to end.

Essentially, it is the focal point of our yogic breathing and physical discipline. It is the most difficult subject to approach because unlike breathing and physical action, we are dealing with an unseeable object; namely the mind.

One of the purposes of meditation is to produce a calm spirit. This is done by emptying the mind of all extraneous thoughts and concentrating single pointedly on one object. In our daily life, we function in a world of duality and opposing forces. When dealing with this duality there is always a subject and object which itself is a duality. Therefore, there must be a good and a bad, an enjoyer and a sufferer, a happy and a sad. By one-point concentration, we can successfully combine the subject and object so that they are inseparably one. Once this power of concentration is attained, all things can be regarded as part of a whole. When the doer and perceiver become one there is no good or bad, or right or wrong. At this level a person has no suffering. There is no sufferer and nothing with which to be suffered. By our ego, which is the subject, ceasing to exist, there is no object of unhappy circumstances that we can experience.

This is total harmony.

However, because our ego consciousness is so strong and our personal desires so great, our selfish ego will not permit us to enjoy this tranquil state easily. When confronted with the idea of meditation a beginner usually sits down and becomes totally exasperated with all the thoughts on his mind. He believes that he cannot meditate. In actual fact, he really is meditating but becomes frighteningly aware of how his mind is in constant control of him rather than he in control of his mind. During the day, we have thousands of thoughts running wild through our mind. This has happened ever since we were born and because it is so much a part of our life, we believe it to be natural. When a student sits down for the first time to meditate, automatically the number of thoughts on his mind are reduced a hundredfold. However, the opposite seems apparent and the number of thoughts seems to be magnified. This is because the person is constantly observing each and every thought, whereas normally, so many thoughts cloud the mind that it is difficult to follow, much less observe.

The pure essence of meditation is to empty the mind so that it can function in its most natural state. Modern science has long recognised that man uses only one tenth of his potential brain power. The great iceberg of the mind that lies beneath the surface remains a mystery, examined by few wise men of our race and speculated on only by religion, science and philosophy. Man acting or meditating as a self existing entity limits himself to a temporary body and a relative mind, created by the limited experiences of his ego in one life time. This is like one drop of water from the ocean. It soon becomes stagnant and evaporates. By man opening himself to the entire universe he can, in meditation, become a great ocean and possess limitless strength and abilities, which defies time and space. Quite obviously this state of meditation, we are talking about here is difficult and uncommon to the ordinary man. Once again, without practice or a tangible working base our experience and understanding of a subject so vast as this is like the individual drop of water.

By intellect alone, we cannot possibly understand the profound ways of the universe. In order to even basically launch ourselves on such a path we must have a firm power of concentration. This is not easy. Mind and body are inseparable in our everyday experiences and when we are feeling down, both are also affected. If a person is depressed, the heart and liver suffer. The feeling of sadness at the loss of a friend has even caused people to die quite literally of a broken heart. When a person is worried they show neurotic behaviour. If a person is nervous their hands and lips shake and quiver. If a person is constipated he is usually slow and tired. A person with high blood pressure is nervous and upset. When a person is healthy his appetite is good, he is full of energy, sexually strong and is generally happy overall. Because our world is based on so much materialism, we often neglect to observe the mind. Often our thoughts and actions are separated. This is unnatural. If we were to cut off our hand, we would remain alive and the mind would still function. The same is true if we were to cut off two hands and two legs also, we would still exist. But we cannot cut off the mind. It is with us all the time. It is the only thing that we cannot change or that is not effected by the material ideas that we place so much importance on. This subject can go very deep and by itself volumes of text can be written. This is not the purpose here however. The purpose is to show that the mind and body must work together for physical and mental well-being. A healthy body creates a healthy mind and vice-versa. Most people agree with this in theory but not in life style. How do we integrate this important balance? This again is a primary function of Tang Soo Tao.

1.18 The Beginner

People begin martial arts training for numerous reasons. Many want to learn self-defense, many want a good way to keep fit, still others lack self-confidence and proper co-ordination. Some people want to learn relaxation and yet others see the need for discipline which they feel is so lacking in our everyday lifestyles. Often parents send their children to classes because they admire the respect that is taught. Quite often the parents hope the physical discipline the child learns in Tang Soo Tao will instill in their children the character traits that they lack the ability to teach by their own example. One often wonders in most cases, if it's really the children who need the training. They are usually healthy, fit and natural anyway.

More often than not, the parents are looking to the children to excel in the cultivation of virtuous traits which they themselves have failed to produce in their own lives. At any rate, the children still make out but the parents are left in the dark.

Another great motivation which drives people to sample martial discipline is the sensationalist attitude. In the past few years violence, having been associated with virility, has fostered in many men romantic ideas of becoming super heroes in 'ten easy lessons'. Spurred on by absurd movies, egotistical whims and bar room talk, many men are drawn into martial art schools in order to learn something quick and easy that will bolster their ego and make them a 'big man' among their friends. They have fantasies of becoming James Bond overnight, and by their Kung Fu virility, hope to attract scores of voluptuous women. This syndrome is nurtured by phoney Kung-Fu schools, with half-rated instructors, who have capitalized on the Kung-Fu fad.

The other half of the sex, women are not without their own delusions. Many lonely women looking for some excitement in life, the chance to meet a man or just to do something different, enter the school because they have nothing else to do. Still others, with more aggressive attitudes who have suffered some mental or physical injury from husbands, boyfriends or love life, search for a quick way to get even. They are willing to pay any amount to learn the quickest possible way to destroy a man's virility. They hope to do this by the independent power they can gain from training or even go so far as to physically harm some person whom they blame for their personal problems.

Lastly, we have the most sincere beginner, the person who desires to learn a logical method to help him cope with his spiritual life and physical well-being. This type of student, regardless of physical capabilities, recognizes the need for self-improvement and is willing to endure any hardship in order to better himself through training. He is an encouragement to both instructor and students alike. As is usually the case, this type of person will not only be an ultimate success in Tang Soo Tao, but usually ends up being a success in almost anything he pursues. This calibre of student is rare to find initially and usually has to be cultivated once he begins training.

1.19 Guiding the Beginner

Regardless of the type of personality and motivation, the valid martial art and a good instructor must be able to adjust the art to satisfy the person's immediate desires for coming. If they are positive, he must provide the necessary encouragement and if they are deluded, he must correctly help the wrongly motivated student, by giving them what they really need and not what they think they might want. This situation requires two things: a perfect and complete martial art; and an instructor with the patience, wisdom, dedication and expertise to communicate his art to others.

1.20 The Beginning

The first basic training term in Tang Soo Tao remarkably provides the answer to all these requirements. By the continual practice of basic co-ordination exercises the student develops poise, confidence and natural movement.

The yogic exercises incorporated at this stage purify the blood, tone the muscles, balance the blood pressure, reinstate the health and produce an incredibly fit body. The breathing exercises involved with these basics help people to relax, concentrate and become aware of themselves. The strict training programme instills discipline, respect for authority and creates an atmosphere of dedication to the instructor and the art. Quite naturally, in a short amount of time the student is well on the way to understanding excellent self-defense. Along the way, he has been able to lose weight, balance blood pressure, gain confidence and has discovered a new and exciting challenge in his life.

For the sensationalist the rewards are not so fine. Having to face the fact that he is not the he-man he thought he was, men who lack insight and fortitude quickly and shamefully shrink away from the training program. When they have to face the real test, which is looking at themselves, men and women alike who desire to harm others, are rudely awakened to find there is no aggression in a true martial art school. With the emphasis based on character development, defense and not offence, these people find that they will *not* quickly learn techniques that will destroy or harm others. The more advanced and dangerous aspects of the art are never revealed to a beginning student until such time he has proved his sincerity to the art and his instructor by dedication, dauntless consistency and practice. By this time, in training the student can easily use any knowledge in a positive constructive manner. The time and sincerity necessary to reach this stage naturally eradicates the type of student formally mentioned. A pugnacious character will always leave the school before achieving anything near this goal. They are the type of people who have rarely concentrated on anything more important than going to the toilet.

Whatever the case may be, martial art training is very difficult. Both the sincere and shallow minded person alike must face some rather humiliating facts about themselves in the beginning of their training. A person who has natural abilities towards sports and athletics find that they are of absolutely no value when trying to perform martial arts movements. Most people are shocked to find that they cannot even fully understand their left from their right. The most seemingly easy technique demonstrated by the instructor is impossible to duplicate. Having to be corrected for the same mistake, literally hundreds of times in the beginning stages, completely exasperates the individual with how unnatural he really is.

The most simple technique as shown by the instructor leaves a beginning student absolutely confused. Some students comment truthfully that they feel like spastics and sometimes joke about mental retardation. Unfortunately, when watching them, it sometimes appears to be true. A person who has not experienced this in actual training is not able to comprehend what is written here. Only the person who has experienced this will understand the truth of what is written and will have to laugh at himself. Every Tang Soo Tao student, without exception, has had to experience these things at the beginning of their training.

Basic co-ordination of a beginner

Perhaps the most humiliating truth to swallow for a beginner student, is how much he hides behind false images. Stripped of make-up, expensive cars and fancy clothes, a person must act and be taught on an equal footing with everyone else. Men, women, children of all ages are treated exactly as equals and are expected to perform to the utmost of their potential at all times. A person cannot hide in his rich home or bourgeoisie status, behind the cloak of qualifications, position or ideas of self-importance. All that he is, is exposed for all to see. Many people who would like to experience martial art know this but are afraid to expose themselves. For those that join, sometimes it comes as quite a shock. If they survive they always emerge stronger, pure and more humble.

All this can sound a bit much to the average reader who has no experience in these matters and actually it is. Fortunately, the situations mentioned do not last for very long. After the initial grace period of several months the Tang Soo Tao student is well on his way to producing skill and coordination necessary to practicing the art. Whether he continues or whether he drops out, although he doesn't quite understand what a martial art really *is*, he certainly finds out what it *is not*. He discovers that it is not a way to bolster his ego. He finds that the respect demanded by a martial artist emerges from humility, not egoism. He finally realizes that the rewards of the art come from the fruits of his labour and cannot be bought at any price.

1.21 Goals of Training

As we have shown, all the preliminary goals of defense, health and confidence, etc., can be developed through the science of Tang Soo Tao. But we must ask ourselves, in Tang Soo Tao, or even in average athletics or sports, what good is it to run faster, jump higher, swim longer or to see or hear better? What have we achieved? If at the end of our study, sport or practice we have done all these things, we have still only succeeded in elevating ourselves to the level of the lower animals. An animal never suffers from ulcers, depression, obesity or similar problems. They don't worry about defending themselves, they do it quite naturally. Even if they lose a fight, they never worry about it once it's finished. Animals are able to see further, run faster, jump higher and do almost any physical action better than humans. Therefore, what, if any value, does this afford man who is supposed to be the 'Lord and Master of Creation'?

Things were not always this way. Man had much more natural ability physically and psychophysically at other ages in his history. Even in the Bible, Adam and Eve had infinitely more paranormal powers. Step by step man has degenerated unquestionably. Even modern day anthropologists confirm that we no longer have the keen senses and awareness of our ancestors. Sociologists must refer to the few existent primitive societies in order to rediscover how man naturally lived in a natural habitat unsurrounded by the distractions of modern civilization. It has been shown that these people do not suffer the common ailments prevalent in our society and they also enjoy a keener sense of smell, sight and hearing, as well as an overall awareness of the environment they live in. They are stronger, more robust and able to live simply and happily with the most minimal utensils, relying mainly on their own natural abilities.

Although we are not advocating the return to stone age existence, there is a lesson to be learned in the observation of the simplicity and adaptability of our ancestors and primitive man. In order to progressively work with our body and mind we must go back to a natural base as a starting point. We must unlearn all our unnatural conditioning before we can attempt to develop a higher consciousness so readily available to a pure perceptive mind in its natural state.

This higher consciousness can be seen everywhere. The harmony and magnitude of nature can be observed in the wind, the rain, the animals, the trees and seasonal changes. No man can control the power of nature in its absolute form, but it can be experienced at all times in all things.

1.22 One Universal Energy

Oriental thought teaches that in some remote time before our universe began, nothing existed. There was no sun, moon, stars or earth. If the sun is now burning it had to start burning at some point and there must have been a time before it began to burn. If there is form, now there must have been a time when there was no form. Buddhism speaks of a void when there was no colour, thinking, moving or seeing. There were no eyes, ears, noses, tongues, bodies or minds. From formless energy, the sun and the earth and all things as we know them came to be. Christians call the force that brought being into the universe God; Buddhists call it Buddha; oriental philosophy terms this Chi.

The cultivation of chi in the life of a martial artist, is of utmost importance. So then, if all things come from universal energy and this energy has no beginning or end, it can neither increase or decrease. Although it can change its external form, its essence remains unchanged. Mankind, the planets and all phenomena stem from a universal source. If something made of chi passes away it can only return to the energy from which it came: Primordial Chi.

A true martial artist aims at transforming his body and mind into primordial chi. This is a difficult task. Before he can do this he must refine the many levels of impure chi within himself. There are physiological chi's which are refined by the internal schools of yoga. There is the chi of spirit and faith which is cultivated by both internal and external systems through diligent training and tenacious perseverance. The desire to strive on against any and all odds and to succeed at one's objective is an important type of chi training, familiar to all schools of thought.

1.23 Harmony

Because our relative world does not promote natural harmony these ideas are sometimes difficult to understand. A man who is one with his environment is immune to life and death. Good or bad, and enemies and friends are one and the same. This total understanding is the basis for eternal life. Christ taught that God was love. The Buddha taught loving compassion. Universal nature shows us love and protection to all things.

This is not just for people but for all creation; from the smallest leaf, to the snail at the bottom of the ocean. The flowers, the forest, the animals and man, receive the same blessings of sun, moon and rain. Nature distributes her fruits equally to all things. By seeing this we can become more unified with the world around us.

Negative people will always point out the suffering they see. They object to the idea of harmony and ask how suffering can be an expression of nature's harmony and love. Suffering exists, but its existence depends entirely on the way we accept it. The same sun that gives light also creates shade. Where there is happiness there is sadness. The sadness itself is part of nature's harmony. If sadness did not exist there would be no cause for happiness. If death did not exist what reason would there be to live?

No man can be happy if he lives against nature's way and even if man can temporarily excel in an evil act, the time will always come when he will have to pay for his ill deeds. We must always strive to perfect ourselves by learning the truths of nature and living in accordance with them. So as we can see, a defense art which protects the physical safety alone is actually quite shallow in relation to all mentioned. Therefore, we must protect all things.

1.24 The Essence of Harmony in Martial Arts

Many people walk into a martial arts training school and have difficulty understanding how the philosophies of harmony and love correlate with what they see. First appearances show a group of people kicking, punching and throwing each other all over the floor. To an outsider it looks as if everyone is practising the fastest way to destroy anything and everything in sight.

Many people wonder what this has to do with love and harmony.

Before we can work with an absolute we must first go through a relative. Before understanding an unseeable object we must first have something tangible to grasp. In training, students are really not trying to harm each other (as it may seem), but trying to use their partner to polish their techniques. Because the defense movements are intensely difficult and numerous in number they take a great deal of time, patience and concentration to master. The perseverance necessary to perfect what is required, simultaneously polishes the personality of the practitioners involved.

To execute a potentially dangerous technique with full power, but controlled, requires an incredible amount of skill. To maintain a calm, relaxed and alert mind in the face of an all-out free-fight taxes the intellectual as well as innate capabilities of a student. The practitioner has to reason quickly; thinking and acting out of knowledge and spirit. In a real situation, no movements in martial arts can be pre-meditated. The student has to perceive experiences and react to situations spontaneously as they occur. This exercises the non-intellectual part of his mind.

In the practice of defense, all the senses must be developed to the utmost. Students learn to develop and utilize all the senses and are not restricted to the belief that the human mechanism consists only of the five senses. Just as cats and dogs can hear and see things not apparent to humans, so we must admit that only our five senses do not show us the whole truth. The defense sense of the bird that will not land on a branch near a hunter's gun sights, clearly indicates a higher sense not included in the five senses.

Each and every individual has different physical abilities and limitations.

In Tang Soo Tao, students learn to recognize and cope with these limitations and also to develop all the qualities they are capable of. Tang Soo Tao teaches that by recognizing one's weaknesses they can become one's strengths.

Training practices exercise both internal and external systems of the human anatomy, which result in keeping one younger, healthier and well balanced for a longer period of time. Since virtually every part of the body is used in self-defense, natural co-ordination and quicker reflexes are assured. This in turn inhibits atrophy of muscle tissue and promotes the autonomic systems of the body. Within each living thing there exists an internal life force which is a necessary ingredient for the perpetuation of life. Tang Soo Tao students do not have to develop this (because it already exists), but they do learn how to be aware of it and how to utilize it in their physical and mental activities.

Martial art is different from sport because mere physical strength is not all that's involved in the practice. Each student strives to develop a means of getting in touch with their inner force, in an attempt to become a more complete being that is a part of and not separate from the universe. This method of practice enables one to grow spiritually by adopting a philosophical approach to life. The character and mental perspective through this system of training is a result of intense concentration and discipline.

The ultimate goal is spiritual awakening of mind and body towards sensitivity, not usually experienced. Practitioners learn to respond to their innermost feelings and become more mature and inner directed.

The proper student of Tang Soo Tao is able to function in situations by using his entire being.

> *'In nature be like water*
>
> *At rest, like a mirror*
>
> *Respond like an echo*
>
> *Be subtle, as though non-existent'*

2.1 One Point

In Tang Soo Tao, all movements are generated from the waist. The concentration rests in the region of the navel.

Students are constantly reminded during breathing, training and meditation to keep their mind centred on this point at all times. All energy known to man is cultivated and generated from this point. This not only holds true physically but spiritually as well.

Logically situated, the centre of gravity rests at the level of the navel. If we tense our shoulders and keep our balance in our head we upset the laws of nature. When the human body is in its natural posture, the centre of gravity will quite naturally settle down in the lower abdomen. This can be experienced when trying to co-ordinate any movement in the body. If we lift something properly, we lessen the risk of injury because all our energy is balanced properly.

The spirit too must also be directed from the lower abdomen in order to function naturally. We unconsciously acknowledge this with our every day expressions.

When someone is together, we call them *well-balanced.* If someone is mentally disturbed we use the slang expression *off his rocker.* To describe personalities we refer to people as being *highly strung* or *low key.* When we see a panicked person or someone who is emotionally upset, what do we see? The face becomes red, the heart beats faster, the voice wavers and they stutter. We usually advise *get hold of yourself,* or *centre yourself.*

The common advice of taking a deep breath and counting to ten is really based on holding the breath in the lower belly to drop the spirit to its natural place.

Almost everyone has suffered headache or stiff shoulders. It is quite common for office workers to collect tension in the neck and shoulders. This is why a good massage is so relaxing. All these examples clearly indicate that the spirit directly manifests itself at certain points in the body.

The balance point of this is the navel.

One point area.

2.2 Tumo

This is not the only reason we concentrate on the navel however, other reasons are deeper and more significant. Oriental philosophy has long expounded that the seat of man's life force is cultivated in the navel region. This energy is called *Tumo* or psychic creative energy. Though it permeates the entire body, it is stored in the navel region. The catalyst for our creative energy lies in the sexual force. Not only oriental religion, but all religions or spiritual paths have been known to encourage celibacy.

Due to ignorance, through the ages people erroneously confused religious advice on abstinence. The result was either sin or suppression. Neither of these was correct.

From our every day experience we can see that sexual energy manifests in the navel region and heat is experienced in this part of the body. Sexual energy is the creative energy of life. The result of male and female energy coming together creates life. We can see the power of strong creative energy in children and youth. They're happy, pure, tireless and easily mend from wounds. If they become sick, their health is quickly restored. The tireless energy as exemplified in youth, shows the power of creative energy unsullied by worldly ways. A sign of health and vitality is a strong sexual drive accompanied by a good appetite.

Both of these centre around the lower abdomen.

When people get older their vitality wastes away. Food looses its taste, the hair becomes white, skin becomes wrinkled and old age begins to set in. It is no coincidence that loss of sexual appetite as well as ability, occurs at the same time as these other visible signs. Sages of old studied well concerning these creative energies and developed many exercises to cultivate and preserve the life force.

Before we get into the next subject, the author would like to state here lest there be a misunderstanding, that when dealing with the subject we are not encouraging celibacy but moderation of all bodily functions. If we are hungry and stuff ourselves, we are equally if not more uncomfortable than we were in the first place. Likewise, if we are hungry and do not eat, we starve. We must find a natural balance to harmonize with nature's laws.

2.3 Life Force

All human beings are the creation of sperm from the father and blood from the mother. These are the gross manifestations of the merging of the cosmic forces of the universe. Although the female can be seen to carry the blood and the male can be seen to carry the sperm, this does not mean that the individual has only one essence. In order to exist, a human must be the result of both the sperm and the blood. Therefore, although not visibly evident, all human beings, male or female, contain the product of both blood and sperm.

The key to the discovery of inner awareness rests in the successful merging of the internal sperm and blood existent in all of us. The union of these forces creates a fundamental spiritual personality expressed by all religions and philosophies. This spiritual integration creates what is referred to as the *Tao*. Therefore the way of the Tao is the total synthesis of the mother and father. In other words, to combine all relative forces of duality into oneness, so they become inseparable is the practice of the Tao. As mentioned before, one translation of the word Tao means *The Way*. Three very important training methods of the Tao are *Chi Gung*, *Nei Gung* and *Wei Gung*.

The Yin Yang symbol representing sperm and blood and all relative opposites which account for all phenomena.

2.4 Chi Gung

Chi Gung is the delicate science of yogas designed to sublimate and purify the primary essences of the body. It incorporates a wide range of breathing exercises which circulate the internal energies into the five major organs. These are the liver, heart, kidneys, lungs and spleen. The practice involves placing the body in various positions while practising various methods of breathing exercises. The position of the body, combined with the breathing, increases energy and blood flow.

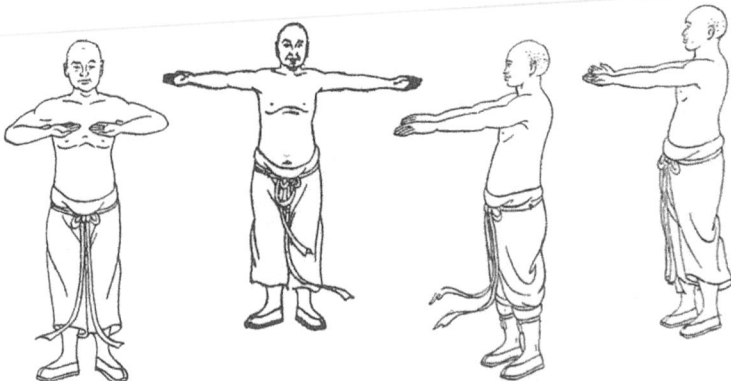

Drawings depict circulation of chi through psychic channels.

2.5 Nei Gung

Nei Gung are meditational exercises done in unison with Chi Gung. They involve changing the body energies by special concentration practices. The male and female sexual fluids are redirected from the worldly course and used to generate energy inside the body. Done correctly and at the proper time these exercises are of tremendous benefit. Done incorrectly and at the wrong time they have a devastating effect on the individual.

In Tang Soo Tao, these yoga methods are incorporated in the forms and basic movements and sometimes in separate yoga practices and meditations. The more powerful internal methods should only be practiced by sincere people who have already cultivated purity of mind, developed from years of training, meditating and cultivating the art.

In this age of degeneration, some martial arts instructors have sometimes stumbled across closely guarded yogic methods which produce incredible internal powers. Though not ready themselves they take the liberty of teaching these to those mentally unprepared to practise them. This is indeed a serious mistake.

Many people try to cover up their obvious lack of pure physical technique with excuses that they train internal styles of martial arts. Tantalized and impressed by tales of super human achievements of famous martial artists, such as flying, ESP, invulnerability, immortality, etc., the foolish plunge themselves into a course of training with romantic ideas of gaining these powers. This is incredibly dangerous. Although these para-normal powers can be obtained they are only the by-products of psychic development. They should neither be displayed nor sought after as a primary objective of training.

2.6 Wei Gung

Where as Nei Gung are the meditational exercises, Wei Gung provides the physical exercises to produce the desired results of breathing and meditation. Wei Gung is a series of very powerful physical exercises to cultivate pure chi. This is the purification of blood, sperm and secretions from all the body organs. It is an integral part of yoga philosophy and of internal martial art study.

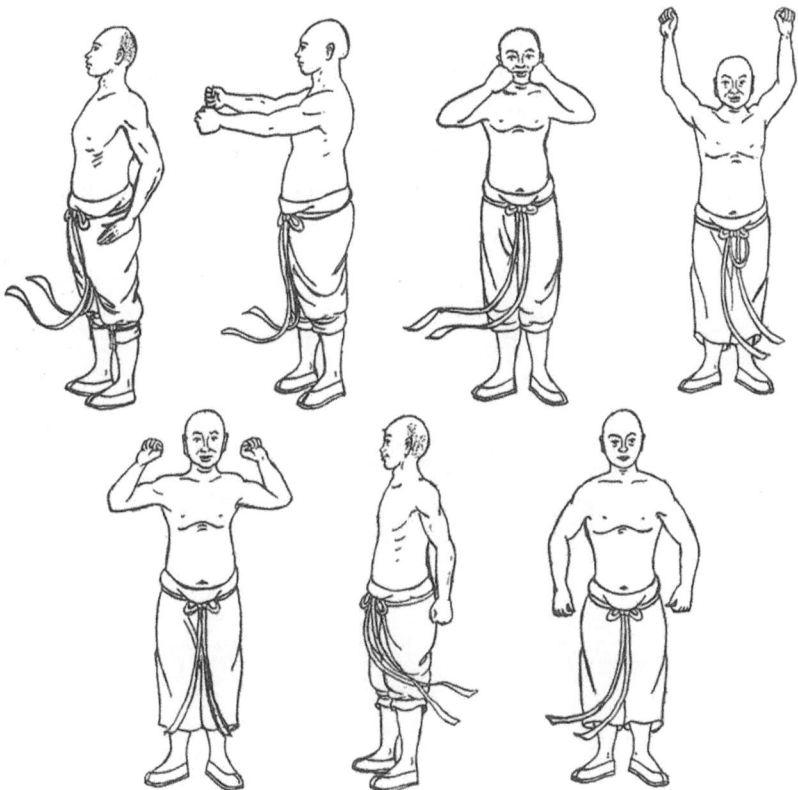

2.7 A Warning

The latent power hidden in the human body can be more useful or destructive than an atomic bomb. Any power released serves to greatly increase any qualities which already exist in the individual. Subsequently, if a spiritually uncultivated person succeeds in releasing some of this energy it will magnify the desire with which it is produced.

In other words, good begets good, bad begets bad.

Spiritually inadequate people desire powers to dominate and control others. Such people are not few in numbers. Although they can achieve temporary results such as invulnerable bodies, withstanding extreme temperatures and mentally controlling others, in the end they will only succeed in destroying themselves. These people are dealing with something closely akin to black magic. Any and all methods used for self-gain alone, without the express purpose of helping others is entirely deluded and against natural law.

2.8 Cultivation of Character

This balance is carefully protected in the training methods of Tang Soo Tao. All forms and basic movements are designed to develop body energies in a gradual way. This takes many years and sometimes a life-time to practise.

Working with a partner instills timing, trust and precision.

Constantly having to use one another as complimentary learning tools enforces our respect, love and understanding for one another. Trust and control is an absolute requirement for students when practising free-fighting and basic motions. Working either individually or alone, strengths and weaknesses are well defined in everyone. By closely relying on each other's energy and example, we begin to experience that none of us are really any different from one another.

We experience that all people are subject to the same laws and suffer the same problems. Many find they are not the self-existent phenomena they thought they were; apart from the rest of the world. These qualities are a direct realization of training and without that experience can only be understood on an intellectual level.

True satisfaction can only be experienced when using our energies for helping others.

It is a wonder indeed that such understanding comes out of a practice which externally appears to be opposite to these ideals. By appealing to man's animal instinct, fear, and the will to survive, Tang Soo Tao training forces the student to take a good look at himself for what he is.

The practices include solo exercises which force a person to compete with himself in order to progress. Mental dullness or self-respect and pride in one's own work show true at this time. Paired exercises with a partner demonstrate his abilities and his inadequacies. All out free-fighting clearly defines a person's spirit and natural responses. Any flaws in a student's character unmistakably show forth in his training technique.

Under close scrutiny many people are actually quite shocked at how totally inadequate they really are. Sometimes they can't face this and quit. Others become totally disgusted with themselves but use this as an incentive to better themselves. Those who pursue never regret it. Those who leave always return at some later date and stand sheepishly at the back of the hall wishing they'd had the courage to continue.

2.9 Misconceptions of Martial Art

Due to the recent success of sensational Kung-Fu movies which glamorise violence, martial arts have temporarily become popular in the public eye. Many *dime-store* instructors have exploited the arts worldwide, for name and fame and to *get rich quick.*

Many instructors have prostituted the art and made it into a sport and a game. Every large city or town is now filled with dozens of various Kung-Fu and Karate schools. Sensationalists glamorise violence and brick breaking and associate these things to martial arts as a course which begins at one point and ends with a black belt. Because of these attitudes the common person approaches a martial arts instructor and asks how long is the course and how much it costs. If one instructor offers him a black belt quicker than another he is considered (by our *instant self-serve* customer) to be quicker and more efficient.

For a martial artist to explain the real truth behind martial arts to a new person is difficult enough as it is. The task becomes almost impossible when an instructor tries to tell someone all the things that a martial art is not, when in actual fact, these things are just exactly what it has become. This can well be paralleled with the art of making love. Two lovers, by their energy and love can, elevate a base act common to all lower animals, to an ultimate act of beauty and harmony. If a man goes to a local brothel he does nothing more than perform the same action as a dog, pig, or any other beast. The infinite quality of the first choice is obviously better than the second.

Although many people try to make a contest of it, martial arts is not a sport and can never be. Sports are entirely based on age, sex, physical ability and pure physical strength. It is limited to age and season.

A sportsman has one objective and this is the desire to win for himself or for a team. The goal of winning, is the object of the sport and when this is achieved the object of the sport is terminated. An average sportsman's life is restricted to his youth and rarely after the age of 30 or at the most 40, is he able to fully engage himself in sport.

Martial art has no winning or losing. There is no finite objective and it is not restricted to size, sex, shape or age. The power which can be cultivated in a pure martial arts technique is potentially the same for woman and man, large and small alike. Historically, it has been proven that a properly trained martial artist enjoys health and perfect control of his faculties until the time he dies. Like a bottle of wine the practitioner vintages with age and although physical ability decreases, it is replaced by psychic awareness. All famous martial arts masters have retained their power and ability to practise late into life, even up to the very time of their death. Because the mind and body are cultivated together, a well developed mind carries on with the work of a martial artist even when the physical body begins to deteriorate. This is because mind is not limited to physical body and material objects. A martial artist's aim is to work for world peace by the development of spirit. The sportsman's desire is to develop ego by the conquest of winning.

There are also other points that greatly differentiate the two. The ultimate objective of the skilled disciple of martial arts is to obtain victory without combat. This is completely ridiculous to a sportsman. Once engaged in combat however, we must win even against great odds. There is no such thing as fair play.

In sports, the purpose of action is hobby and recreation. Games result in victory or defeat. In martial arts the purpose and result of action are very serious and a man's destiny can rest in one motion. The result is not to win a game but to succeed in the actual struggle between life and death. This is why people who practise the art must do their utmost to train in the mental aspect of the art. We must cultivate courage and bravery and be ready to look in the eye of death at any time. If we keep the reality of death constantly in front of us, then all our actions, speech and conduct will always be affected.

This is incredibly different from sports, as we can see. The question of winning or losing perhaps is explained in a quote from an old martial arts saying. 'The winner in combat will have another test to face, the loser has already faced his test.'

2.10 Tang Soo Tao and Other Martial Arts

There are many different varieties of martial arts designed for various purposes. A whole book can be written simply on the types of martial arts. This section is to provide a key to understanding the particular characteristics of the major classifications of arts. There are too many separate art forms to deal with individually so all the art forms have been categorized into some very general categories. [The writer apologises to any artist who feels insulted if his particular art has either been deleted or not explained adequately. The goal here as expressed, is to provide a guide line to see the differences among the arts.]

Judo

A form of defence based mainly on holding and throwing a person down with bare hands and feet. Adopted from the older form of Jiu-Jitsu, it is now mainly a sport and it is usually limited to weight classifications. Primary country - Japan.

Jiu-Jitsu

The Mother form of Judo, based on throws and take-downs with hands and feet, methods of choking and some bone breaking techniques. It also specializes in dislocations, basic practice of striking specific points of the anatomy and bone and joint locks of various sorts. Primary country - Japan.

Aikido

A method of defence for throwing a person, either attacking in close or from a distance. A systematic way of throwing or downing a person using the inertia of his own attack against him. The art was devised from the movements of the samurai sword. It specializes in throwing, takedowns, joint locks and arrest techniques. The art has no offensive motions. All techniques are defensive and unusable if not first provoked. Primary country - Japan.

Kendo

Main defence art of the sword. Attack and defence art based on cutting, stabbing, striking and deflecting an opponent's sword movement. Can also mean a form of stick defence. Primary country - Japan.

Karate

Systemized method of attack and defence using bare hands and feet. The art contains kicks, blocks, chops and strikes. Karate movements though sometimes circular are generally characterized by straight, direct, linear movements. Primary country - Japan.

Tang Soo Tao

Chinese defence form based on attack and defence with bare hands and feet. Study of special anatomy points and special pushing techniques. Blocks, strikes, kicks and punches, used as progressive adaptations from the mother arts, Tai Chi Chuan, Hsing-I and Pa-Kua.

Kung-Fu

Chinese forms related to north and south China. Various systems practise hard techniques, various systems practise soft techniques. Many schools internal, many external. Although linear attack practised, primary emphasis focused on circular, round, flowing motions. Practise of low leg manoeuvres and leg sweeps; also use various types of weapons.

The majority of Kung Fu stress study of herbs, diet, medicine, acupuncture and various types of yogas.

Tai Chi Chuan

Slow motion health or defence form. Can be used as either or both. In modern times it is commonly used more as health by common people than as defence, Emphasis is on breathing, slow fluid motion with defence motion. Defence is based on pushing exercises in unison with chi development. Primary practice is one long dance form. Can also be included under Kung-Fu. Primary country - China.

Yudo

The art of archery.

Tang Soo Do

Form of self defence using bare hands and feet. Depends mainly on kicks, punches, blocks and strikes in systematic movements. It has some similarities in Karate. Advanced specialities include many intricate varieties of kicking techniques. Basic combination of Okinawan Karate, with traditional Korean Soo Bak Do. (Foot fighting art native to Korea). Primary country- Korea.

Tae Kwan Do

Off-shoot of Tang Soo Do active in Korea since 1961. Basic foot fighting skills emphasizing free fighting as a form of sport. Primary country - Korea.

Kempo

Chinese style art form as spread to Japan, similar to Karate, but with more emphasis on circular movement. Also some specialities of bone locks, striking points and take-downs, similar to Judo throws.

Nin-Jitsu

Commando form of self defence of ancient times. Specialities include sabotage, espionage and use of all sorts of weapons. It developed the art of throwing various kinds of missiles, including knives, darts, hatpins, chopsticks and almost anything imaginable. Also professional arsons. Ninjas relied heavily on the defence of secrecy and hidden identity. Primary country - Japan.

2.11 The Best Martial Art

Because there are many varieties of martial arts many people like to put one style against the other. Someone always tries to speculate on the superior technique and the development of the ultimate weapon. Because we are using martial art as our vehicle, defense is an important goal which should be conscientiously developed.

A defense art must not lose its effectiveness or it loses its value as the vehicle to obtain our training objective.

A person however, who worries about which art is superior has no real understanding of martial virtue. Just as all men are equal so is it with true martial arts.

The validity of a true martial art depends on the spirit of the instructor, the spirit of the student and the interpretation of experience of life gained in training by both instructor and student. The oral transmission of energy passed down from instructor to student successively, is also an integral part of a martial artist's experience which is often times over looked. Any art regardless of depth can be developed to a very high degree by a practitioner with insight and dedication. Even an intrinsically strong art can be reduced to very low standards by inferior instruction and training. The student who is practising any martial art technique to the utmost of his understanding with the desire to perfect himself through the perfection of his technique, is practising the best martial art.

The superiority of any martial art can only be evaluated by the purity of character in each individual practitioner.

2.12 Yin Yang

As we have stated earlier, Yin Yang are the oriental counterparts for the positive and negative aspects of our world. Male is Yang, female is Yin. Yang is hard, Yin is soft.

The Tang Soo Tao art is a total integration of the Yin Yang philosophy. The physical art form clearly and progressively works on the Yang style movements until they totally become Yin. This means a progressive training from hard to soft. Many schools advocate softness. Unfortunately, they develop so much softness they lack the strength and power of the hard. Hardness in turn has immediate strength and power but too much hard develops imbalanced energy. People who only practice hard style often develop similar personalities. Driving force, power and speed are fine to develop in early years of training as long as the practitioner gradually integrates soft movements into his hard movements. If he cannot do this successfully the hard chi that he has created will cause his body to become stiff and rigid. In later life he may have difficulty training at all. If he does not find some way to balance the chi he definitely will not be able to continue with higher levels of training.

Basic co-ordination movements combining external movement in Yang chi development, (or hard style).

The type of chi that is developed in hard-style only martial arts, limits the art to a finite state. In progressive martial arts, we must successfully integrate the balance between these two; hard and soft. Softness should not be equated with weakness. The female energy is the subtle complimentary to the Yang, without which the Yang could not exist. The vice versa also holds true. This can more easily be explained with an example rather than philosophical jargon. A raging hurricane has a devastating effect and an awesome power. It can devastate the huge powerful oak tree but it cannot harm the blade of grass that gently bends beneath its raging movement. In Tang Soo Tao, the beginning student is taught basic external movement which emphasizes power, speed and technique. The hard style moves are designed to develop coordination, spirit and a feeling for the power of technique. It is not until the student thoroughly masters and has an understanding of co-ordination of external powers, that he can begin to be introduced to the soft, subtle ways of the soft forms.

The soft forms are flowing and infinitely more complex. To effectively deliver the soft power in the Tai Chi art form, compared to delivering the hard power in the external arts, easily takes twice the number of years to cultivate. By systematically working with styles, the student has a practical application of his more basic training while he works on difficult more advanced technique. This is important for the student for he must have something tangible to work with. If he works with hard all the time he will only develop good attack, but not good defence. If he begins with soft too soon his power will always be weak and he will not be able to focus power when he needs it.

Whether hard or soft forms, it should be remembered that the primary purpose of forms after basic coordination is the development of chi. Chi cultivation is the most important part of the martial artists' experience. Without chi, or the generation of intrinsic energy inside the body through appropriate training exercises, the art remains only a physical form of exercise.

Soft forms develop passivity and relaxation. They teach the art of gradually yielding in order to overcome. Ultimately, they are infinitely more powerful than the hard forms.

If two people are in a conflict we have an even battle where the stronger will always prevail. If only one person is angry however, and the other refuses to argue, there is no one for the other to fight. If there is no object there is nowhere for the subject to test his strength. Tired of fighting with himself, the angry man will eventually burn himself out.

The same holds true for hard and soft technique. As was the case with the hurricane and the blade of grass, even the most powerful cannot defeat the strength of nothingness (yielding).

Tai Chi classics use the phrase *move a thousand pounds with four ounces*. The progressive movement from hard to soft also has a practical application in daily life.

First basic movements are in the form of blocks, straight, hard and to the point. The defender meets the attack head on and forces the aggressor out of the way. Physical contact and direct confrontation are involved. Movements must be strong, hard and fast. Our social upbringing is much the same way. We are always told to fight back and to stick up for our rights. Parents want their docile children to be more aggressive. We are brought up in a world where muscle and strength always win. We attempt to influence and in turn are dominated by displays of power. Our competitive education system teaches us to push forward and never take no for an answer. These points of life style can be seen anywhere from domestic arguments in our own home or our neighbours, to the way with which our politicians handle foreign policies.

Soft style cultivation of Yin chi.

The next up from basic blocking is deflecting. This involves more circular movement and better timing so as not to meet the opponent head on. It involves less force and energy and is much easier and more effective. The highest form of defence movement is just like meeting a guest at the door and letting him in. By sensitivity, combined with perfect timing and relaxation, the purely soft practitioner can receive any attack at the same speed it is delivered. Rather than struggle he simply moves with it until the attack has lost its momentum. At which time the offensive is at its weakest. To upset the balance of an aggressor at this point is as simple as pulling a chair out from underneath somebody as they are committing themselves to sitting down.

In everyday life, only an ignorant selfish person argues in order to get his way all the time. If we know we are right we shouldn't force our opinion on others. If others wish to force theirs on us and we know that we are right, what harm can they do us. Only the person who doubts himself feels it is necessary to defend himself all the time. As has been proven by the wisest sages in history, the strongest most influential way has not been in resisting, but in demonstrating by example. Christ certainly was not promoting cowardice when he urged mankind to *turn the other cheek*.

The soft 'pushing hands' practice of Tai Chi Chuan.

2.13 Forms

It should be noted that the forms illustrated in this book are for the progressive development of a beginner student. They are for basic co-ordination only and to give a student the most rudimentary understanding of defense movement. Though they appear similar to forms illustrated in most other books such as Karate, Tae Kwan Do, etc., there is an important difference.

Tang Soo Tao art forms begin with forms such as these and gradually progress into the master form of Tai Chi Chuan which is not demonstrated in detail in this particular book. An average martial artist will obviously recognise some basic similarities with these forms to other art systems. He may feel that the only difference is a wider stance, squarer stance or slightly more refined or rougher movement. The difference however, though visibly not apparent in the pictures, is the method in which the students are introduced into the forms. The method is by constant exposure and demonstration of the master Tai Chi Chuan form. As has been explained elsewhere in the book, the softness in this form is not practical or applicable as a martial art in the fundamental years of a martial artists' training. External systems have little difference in their forms after first and second Dan levels. The difference between a senior Dan holder and a beginner black belt in these associated arts, rests in the fluidity of the movement and the number of times the senior member has practised the basic movements.

The focal point of external art forms stresses defense through repetitive practice of basic motions done thousands and thousands of times. This instills in the practitioners the ability to use these forms without thinking so that they become automatic. Although this partially holds true for development of techniques in Tang Soo Tao, it is not the main focal point. Integration of non-structural form or formlessness as introduced gradually in the Tai Chi Chuan form through the basic forms, gradually produce in the student a formless innate movement which is beyond description or structure. Though correct external movement is initially necessary, most important emphasis is placed on internal yogas done in connection with the forms. The primary focal points of the movements is the internal control of the secretion glands. This in turn develops an internal power source for purification and defense. Though external systems can produce effective conditioned response, their philosophy of movement rests on the refinement of basic techniques which are founded on highly structuralized external body movements. External art forms were primarily introduced during times when hand to hand combat was the mode of the day. Military experts who desired a quicker more effective way to teach martial arts, often adopted basic fighting techniques so they could be taught to the common soldier. Though they undoubtedly had practical application in basic defense, these forms lacked fundamental depth in developing the esoteric sciences, progressively through martial art forms.

Although practitioners of any martial art can develop a relatively high degree of defense, awareness and general well being, there are several points which differentiate internal and external systems. External systems developed emphasizing defense using the limbs of the body. Effectiveness was based on speed, strength and body size. Practical application of the art was quick though rudimentary and limited to human levels.

The internal systems placed much less emphasis on external structure and took much longer to develop practical self defense. Defense when cultivated used an unseeable element termed chi. Because of this unseeable element it was more difficult to understand and so less popular. Although practicality in defense took much longer and was more difficult, the internal systems were not confined to relative body size or strength and powers developed bordered on the supramundane.

2.14 Tournaments

Tournaments are not an integral part of martial arts. Although they are ultimately not very important in a student's training experience, like anything else, they can be used as an advantage or a disadvantage. The disadvantages of tournaments are that they make a game out of martial arts. Games must have rules. If we must follow certain rules then we must limit our technique and natural fighting methods. This creates a conditioned response that can be practiced. This inhibits natural formless movement.

In addition to this, there are rules for contact in many tournaments. In some tournaments there are points given for effective technique. In other tournaments a person is awarded points for damaging contact. If we have no contact ruling then it is difficult to gauge a person's ability to execute effective technique. If we allow excessive contact in a competition people can become seriously injured. True martial art encourages the perfect development of each and every technique used. A maximum potential of any and all techniques can kill, cripple, paralyse or seriously injure another person. But to encourage this type of conduct is the antithesis of the philosophy in any true school of martial virtue.

The only practical way which is remotely feasible is a controlled free match for a designated time between two people. There should be four judges and a centre judge. At the end of a specified amount of time there should be a unanimous decision as to which practitioner displayed the best qualities of defense, (not offense), technique, art, skill and demeanour. This is the only logical way acceptable to conduct a competition. This has it's drawbacks however, in that it allows the students to demonstrate a defense ability for a long period of time. The first technique scored could be the last and in a natural situation there would be nothing left to judge. So although this is a constructive way for students to compete and learn from one another it is by no means a one hundred percent sure indication of the superior martial artist.

Which brings us to another point, being; the superior martial artist. The word *superior* has connotations in a martial arts world of being physically better than someone else.

Many tournaments rarely have much to do with character attributes. Tournaments also stress winning and losing. There is no winning or losing in a real martial art. Real martial art is yielding, not dominating. It is helping others, not winning over others. It is humbly demonstrating life by pure example, not by public displays of strength. Winners often develop incredible egos. The ego usually substantiates a very self existent I in the heart of the person involved. This limits his ability to accept others as his equal and to really generate himself to benefit others. He becomes worried more about himself and of preserving his ego.

The advantages of tournaments are that they promote courage and confidence in the individual. They give a student a chance to examine his own technique in a strange environment. He has the exposure of training and practising techniques on different styles and personalities than he normally is accustomed to in his home training hall. Tournaments can sometimes encourage sportsmanship and respect for one another if they are organized constructively and entered into with proper motivation.

2.15 Five Problems Associated With Organizing A Tournament

There are five points that create difficulty in trying to organize a tournament.

- Full understanding of the art by the public so that participants are not degraded to the level of gladiators.

- Tradition is sometimes endangered by the extreme emphasis on winning or losing or attempting to prove the best style.

- There is a problem to determine method, regulation and system to use.

- Prevention of accidents.

- How to conduct a fair situation which shows the full ability of a competitor based on the art during the competition.

3.1 Diet

We are what we eat.

We should eat foods that are in season, in accordance with what nature produces for us. We should chew our food well and think about what we are eating. It is better to go without food than to quickly gulp down any old thing on the run. If we do not chew our food well we cannot digest properly, therefore we do not get the nourishment from the food because our body does not have the time or the energy to assimilate food eaten in this manner. It simply goes into the intestine where it also causes problems of constipation because it has not been processed properly. Constipation is one of the main factors for all diseases of the body. The blood becomes contaminated when the faecal matter is reabsorbed into the system because it is not discharged properly.

Eating between meals also causes problems of digestion because it also takes at least two hours and often more, for the body to assimilate the food. Piling in more food before the stomach is ready causes an overtaxing of the system and works just like a traffic jam.

We should relax when we eat and enjoy our food.

3.2 Exercise

Modern conveniences weaken all our natural muscle tone and hasten atrophy in the human body.

We should adopt a moderate program of consistent but not strenuous exercise which keeps our muscles toned. Muscle tone is not muscle bulk. Exercises that create bulk in the tissues usually impede circulation of the blood and encourage rigidity in the body. We should all adopt a practical exercise program befitting our abilities and age.

3.3 Breathing

Man can live weeks without food, but he cannot survive more than a few minutes without air.

Air contains the most important essence of energy, not only necessary for survival, but also for correct functioning of the organs. Most people use only one third of their potential to absorb this energy. We should not breathe with the chest but from the navel area. Breath should first inflate the lower belly into the solar plexus, up into the chest and finally into the head. When most people inhale, their lower belly contracts and their chest expands. This physiological movement fills up the top third of the lung and collapses the other two thirds. After many years of this, man's fullest capacity to breathe in air becomes greatly impaired.

People who breathe long and full enjoy long and harmonious lives. Shallow breathing is a sign of sickness, heart condition or nearing death. We should concentrate on our breathing at all times and strive to breathe calmly and deeply in all things that we do. If possible, we should combine long deep breaths with our meditational exercises. This calms the body and mind simultaneously. The best time to do this is at dawn and dusk when the energies of the universe are changing with the sun and the moon. Breathing at this time is very beneficial because the energy given off by the sun at this time is purer and stronger than during the rest of the day. Breath is life, make the most of it.

Meditation is not an exercise for hippies or yogis in the desert. In the context of medicine, it is a prescribed method of relaxation. We should reserve the time often, when we can have a few moments to ourselves and empty the mind of extraneous thoughts. We should breathe deeply and slowly and concentrate on an object.

We can let the mind drift or let the mind meditate on some pleasant thought. Meditation for the common man means consistently making a small space for himself each day. It does not have to be long, only consistent. We should not wait until we are entirely neurotic, saving up for our annual holiday, when we think we will escape.

The same mind and problems will follow us everywhere.

3.4 Fasting

It is difficult to think on a full stomach.

Usually, after we eat we feel sleepy and do not feel like working. This is because the body's energies are engaged in digesting the food. While this is happening the energy that stimulates us to be active is temporarily deficient. Everything slows down. When we are hungry we are usually very speedy. This is because the energy is freely moving all over the body and the energy used by the digestive system is free for our disposal. The organs directly related to food are the stomach and large and small intestine, although all the organs are interrelated when food is in the body. Just as an automobile engine overheats, if we run it too hard and too long, so it is with our digestive system. From time to time it is very advantageous to give it a short rest which helps us to balance our energy. Think for a moment of how often in the day we are engaged either in eating, drinking or going to the toilet. In actual fact, it encompasses a great part of our waking state. If we combine sleeping time with eating, drinking and toilet activities, we would find that over half our life is used before we even start.

Imagine even one day of rest for our digestive system. Fasting is not an extreme idea. All great men have fasted just prior to great spiritual attainment. Our animals as well as ourselves, lose the appetite when feeling ill. Either in sickness or spiritual matters there is a natural mechanism that stops us from eating. Though not to be taken to the extreme, fasting in moderation can be conducive to sound physical and mental well being. Chinese meditation encourages fasting just prior to the change in each season.

3.5 Chinese Medicine and the Martial Artist

Oriental medicine has always worked on the level that an ounce of prevention is worth a pound of cure.

Four principals are outlined in all medical books as the foundation for preventive medicine. These are diet, exercise, meditation and rest. The four must work together equally. Many people pay attention to diet but they sleep at all odd hours. Many people sleep but feel more tired when they get up than before they went to bed. Many people sleep and eat but rarely exercise. The body is just like a door hinge. If oiled it works fine and if left alone it becomes rusty and non-functional. The conscientious balance of these four areas will undoubtedly provide a long life free from ill health or mental agitation.

By becoming proficient in understanding the methods of preventive medicine the Tang Soo Tao student should be able to adjust his lifestyle properly and advise others how to stay healthy as well. Should something happen however, to upset the healthy balance, he should know how to remedy the situation. Also, because there is a great deal of physical exercise and contact in the art of Tang Soo Tao, small mishaps are bound to occur occasionally. What good would it do to take something apart if one couldn't put it back together again. In defense we learn techniques which can dismember or destroy a person in many ways. In medicine we learn how to fix it up again. Neither of these is better than the other. They are complimentary. The extreme sensitivity and awareness developed in training cultivates the finest energy in the learning and understanding of sickness. The Tang Soo Tao combines defense and healing into our most important experiences of existence, i.e. life and death.

As explained previously each of these five elements, metal, water, wood, fire and earth, directly correspond to the five main organs of the body: lungs, kidney, liver, heart and stomach. Therefore if a person's fire element is blazing out of control we must use water to put out the fire. Medically speaking, we must sedate the heat energy and stimulate the kidney in order to produce the water to put out the fire.

The use of moxibustion and herbs are auxiliary aspects which are an integral part of the whole science of acupuncture and Chinese medicine and operate on the same principals.

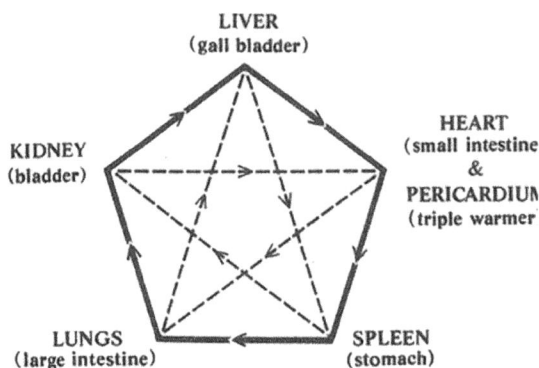

Chinese counterpart of diagram below, showing chi flow.

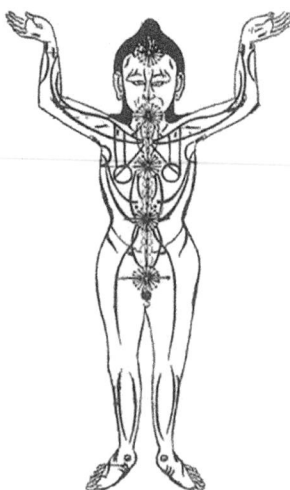

Tibetan medical chart designating chi cultivation areas.

If, for some reason the mainstays of Chinese medicine fall short, the fundamental back-up systems include: acupuncture, moxibustion, massage and herbal remedies. These subjects are pertinent to Tang Soo Tao in that the fundamentals of how they work are exactly the same as the principals of the defence art. In acupuncture for example, we have meridians or highways of energy in which the life force travels. On these highways are various points which can be stimulated or sedated according to sickness in the body. If we acupuncture these points, we have remedial medicine, and if we strike them, we have self defense.

Furthermore, each of the highways in the body are named after one of the five elements.

3.6 Din Mak

No thorough history of Chinese medicine or martial arts is complete without a brief mention of Din Mak theory. Din Mak, commonly referred to as the *Death Touch*, is a method by which the martial artist can cause death or paralysis, instantly, permanently or temporarily, by lightly striking or sometimes merely touching vital energy points on the body.

It is a science based on the periodic circulation of vital energies throughout the major organs.

As explained before, every two hours the vital energies circulate into different organs. There is a particular time in each day when the energy is at an excessive or deficient level in each organ. By understanding the basic flow of the bodies vital forces, the martial artist can ascertain the weakest point of his opponent at any time. By this knowledge he can successfully destroy his opponent without even leaving visible signs. This however, is not the fundamental reason for studying the science. By understanding death, the martial artist can also give life. By understanding where energy is weak in the body, we can also use these points to draw energy into the weak points of an ailing person. This can be done as a medical practice or on the occasion of accidents during training which happen from time to time.

Start
of
cycle
3 a.m.

2 a.m.   4 a.m.

Midnight   6 a.m.

LIVER   LUNG

GALL BLADDER   LARGE INTESTINE

10 p.m.   TRIPLE WARMER   8 a.m.

STOMACH

PERICARDIUM   SPLEEN

8 p.m.   10 a.m.

KIDNEY   BLADDER   SMALL INTESTINE   HEART

6 p.m.   Noon

4 p.m.   2 p.m.

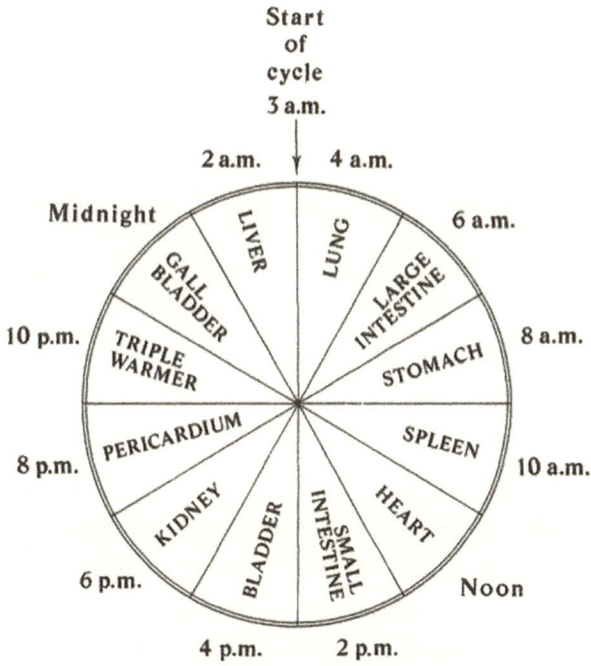

Time clock showing flow of life force.

3.7 Buddhist Meditation and Martial Art

There are two types of meditation of fundamental importance in Buddhist philosophy which relate to a martial artist's meditation. These are Mahayana; and Zen.

Mahayana meditation involves cultivating all activities of the body, speech and mind, not for self gain alone, but for the benefit of all living beings. It is a noble path, difficult to follow, but with indescribable rewards. If we examine closely all things that we see, we can find that nothing we can experience through our senses has a self existent nature. All things are inter-related. Matter can not be created or destroyed, it only changes form.

If we look at a wheel, what really composes the wheel? Is it the spokes? Is it the hub? Is it the round part connecting the two of these? A spoke is not a wheel, a wheel is not a spoke. The combined parts create a wheel.

Such is the case with all things including man.

If we examine ourselves closely, what is a human being? Is he an arm? Is he a leg? Is he a head? The obvious answer is no. If we take the blood from a human being he will die. If we cut out the heart or lungs or any important part, he will die. But though all these things are necessary requirements to keep us alive, none of them can be called a human being. Blood is not a human being, a foot is not a human being. Even that which we cannot see, our soul or spirit, is not the human being.

So as we can see, there is no one single part of any mans make-up that can be called the human being. It is a combination of many things all of which are inter-related, but none of which are self-existent enough as to be called the human being.

If we go one step deeper we can even examine the parts in themselves. Is the blood, for example, self existent by itself? The answer is no. Blood does not exist by itself. It is composed of many elements. It has water, fat, acids and many constituents. Let us examine one of the constituents, water. Is water self existent alone? No, it is composed of atoms, which are composed of protons, neutrons and electrons.

And so it goes on infinitely.

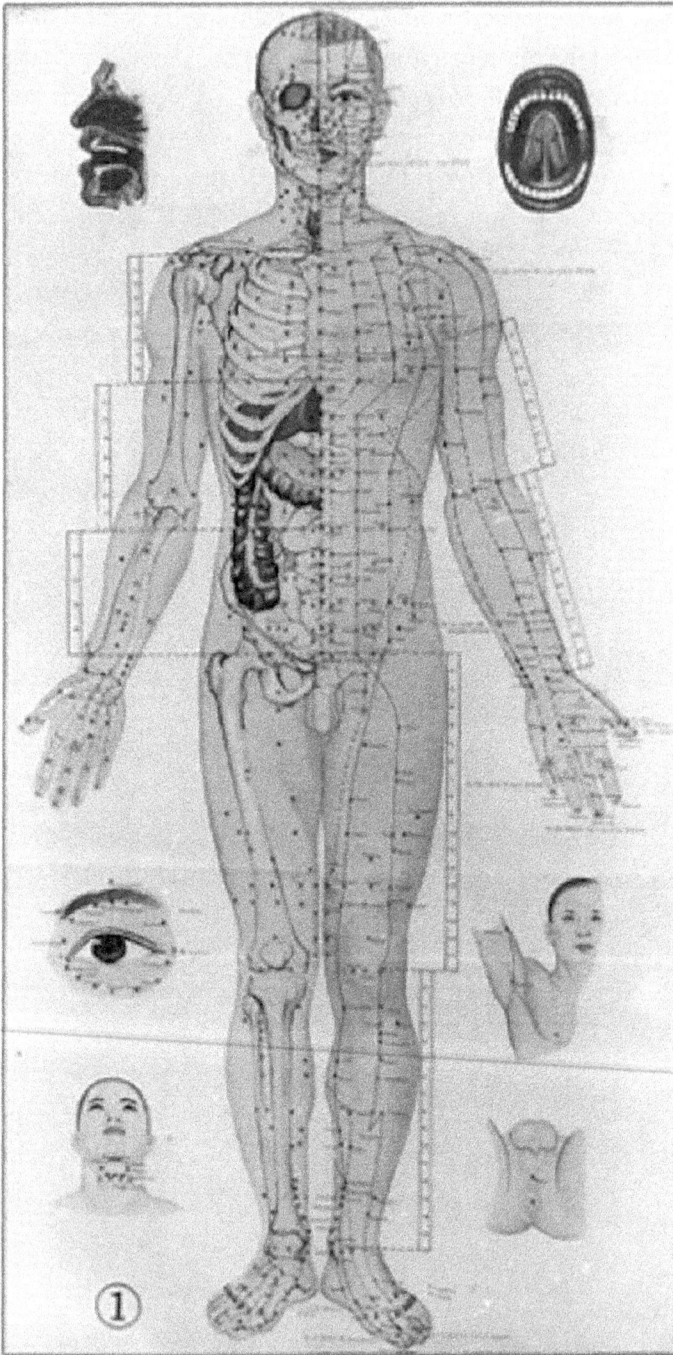

*Charts 1, 2 and 3 illustrating Chinese acupuncture meridians and points used in healing,
Din Mak Kung Fu and meditation.*

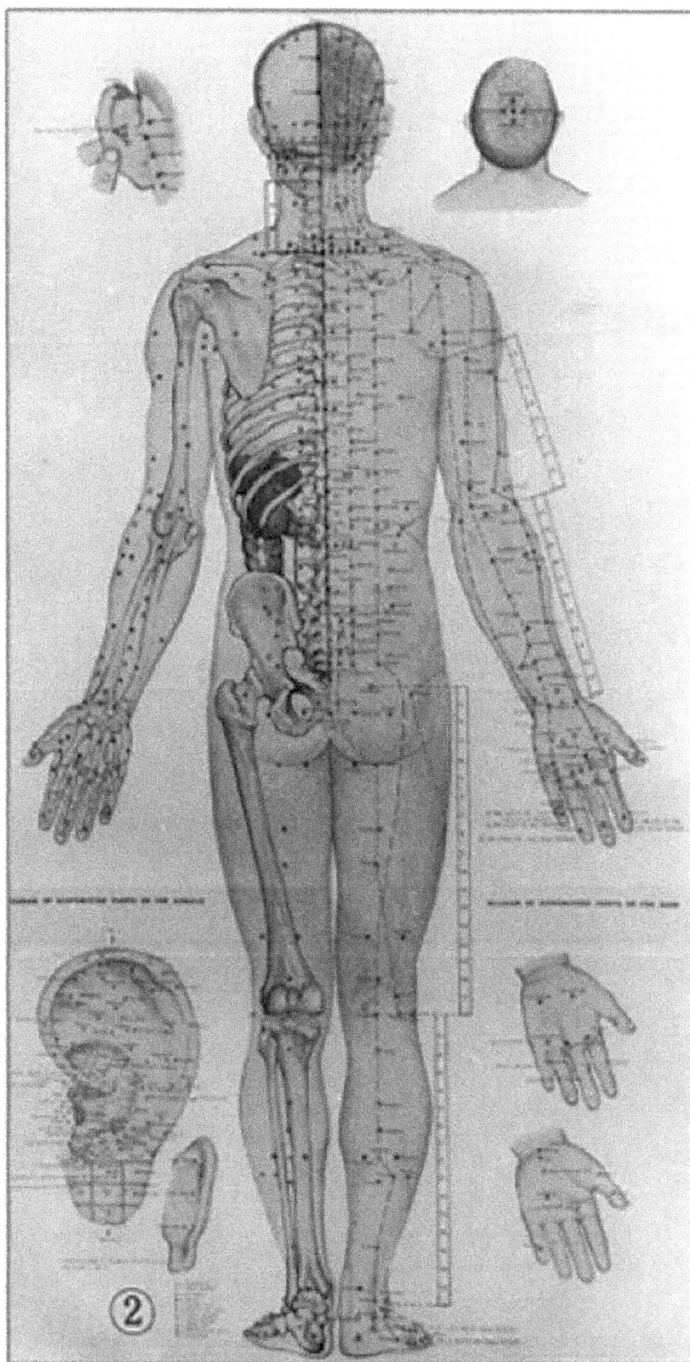

Chart 2: Rear aspect of major meridians

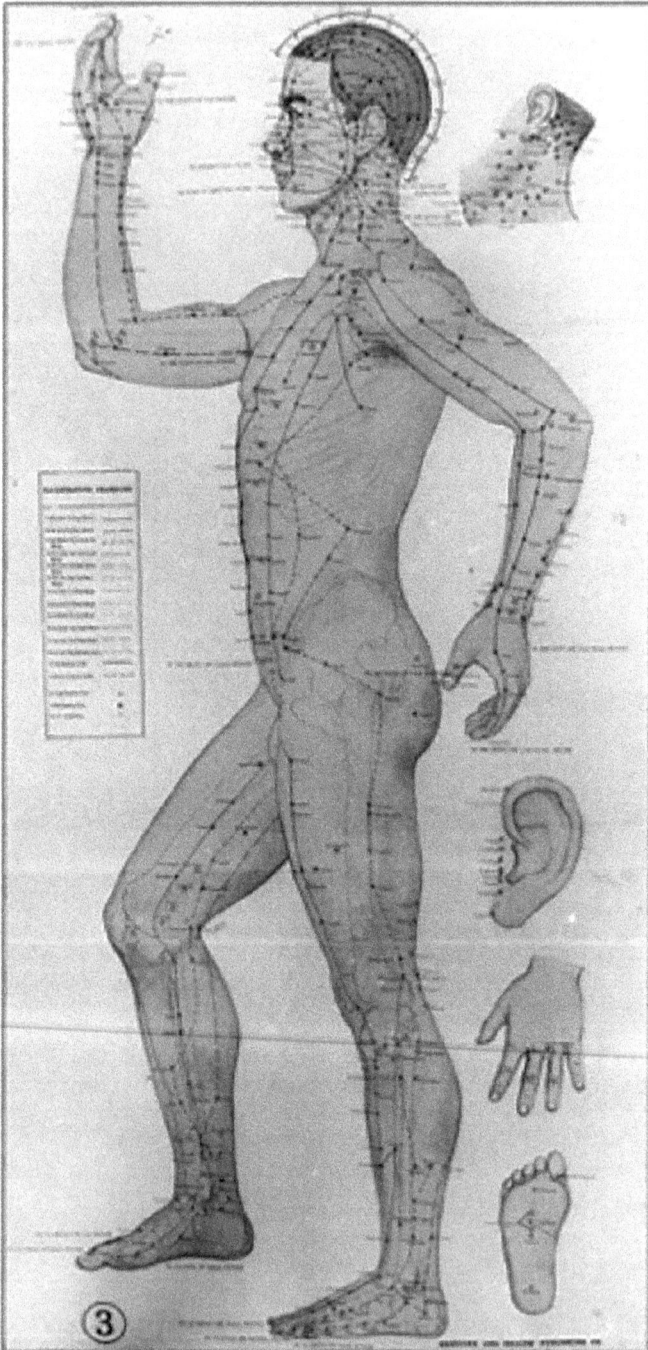

Chart 3: Lateral view

What we can logically determine from these examples is that no matter what we are talking about in our relative world nothing exists inherently of its own nature.

Mahayana means *greater vehicle*. Greater vehicle refers to a greater way of thought. If indeed all things are subject to the laws outlined here, then they must all be subject to a common law of existence. Since all existent phenomena are subject to the same laws of cause and effect and inter-relationships, nothing is independently separate from anything else. Because of this, Mahayana Buddhism encourages mankind not to be driven by greed and hatred, but to love one another in harmony as in accord with the natural law. Self cherishing motivations have no logical foundations. Since all men are equal, why do men always try to define their individuality and set themselves apart from each other? Many people try to set themselves above others. No creature has any desire different to any other, other than to be happy, to spend our lives catering only to our personal needs, whims and desires and ignoring the feelings of others, is a useless, pointless life. The only way to liberation is selflessness and dedication to the ideal of the equality of all mankind and actually all living beings. One who meditates on these points and tries to incorporate them into his life, finds them to be incredibly logical and liberating. By separating ourselves from others, self cherishing lifestyles separate an individual from the rest of mankind. Just as the famous writer John Dunne, expressed 'no man is an island', so too it is with any creature that suffers the delusion of having a self-existent nature. When we work only for ourselves we become like the tributaries of a river when cut-off from the main source after a long drought. The water becomes stagnant, polluted and gives sickness to any creature that drinks from it. It finally evaporates and dries up all together. Let us abhor the idea of self existence and self-cherishing and keep our entire consciousness in the main stream of the universal river.

In order to do this we strive to create all actions for the benefit of all sentient beings through meditation on the Mahayana. This is not unlike *'love thy neighbour as thyself.'* Man's problem is ego of self which is caused by grasping, remedied by wisdom which comes from concentration, which in turn is produced by morality.

3.8 Zen Buddhism

In the world of martial arts, Zen Buddhism is often talked about and expounded as the most prolific part of a martial artists' spiritual development.

Zen talks about the absence of thought, action, desire and of a great emptiness.

Often people think of Zen as having no conscious thought. Because many martial arts men of ancient times were involved with Zen, especially the famous Samurai of Japan, many people relate this aspect of Buddhism to martial arts. Immature martial artists, romantically examine impressive fighting histories of dauntless heroes – they are wrongly impressed and influenced by stories of pugilists who successfully defended themselves against scores of attackers, often killing many of them. The power and mental concentration is impressive, however, this is not the focal point of Zen meditation.

Zen meditation was developed in China and cultivated in Japan, as a method for emptying the mind in order to prepare oneself for the deeper aspects of meditation. It is not an end in itself, but a preparation. Some martial artists historically and of modern times, have sadly mistaken the emptiness of mind with blanking out a person's fear and morality in order to substantiate and rationalize merciless killing. This is entirely wrong and against the true meaning of Zen.

If we try to read a book, watch television, answer the telephone and talk to a friend all at the same time, we are not only scattering our energy but failing to succeed in one of these actions properly. If we want to practise exercise in a room we cannot do so when it is full of chairs, tables and miscellaneous furniture. We must first remove the furniture from the room in order to move about freely. Likewise, in the brightest part of the day we cannot enjoy the light of the sun in a dark room unless we open the blind. We do not have to make any effort to draw in the sunlight, it comes in happily all by itself. All we have to do is open the window. The Zen masters often used the example that the usefulness of a pot is its emptiness. That the sound created by a bell is obtained from the emptiness which lies inside the bell. In the development of mind we must eliminate all obstacles to our training. As in the case of removing the chairs from the crowded room, we must first remove useless distractions from the cluttered mind. Only then can we perceive the clarity of the true nature in the mind. This is the basic attitude of Zen philosophy.

By understanding the true nature of self, through the examination of the true mind, a Zen Buddhist cannot possibly differ from a Mahayana Buddhist. The end result will always be reverence for life and harmony with all creation.

Zen aims at the most direct method for obtaining pure clear insight into the absolute nature of self. Often Zen refers to seeing the original face. Often a Zen master asks his student what was his original face even before his parents were born. This complex riddle often caused a meditator to plunge into the question; the origin of his very existence, Zen masters often urged that unless a man could observe his true face, before he was actually born, he would never be successful in obtaining Enlightenment (Divine Wisdom). To get to the root of this problem, a serious Zen man must examine in depth and detail, the experience of life and death. Experiences of life are relatively tangible but experiences of death are not so easy to examine. A true Zen man, or any good Buddhist, must clearly understand not only how to accept life, but how to die correctly. The art of dying is one of the most important links connecting martial arts and Zen Buddhism. Before we prepare ourselves for death, we must know what happens to us when we die.

3.9 The Death Process and Dissolution of the Elements

Cycle	Factor Dissolving	External Sign	Internal Sign
I	Earth Element	Body becomes very thin, limbs loose; sense that body is sinking under the earth	
	Aggregate of form	Limbs become smaller, body becomes weak and powerless, sight becomes unclear and dark	
	Basic mirror-like wisdom		
	Eye sense	One cannot open or close eyes	
	Colours and shapes	Lustre of body diminishes; one's strength is consumed	
			Mirage-like vision
2	Water Element	Saliva, sweat, urine, blood and regenerative fluid dry greatly	
	Aggregate of feelings	Body consciousness can no longer experience the three types of feelings	
	Basic wisdom of equality	One is no longer mindful of the three types of feelings	
	Ear sense	One no longer hears external or internal sounds	
	Sounds	'Ur' sound in ears no longer arises	
			Smoke or Fog-like vision

3	Fire Element	One cannot digest food and drink	
	Aggregate of Perception	One is no longer mindful of the affairs of close persons	
	Basic wisdom of remembering Individual things	One can no longer remember the names of close persons	
	Nose sense	Inhalation weak, exhalation strong and lengthy	
	Odours	One cannot smell	
			Spark-like vision
4	Wind Element	The ten winds move to the heart; breathing ceases	
	Aggregate of Mental formation	One cannot perform physical actions	
	Basic wisdom of achieving activities	No longer mindful of external worldly activities, purposes and so forth	
	Tongue sense	Tongue becomes thick and short, root of tongue becomes blue	
	Tastes	One cannot experience tastes	
	Body sense and tangible objects	One cannot experience smoothness and roughness	
		In worldly terms, we would say this person is dead.	Dying flame in the distance
5	Eighty conceptions	Winds in right and left channels above heart enter central channel at top of head the white 'drop' that has come from the father and has remained at the crown, begins to come down the central channel towards the heart centre.	
			Clear vacuity filled with white light

6	Mind of white appearance	Winds in right and left channels below heart enter central channel at base of spine now the red 'drop' obtained from our mother, which has remained at about the level of the navel, begins to rise up the central channel towards the heart.	
			Very clear vacuity filled with red light
7	Mind of red increase	Upper and lower winds gather at heart; then winds enter drop at heart	Vacuity filled with thick darkness; then, as if swooning unconsciously
8	Mind of black near-attainment	All winds dissolve into the very subtle life bearing wind in the indestructible drop at the heart	
			Very clear vacuity, the mind of the clear light of death

The Eight Stages or Cycles of Dissolution in the Death Process

This death process is studied and observed by all serious meditators. It is helpful for a meditator along the path to understand his experiences in meditation after they have happened. Intellectual understanding of these without any actual experience of meditating is relatively useless. To understand life is to understand death.

The true object of the meditator in Zen is to live in the absolute all pervading presence of time and space. This means he must be totally involved and aware of death and life simultaneously, at all stages of his practice. Unless he understands where he came from before his life, he will never understand the riddle of his original face. He must go back in the consciousness before the time of his existence.

This is the true death.

After making this journey he must then emerge again from the former self back to the present, inside his present body. Through his meditation the person can actually experience the entire process of death and rebirth before he actually physically dies. Thus he is able to understand the relativity of his own existence to the absolute nature of his own mind.

In comparing the similarities of this form of mind cultivation with Western spirituality we can again refer to the teachings of Christ when he said *'Unless a man be born again, he cannot see the Kingdom of Heaven'*.

Meditation

Three requirements:

1. Meditator

2. Subject of meditating

3. Object of meditating

Self Existence

1. If no meditator, then no object of meditation.

2. If no subject, then no meditator.

3. If no meditator, then no subject.

4. All are non self existent, as are all things.

5. They are void of true nature and true self existence.

6. The true nature of all things is voidness.

7. The larger the bell, the bigger the sound.

3.10 Tantra

Another important path of Mahayana Buddhism is an area called Tantra. Tantra has two main methods. First is the conversion of and sublimation of all the energies of the body. This is exactly the same as principles and methods outlined elsewhere in this book. The second method of Tantra is for the practitioners to use their desires and attachments as a path to self liberation by which they find that what the God man searches for is really in the self.

Meditators learn to use the energies of lust, greed, hatred, fear and anger, which arise from desire and self cherishing motivation. The essence of these energies are extracted and turned into good. This approach is significantly different from other religions, which promote only righteous thought, word and action, but usually give insufficient method to accomplish this virtue and even less to overcome the vices and temptations of life along the path.

The Tantric method of turning a weak point into a strong one, has something highly in common with the ways of martial virtue. Many people first take up training in a martial arts school because of fears and inadequacies in themselves. There are people, not few in number, who want to learn to fight and to learn martial arts for evil purposes to gratify their more base desires.

Most people who begin training have no thoughts of higher spiritual nature, nor do they want any. If they did, a Karate or Kung-Fu school would be the first place on earth they would go to look. Probably the single most magical aspect of martial arts training is that although people come to learn how to be tough or to handle themselves in any situation, by the time they have gained the ability to do this, the initial thoughts, desires and motivations for joining are usually long gone.

Instead, they find themselves engaged in higher levels of thinking and life style, even to the point of questioning basic values they have been raised on. This occurrence is so strong, it happens so naturally, that even if a person fought against it, it would gradually seep into his character anyway.

This is the fundamental importance and magic of both the Tantra and martial virtue; to change gross base motivations to ideals of high worth and to discover truth by self-realization.

A tantric practitioner.

4.1 Meditation in the Training Hall

It is difficult for a beginner student to understand why he should sit down and do nothing when his objective for joining a martial arts school is to do plenty of something! Because the art is so complex and involved, it is ridiculous and sometimes even dangerous, to imagine trying to begin to learn the art when the mind is not concentrated properly on the subject.

Basic meditation before class is designed to relax the mind, filter out distracting thoughts and consolidate the wayward energies of the daily activities engaged in before coming to class.

The first and most important martial art movement taught to all students.

Students practising sun and moon meditations of Yin Yang.

The student is encouraged to sit with his back erect, his neck straight and mouth closed. The tongue should be resting behind the two front teeth touching the upper palate. Eyes partially or fully closed and gazing towards the centre of the nose and slightly downwards.

In kneeling position, the heels must be pushing against the top of the buttocks and in cross legged position the left heel should press to the inside groin. The arms should be slightly bowed with the right hand resting on top of the left at the centre of the navel.

(There are several Mudras or hand positions common to sitting meditation. Outlined here is only one. Students should practise whatever is demonstrated by the instructor.)

The meditator should focus his breath in the lower abdomen and visualize a white dot. In the forehead he should visualize a red dot. With a long inward breath he should raise the white dot towards the heart centre, while breathing to the top of the head and raising the breath up from the base of the spine. With an outward breath, slow and long, he should imagine the red dot in his forehead floating down towards the heart centre and meeting the white one. This simple meditation has very profound effects to relax the nervous system, produce one point concentration and to activate the psychic energies of the body.

The postures are designed to stimulate circulation of blood and energy. Sitting in a proper meditation position increases our concentration ability and the harmonious balance of the body functions by 500%. This posture is so profound that this begins when the meditator sits down even before he begins the actual meditation. The visualizations are symbolic of the sun and the moon which are the opposite coordinates of our everyday experiences. The red and the white are also symbolic of the blood of the mother and the sperm of the father which is the basis for not only our existence but the existence of all life force. Physiological symptoms gained from meditation provide relaxation, added strength and prepare the serious martial art student for the severe disciplines of training and guard against the fears of injury and death in actual combat.

When sitting meditation is finished, the martial art practitioner begins his physical training involving forms, basic motions and one-step exercises as well as free fighting. The format of physical training is actually a continuation of the meditation he has entered into while sitting.

In order to train, learn and function correctly, whether in actual motion or in utter stillness the students' mind must be calm, relaxed and one pointed in concentration. Many students often comment on how relaxed they are at the end of a training session. Sometimes they are quite surprised to find that although they have spent two hours in a completely exhausting physical workout, they are not tired. Often times, they comment on feeling tired before class and in spite of the hard physical discipline are more energetic after practice than before they started. This is because during normal everyday activities our mind and energy is scattered in a thousand directions at one time. This results in tension and mental as well as physical exhaustion. During training, a student's entire energies are concentrated on his practice. The training is usually so intense that even if he wanted to he is unable to concentrate on anything else.

This one-point concentration consolidates all the energies of the body into one force for a certain period of time. This concentration, regardless of physical expenditure of energy, results in a calmer more energised body as a whole.

After class, again, all students sit down to meditate. It is at this time that we receive the benefits of all our work. Sometimes, an entire class of two hours of sweat and blood is conducted to give the student the experience of a few seconds of blissful experience with his inner mind. It is sometimes a glimpse of formless time and space. For some it is only a relaxed feeling of peace. Regardless of the experience, students always leave each and every practice session with a feeling of satisfaction and accomplishment. Each training session is an individual experience which when over leaves a student with a closer realization about himself through his art.

In relation to mind, I would like to take the liberty to quote one of the great Indian Saints of our time; Ramana Maharshi.

'Man longs for perfection in finitude and permanence of happiness. He seeks to find his real nature, his true self. Tired of seeking outwards he turns inward and finds it within. This turning inward and seeking, are intellectual functions. After long continuous practice, the intellect discovers that it is unable to function by some higher power, which now abides all alone. The purpose of the intellect is to realize its dependence on a higher power. It must annihilate itself before the goal is reached. With firm conviction, one must persist and gain direct experience, remembering that intellectual conviction is one thing and realization is another. Everyday life is part of our spiritual practice. As one practices, one experiences greater friendliness, bliss or service, a strong assurance that one is in the keeping of some higher power.'

True mind has no duality – no subject/object relation. Mind can only reflect itself when observing other things. Slowly eliminating duality the mind will automatically exhaust delusions and defects. The discipline of body, speech and action is to control distracting phenomena in order to give mind proper conditions to work.

Leaving all I shall be part alone,

yet though not having understood this

I have committed various kinds of evil

For the sake of friends and foes.

My foes will become nothing,

my friends will become nothing,

I too shall become nothing,

likewise all shall become nothing.

Just like a dream experience,

Whatever I do or have

Will only become a memory.

Whatever has passed will not be seen again.

4.2 The Instructor

Although supersonic airliners can take us all over the world, it is useless for us to sit behind the controls and learn how to take-off, if we don't know how to land.

The intricate art and philosophy of Tang Soo Tao is impossible to begin without a proper instructor. Just as you would not like to get into an airplane with a drunk pilot, it would likewise be a disadvantage to begin Tang Soo Tao practice with an incompetent instructor. The instructor is of utmost value and importance to students at any and all levels. Without a proper instructor, it is difficult to learn anything quickly, if at all. Because the subject is intricate, the martial arts instructor must possess unusual qualities, not necessary for instructors of other fields.

An instructor must have a total understanding of the level of the art form he is teaching.

In olden times, a disciple had to search far and wide for a knowledgeable instructor. If he found one he faced another problem; being accepted. Often times, disciples were forced to endure great hardships in order to prove their sincerity to train. Only after he was totally convinced of the sincerity of the student would the master consent to teach. Once accepted, a long difficult road was assured. The true secrets of a martial art were once only handed down from father to son, or from master to student. A master usually picked one, sometimes two and at the very most three students to pass on the entire lineage of his art. Students were rarely taught much at any one time, but were rationed knowledge like sips of water over many years.

Although this is not quite the case today, there are still some obstacles a student must overcome to locate a good instructor.

The instructor must be able to communicate his art to students at all levels of training.

This is as difficult today as it was in ancient times and perhaps more so with the degeneration of martial arts. To find a good teacher we must look for certain qualities. A good teacher should have all the practise and experiences every aspect of training he is trying to teach us. This knowledge in turn should have been passed on to him by his instructor.

The energy cultivated in this way helps to preserve the spirit and heritage of martial art systems. It also aids in maintaining proper standards. Needless to say, it is seriously lacking in many schools of modern times.

A good instructor must understand the physical and mental progression of ideals at every stage of the art. He must be patient, kind, responsible and well disciplined. His judgement must be fair and correct at all times. A good instructor must have perfect experience through training and meditation in all aspects of the art he is instructing. He must be totally dedicated and willing to sacrifice himself for the art. He should be willing to do anything in his power to aid his pupils, inside or outside of class.

A proper instructor should be a shining example of the discipline and philosophy expounded in martial art. Through discipline, an instructor should be able to conduct a class which elicits discipline from love and respect, not from fear or regimentation.

An instructor must be responsive to the needs of his students and have a keen sense in judging the abilities and attitudes of others. He should always give the student what he needs, not what the student wants and must have the ability to know the difference.

In teaching class, he must show no favouritism towards any student but at the same time should be able to extend an energy to assist those of limited ability. He must come to understand each and every student's individual personality and be able to vary the classes so they suit all of the students.

Martial art instructors must have an impeccable faith in life and a strong desire to help others. They must be able to instantly pinpoint the most minute error on the part of each student. They must understand when to correct and when to teach.

A mindful instructor should see the problems of students inside and outside of class and aid them accordingly.

He should be able to gauge the level of progress, in direct proportion to the ability of the student and teach accordingly. Any instructor must be a power package of inexhaustible energy. His presence should command respect and admiration inside and outside of the training hall.

In addition to all these points, a qualified instructor should have some formal instruction himself in basic first aid and medical experience to handle any unforeseen accidents or problems.

From personal training and experience, a good instructor must be able to extract the maximum output from all students at any time. Failure to do this can result in disrespect and a decline in spirit. No instructor should ever put money or quantity of students before his art. The quality of a student and the self respect for himself and the art must always take priority with any decisions dealing with these matters.

A beginner entering the path of Tang Soo Tao is a foreigner in a strange land. The instructor is the guide with the road map. Though he can show you the quickest and the best way to reach the objective, the instructor cannot walk the path for you. Like all real experiences in life, the real understanding of Tang Soo Tao must be discovered alone, as in the old saying, *Born alone, die alone.*

In all aspects, the advice of the instructor should be strictly adhered to. If we do not follow the guide with the road map, we will undoubtedly become lost.

About half way down the path, some people ignore the guide and foolishly run off looking for a better way. This is akin to trying to fly the airplane after learning only how to take-off and not to land. The instructor's teachings should be followed unquestionably. To doubt an instructor is to doubt the fundamental roots of the art. If we do not respect others we cannot respect ourselves, nor can we ever expect anyone to respect us. An instructor holds the position for a very definite reason. He has earned his position by endless hours of practise and dedication required to reach the level of his position. Because he is human, there are apt to be times when he could possibly make a few mistakes. Mistakes in the life of an instructor are negligible. They should be overlooked and forgotten by students. In a student/disciple relationship, even when an instructor is wrong, he is right. What is important is not the issue, but the discipline and the respect for authority. We must have faith for our instructor at all times and overlook any apparent weaknesses. We must always appreciate his rank and remember that the good qualities of what we have learned incredibly outweigh a few minor discrepancies that he may not have yet had time to work out himself. Often times he hasn't had time to work out minor points, either in technique or philosophy, because he is giving his time to the students. If we don't feel this way we shouldn't be there and instead should be looking for another instructor.

An instructor is not a friend; nor can he ever be. He is an instructor. From the time a person walks into the class until the time he is no more, the relationship between the instructor and the student must remain the same. It may deepen, but should never become distorted. To ingratiate yourself with your teacher is of no use for the development of your art. An impartial instructor will take no notice of this kind of attitude and it will only serve as a distraction to your training. This does not mean that you should not be friendly towards your instructor or that he should not show a friendly attitude towards you. He should be happy, friendly and courteous. If he is not, then the art is working against and not for him. We should not however confuse happiness, friendliness and kindness with a smiling face and sweet compliments. This is not the way of martial virtue. An instructor may be jovial all the time or may appear grumpy and sometimes he can be a combination of both. This has no bearing on the sincerity with which an instructor teaches. People who are looking for smiling faces, compliments and good buddies, are not seriously interested in developing the qualities outlined in this book.

We can never know the instructor's primary motivation for extending any attitude towards us. We should always believe we will get from him what we need and deserve and not expect to hear ego pleasing things. An instructor is not your friend. To treat him differently from the point already outlined is to take from him the vital tool of his trade which he uses to instill in the student the necessary traits befitting a true martial artist. It destroys the energy with which he can create in the student, the drive to be successful in his endeavour.

4.3 The Training Hall

There are no intrinsically redeeming qualities of any building.

A building is just an empty space with a roof and walls. If we go into different sorts of buildings however, we encounter different types of feelings. Everyone is familiar with the energy they feel when they go inside a hospital. If we walk into a newspaper office, we are overcome by busyness. Many people have expressed the feeling of serenity when walking into an old church or cathedral. In all of these places, it is not the place, or the building or what we find materially that gives us these feelings; this is the energy of the people and the work. In the church, one can hardly have attachment to a lifeless statue, but the energy with which the church was constructed and the work and feelings of the people inside create the vibration which effects our feelings.

So, as we can see that the feeling of a place can have an influence on our energy, this is especially true in Tang Soo Tao.

The To-jang plays an important role in the life of a martial artist. Roughly translated To-jang means *training hall* but this is a gross understatement. The To-jang is the place where we come to develop the physical and mental spirit of the Tao.

Any person who has trained knows the feeling of walking into a martial arts institute. It is unlike that of any other place.

A student must regard his training hall with a respectful attitude as a source of energy and learning. The person's attitude towards his training centre should be so strong that even when he nears it on his way to practice, his thoughts of the day quickly fade and his mind and attitude turn towards discipline. Regardless of whether it's only a high school gym, storage area or a proper institute, the To-jang should be regarded with respect and love for the time that it is used. To set this attitude is to create an impressive atmosphere which is conducive to practice and essential for learning.

Respect and conduct towards the training area (temporary or permanent), should be second only to that of the instructor.

4.4 General Rules for Class

In order to co-ordinate any activity it is necessary to have order and discipline, otherwise everything will be in chaos.

This is certainly important in Tang Soo Tao when we are practising the practical application of potentially dangerous defense techniques on one another. To avoid any injury or disturbances of any kind, we must follow certain rules.

Traditional formalities in class.

1. Entering the To-jang

Students entering the To-jang (training hall) either in Tobok (training uniform) or in street clothes, shall salute the flags and bow to the instructor as soon as they enter the gym. This should be done without exception. Students do not have to wait for the instructor to acknowledge the bow if he is busy.

2. Bowing

Bowing is a sign of respect.

It is a custom and a ritual of the countries from which we received the arts. To disregard tradition is to disregard the spirit of martial art. When bowing to a flag, one's feet should be together, left hand by the side and the right hand in a fist covering the heart. Bowing to an instructor or senior, both hands are at the side with the eyes gazing down. Bowing should always be done with respect and thoughtful action, not hastily, as a routine.

Beginning students should not regard bowing as part of 'the trip'. When bowing to the flag we should regard it as something which represents the philosophy of the goodness taught in martial art.

Although the flag is oriental in origin, it is not there to represent any country. We should not mistake bowing to the flag as pledging our allegiance to any country. We bow to what the flag represents, which is the ideal of Tang Soo Tao.

3. Opening the Class

1) Students will line up according to rank and seniority. The highest ranking member will be on the right.

- Seniority is determined by belt colour of the student.
- In cases of students with the same belt level, the student who has trained in the school longest is considered senior.
- If this seniority is the same, then the senior is determined by age.
- In cases of male and female of the same belt level, the male will always take the senior position.

2) The instructor will take position in front, centre of the class.

3) The highest ranking member of the class will call the commands.

- Turn to salute the flag.
- Bow to the instructor.
- Meditation.

During the Class

1. Proper respect and discipline will be maintained at all times and all rituals will be performed in the proper manner. When the master instructor of the school enters the Tojang, the instructor on the floor or the highest ranking member of the class should call everyone to attention and have the class bow. After this respect has been paid, the class should immediately return to training.

2. When a student comes late to class he should wait until he has been recognized by an instructor then approach him, bow and receive permission to enter the class.

3. When a student must leave the gym during training he should first receive permission from the instructor.

4. If a student has a question, he must first refer to a senior member. If a senior cannot answer the question he should then be referred to the instructor. A chain of commands should exist and not be broken without sufficient reason. A student should never approach an instructor unless he has something important to discuss.

5. There should be no unnecessary noise in the To-jang or any activities unrelated to training.

6. Students should remain silent, especially during forms and free-fighting.

7. Absolutely no smoking at any time.

8. Students seated on the side lines shall remain still, so as not to disturb others on the floor.

9. Students are not permitted to chew gum.

10. All jewellery must be removed before class.

11. Toenails and fingernails must be clipped and trimmed to avoid injury.

12. Students should be clean and showered before coming to class.

13. Any student who uses alcohol within two hours of training time will not be permitted to train. If he comes to the training hall he will be severely reprimanded.

14. No students should train under the influence of any drugs.

15. Students and instructors should have clean tidy uniforms.

16. Students and instructors should use proper terminology in practice.

17. No student should seek instruction in any technique unrelated to his belt level.

18. Students who have trained in other arts should not practise them before the formal class begins. This causes confusion to other students.

19. Any student who has trained and obtained a grade in another art, will be permitted to wear his belt as a guest in the school for a grace period of six weeks. After that time he must join the school and must wear the level of belt appropriate to his ability to perform techniques in the style of Tang Soo Tao.

20. One should never lose self control or patience. Before and after exercises and combat, the student should turn around, adjust his uniform and make the correct respects to his opponent and/or instructor.

Closing the Class

1. Students should line up by seniority and rank, the highest on the right.

2. The instructor should be centred up front.

3. The highest ranking member will call the commands.

   a. Turn to salute the flag.
   b. Bow to the instructor.
   c. Meditation.

4. At the end of meditation, students should create the symbol of the flag with their hands on the floor and say thank you to the instructors and all the fellow students they have trained with. After this they should leave quietly and discreetly and bow when leaving the hall.

Meditation

While seated on the floor members should sit with their backs straight, necks straight, eyes closed and hands in the proper position as demonstrated by the instructor. Tongue should be behind the two front teeth and mouth closed. If sitting on the knees, the buttocks should rest firmly on the feet with space of one to two fist lengths between the knees. If cross legged, the student should sit with the left leg tucked under the groin with the right leg resting on top of the left calf. If this is not possible, any comfortable position which keeps the back straight, is permissible.

The student should always pay attention to all the details explained by the instructor in regard to the meditation. It should always be remembered that meditation is an integral part of a martial artists' experience and training. The body dies but the spirit does not. Without the cultivation of proper spirit the practise of Tang Soo Tao or any other martial art becomes mere exercise that is no different than washing the dishes or sweeping the floor. The cultivation of spirit in the life of a martial artist is of utmost importance at all times.

Ten Points of Character Training

1. Every member should always seek truth and practise it.

2. Every member should always promote the highest moral character through the training of Tang Soo.

3. Every member should respect and obey his parents, teachers and superiors.

4. Every member should love his country and help in the community.

5. Every member should develop confidence and humility and practise them both inside and outside of class.

6. Every member should always do his best to promote intellectual understanding.

7. Every member should not hesitate to sacrifice himself for justice.

8. Every member should do his utmost for the development and spread of his art, universally.

9. Every member should develop endurance and be calm and humble in mind.

10. Every member should remember that the ultimate purpose of Tang Soo Tao is to promote physical and mental growth.

Basic Points for Practice

The following are excerpts from points outlined by the author's Korean instructor, Mr. Hwang Kee. Mr. Hwang Kee's points were so thorough that it was difficult for the author to compose anything more complete. So they are presented as received.

Reverence for life is as important as offense and defense. A martial artist has the obligation to protect all forms of life, even that of an enemy. Reverence for nature, respect for beauty and rightness of action are primary goals of training.

Five Requisites

1. Oneness with nature

2. Complete awareness of environment.

3. Experience.

4. Conscience.

5. Culture.

Emphasis

1. Reverence for nature.

2. Physical control.

3. Courtesy.

4. Modest heart.

5. Thankful heart.

6. Self sacrifice.

7. Cultivation of courage.

8. Chastity, or moderation of appetite.

9. Strength outside, mildness inside.

10. Endurance.

11. Reading ability.

Ten Points of Faith on Mental Training

1. Be loyal to your country.

2. Be obedient to your parents.

3. Be lovable between husband and wife.

4. Be co-operative between brothers.

5. Be faithful between friends.

6. Be respectful to your elders.

7. Be faithful between teacher and student.

8. Be discreet in killing.

9. Never retreat in battle.

10. Always finish what you start.

Five Physical Development Requisites

1. Contact with natural surroundings.

2. Contact with diverse physical conditions.

3. Suitable nourishment.

4. Suitable rest.

5. Emphasis

    a. Vocal exhalation for thoracic strength (Ki-aup)

    b. Eyeline of sight

    c. Continuous balance during movement

    d. Flexibility

    e. Correct muscle tone for maximum power

    f. High and low speed techniques

    g. Exactness of techniques

    h. Adjustment for proper distance

    i. Proper breathing for endurance

    j. Conditioning of body limbs

Attitude Required for Training

1. Purpose for training should be cultivation of mental and physical character.

2. Sincerity is necessary.

3. Effort is necessary.

4. Consistent practice schedule.

5. Do one's best.

6. Train with good spirit.

7. Obey without question the word of instructors and seniors. Look and learn.

8. Don't be overly ambitious. Pay attention to every aspect of training. Get instruction step-by-step on new forms and techniques. Try to conquer feelings of idleness, depression or mental agitation.

9. Cleanliness is desired after practice is finished.

Characteristics of Tang Soo

External displays of power are only outward signs of mental power achieved by inward working of the body. The real purpose of training is to develop spirit and pride of a martial artist. We should constantly think of justice, effort and faith in mental training and cultivate this through training. In attack and defense we use scientifically applied punches, kicks, chops and evasive action, which fully utilise virtually all parts of the body.

1. It is natural and reasonable to practise Tang Soo as a martial art.

2. It is a good practise for mental and physical well being.

3. You can practise anywhere and it is inexpensive.

4. You can practise individually or in groups.

5. Anyone can learn the art with effort and faith.

6. It develops your body and sense of balance.

7. No external objects are required in order to practise.

8. Tang Soo Tao is an instinct unique to man, eternal and inseparable to the human body.

4.5 The Belt System

The awarding of belts is to encourage the student and serves as a sign of his progress. Advantages of being upgraded are:

1. It serves as a sign of progress.

2. Is an encouragement to the student.

3. Is an incentive to fellow students.

4. Also it is encouraging to the instructor.

5. It establishes seniority.

The disadvantages of the belt system are:

1. It encourages jealousy and rivalry among students.

2. It bolsters the ego.

3. It can produce a false sense of achievement.

Any upgrading of a student, big or small, should produce a sense of accomplishment but not encourage a lack of humility. If a student passes his test he should not be satisfied and stop there. He should treat a new belt as another small step along the path of his training. He should regard his belt level, however menial, with respect and authority.

Students are graded on three levels. Character development, natural achievement and physical ability. All people are different. People who practise Tang Soo Tao vary in age, sex and ability. It would be unfair to judge them all equally.

Receiving a black belt is a rewarding experience. Shown here are the new black belt awards presented by guest Tibetan Lama, Ratto Rinpoche, spiritual advisor to the Tang Soo Tao School.

Each student is expected to perform basic physical motions to the best of his personal ability. They are not judged in comparison to anyone else.

With each belt level a student is expected to improve in character and technique. From term to term, the student is expected to consistently develop in character and technique according to his capability. It is quite obvious to some students, especially younger ones, that their physical adeptness is more superior than others.

Sometimes, students think because they can do a technique better than someone else, that they should have a position higher in the class. This is rarely valid. We must respect each other for our weaknesses and strengths and for how hard a person tries.

A person gains seniority from practise, physical technique and time in the school. Consistent attendance is an absolute must. Without proper attendance even a person who can easily pick up the physical aspects of the art lacks the psychological conditioning which comes from consistent and diligent practise.

Sometimes, when free-fighting a lower belt student occasionally is able to get a technique in on his senior. Immature students sometimes erroneously regard this as making them equal to their senior. This is against all principles of seniority and common decency. A person who thinks this way not only is not equal with the other person but does not even deserve the level of belt that he is, or the privilege of practising with a senior in the first place. We must respect all others for the efforts they have put into their practice.

We must not only appreciate what we can see.

As has been explained many times, all material things must pass away. All the physical technique in the world will not help a person at the time of death. All the best technique will not give happiness to anyone. What will bring happiness, what will help us to face our problems with conviction and courage is the spirit we cultivate from the practise, not the practise itself. Every senior has a special quality to teach any junior. We must always respect our seniors. If we do not respect others we can never expect others to respect us.

Without these principles there is no martial art.

There is another interesting point in relation to free-fighting among juniors and seniors. Often a junior's technique is so inferior to that of the senior that the senior has absolutely nothing to work with. He can either knock the junior out or strike the junior so hard as to render his techniques non-functional. A senior cannot gain much from this and out of his kindness usually does not choose to be so harsh. A junior must learn to appreciate greatly this painful compassion on the part of his senior. A senior has cultivated a substantially higher level of control than his junior. The junior in turn is much less able to co-ordinate his hands and feet. Because of this it is usually the senior, not the junior who sustains the worst *off the wall* mishaps.

Breaking technique is never practised but is a requirement when taking 1st Dan grading.

He can either wipe out his junior or help him learn to spar. Since there are few redeeming qualities of the first choice seniors usually adopt the latter. In order to do this a senior allows himself to be a target dummy for the wild unrefined skills of his subordinates, while he himself controls his own physical actions with utmost care.

A junior should never underestimate a senior and always be thankful that he has someone to work with who knows more than him. It is always more conducive to learning to work with someone more experienced than ourselves.

Belt gradings are given in ten basic stages for the beginner student. These stages begin at 10th gup white belt and progress to 1st gup red belt.

Gup testings are held every three months. Relative to proper attendance a student is allowed to gup test once each term.

For higher levels of training after advanced levels of red belt, the time required in each grade ranges from six months to four years between gradings.

The minimum time required for a student to reach the beginning stage of black belt is three to five years.

At black belt level the belt level is referred to as Dan.

A 1st Dan black belt must remain in that grade for a minimum of two to four years before taking 2nd Dan test.

A 2nd Dan must remain in that grade for a minimum of two to four years to take a 3rd Dan test.

A 3rd Dan must remain in that grade four years to take a 4th Dan test.

At 4th Dan martial artist should be at the master level. By this time he should have learned and perfected all physical characteristics as well as the basic philosophy of his art.

Various schools have all sorts of levels of Dan gradings. Any rank after the rank of 4th Dan is given in regard to what a person has done to promote the art universally. All significant developments from this master level onwards are on the levels of personal research, psychic awareness and spiritual development.

Meaning of Belts

White	White is significant in almost any culture or time, as a sign of purity. It is an absolute colour. The beginning student knows nothing and because of this has done nothing in relation to martial art. In this respect he is pure, untainted and open to receive proper instruction. White is also the sign of male creative energy the beginning of life.
Purple	According to ancient mythology purple was the colour of the under-world. At one time creatures were believed to live at the centre of the earth. There were many kinds of spirits who ruled all life beneath the earth.
Green	Green is a sign of life. As we rise from the centre of the earth to the surface, we find growth. We emerge from darkness into life. It is a sign of happiness, youth and growth.
Blue	Blue is the colour of the sky. As our mind and consciousness develop our thoughts are lifted upwards towards heaven.
Red	Red is the colour of the sun. It is beyond the sky. The sun is the life force in our solar system. Without the sun we would die. Red is the colour of female creative energy. Red is also the colour of the fire element which lies in the heart. The red belt is the beginning of an advanced level of training that requires a strong heart and a firm will.
Black	Black is the opposite of white. It is the complimentary factor to the beginning stage. At night all becomes black. Just as the coming of the night signifies the end of the day, so does this belt level signify the end of a student's basic stages of development. Black is the colour in the universe which signifies endless time and space. It is the beginning of the end.

4.6 Basic Movement

Success in any form of learning depends on a firm foundation. If a man builds a house with a weak foundation it will never last or survive a bad storm.

The cultivation and perfection of basic technique is of paramount importance to any level of martial arts training. The development of basics takes constant, consistent practise for many years. Basic motions promote balance, coordination, power and fundamental understanding of defense motions.

All basic movements are scientifically designed to produce maximum power with minimum effort. They must be repeated thousands of times in order to vaguely understand how they work. Weight, speed, distance, timing and breath are all essential factors co-ordinating basic motions. Careful detail must be observed, such as stance, hand positioning and poise, in executing any basic technique. Basic motions include co-ordination and defense movements of hand and foot in union with stances.

Hand Motions

There are two kinds of hand motions, closed and open. Together they comprise dozens of various methods of blocking and striking. Closed hand motions involve methods of striking with front or back fist, to specified points of the anatomy. The power must be concentrated at one small point of the striking area, not the entire surface.

This we call *focus*.

Focus in martial arts technique is similar to the effect produced by being struck with a pointed end of a knife or slapped with the flat edge of the blade. The power lies in the concentration of energy into a small concentrated force. A beginning student learns three fist motions: lunge punch, reverse punch and backfist. Though they can be used in a myriad of ways the fundamental principals of the punches remain the same.

Open Hand

Open hand is used in striking or blocking with either inside or outside of the hand. There are more varieties of open hand technique than closed hand technique.

Application of open hand technique.

Foot Techniques

There are dozens of varieties of foot techniques. Of these, four are of utmost importance to the beginning student. They are front kick, side kick, round kick, and back kick.

The quality of the power displayed in the kick is the same as the hand. Proper focus, timing and form, are essential in the execution of foot techniques. Foot techniques involve more balance than hand techniques. Though the legs have more power, they are slower and require more co-ordination and concentration than do the hands.

Some students are quite natural to kicking and for others it is extremely difficult. Kicking can be effective in defense but it can also be used to develop better punching habits. The person who can balance himself perfectly when kicking can use this skill equally well when developing punching techniques. There are no techniques, hand or foot, that are practised for the uniqueness of that technique. While practising any technique in martial art we are simultaneously developing certain qualities which effect all our techniques. Sometimes, motions lack appropriate application but all of them are conducive to the poise, balance, focus and concentration necessary for all Tang Soo movements.

Three basic stances to settle the one-point.

Stances

Of all the stances there are three of fundamental importance. These are forward stance, side or horse stance and back or cat stance. These three stances incorporate the scope of all the dynamics required to defend from any position at any angle. (Stances as well as feet and hand motions are innumerable. The ones mentioned here are basic and fundamental to all martial systems).

Posture

Basic posture should be erect, well centred, balanced and natural. A person should be able to move and change stances without wavering or failing. Perfect stance is necessary to execute any hand or foot technique. The coccyx, backbone and the neckbone must always align to promote proper chi flow.

Defence Positions

There are three positions of defence which cover the area of the human body. These are low levels, high levels and medium levels. Perfect understanding of these three positions enables a person to successfully develop beginning or advanced techniques at any stage of the practice. By combining the three defense areas of low, high and middle with the three defense stances we can begin to adjust ourselves to meet any attack, from any angle.

Three basic blocks for co-ordination.

Forms

Forms are the heart of the martial art. There are co-ordination forms based on man's movements, animals forms, free forms and even mind forms. The forms contain the philosophy, meditation and metaphysical yogas inherent in martial art. They are the spirit and nucleus of creativity. They contain every single martial art technique conceivable in the realm of human defense. The secret to forms rests in endless dedication to their development and proper interpretation of the techniques and philosophies they represent. Forms help a student appreciate his basic training. The form is not an end in itself however. To adhere too strictly to form can actually block a student's progress. The form is only to be perfected so that the student can progress to non-structural movement and formlessness.

Before we can talk at this level however, we must have a foundation to work from. From learning the basic alphabet we can learn to write. From reading and writing we can learn shorthand. But first, we must have a ground on which to communicate. Performing with hands and feet and conditioning the body is the beginning of the study of our art. In actual combat, form does not appear to be a necessary part in the martial art. However, practising forms perfects the ability to perform hand and foot techniques freely which is important to make the best use of one's body at all times. After basic movements are learned they are applied to and transformed into forms. Traditionally, forms are a clearly defined set of movements involving blocks, kicks, thrusts and evasive actions from all basic angles from which a person can be attacked. These are the four cardinal and four intermediate directions.

Each form has unity and purpose. Basic forms consist of one block, thrust or strike. They involve basic turns which develop control, rhythm, power and speed in the early integration of basic technique. As they progress the forms become increasingly complex in variety of techniques, combinations and sequence of movements. One form can take many years of daily practise and intense concentration in order to master. Perfect form, the ultimate union of mind and body, is the highest of art and an object of intense beauty.

Forms however do not exist for their own intrinsic qualities. They are an exercise of the art that produce a progressive integration of the mind, body and reflexes for the stresses of free-fighting and ultimately for the reality of a real defensive conflict. The sequence of moves in the form may stimulate counter movements to many different kinds of attack and strategies against one or more attackers. In different forms many subtle movements are combined into intricate sequences and a variety of patterns. A practitioner should not only remember the order of the form, he must develop balance, rhythm, breathing, speed, variation, power and control. By paying attention to these things the form becomes a practical approach to a living ideal. It is foolish to believe that one knows the form simply by having memorized the sequence of individual movements. We cannot appreciate any great work of art by bits and pieces but only by observing the entire work as a whole.

The beauty of the form is the union oneness of all the moves in harmony with the practitioner. If while watching a form we are aware of the different parts of the individual movements then we see physical skill but certainly not the art. Form is the mother body and pure essence of all aspects of technique in martial arts. They must be practised with sincerity and deep commitment. The doer must only practise forms for which he is mentally and physically prepared.

It is ridiculous for a low level student to practise a senior grade form. He will gain no understanding value, purpose, unity or meaning of the form. The person who attempts a form beyond his reach debauches the art and weakens his own practice by overestimating himself. Each martial art system contains a complete set of forms which develop all technique pertaining to that art. Body of traditional forms are so extensive they leave little room for changes or additions. One art form has enough forms to practise for a life time. Each form has its own particular character and personality which effect certain traits in the individual. By practising various types of forms a person can not only develop excellent defense but also effect great changes in his personality, external body structure and internal secretions.

---

1. FORM AND SEQUENCE

Correctness in sequence of moves.

---

2. POWER CONTROL

Command of the release, restraint and relaxation of explosive energy of focus power.

---

3. TENSION AND RELAXATION

Mastery of breath and timing.

---

4. DIRECTION

Certainty of balance and confidence of step when changing directions.

---

5. SPIRIT

Evidence of a sense of calm and humility based on self knowledge and dedication to the perfect form.

---

7. POWER OF TECHNIQUE

Focus and power equal in attack and defense.

8. UNDERSTANDING

Demonstration in the form that the sequence of moves has been internalized and flows with the naturalness and ease of reflex response that is without the obvious intervention of conscious thought.

9. DISTINCTIVE FEATURES OF THE FORM

Obvious awareness for the specific times of attack, the number of attackers and the direction of attack for which the form was designed.

10. PERFECT FINISH

Additional evidence of concentration and control. The last move of the form ends at the starting point and the doer remains frozen or fixed for a few moments upon completion of the form.

11. PRECISION

Utmost accuracy which reflects the co-ordination, balance, power, ability and total control from beginning to end.

12. INTENT

An obvious gaze of intent without emotion, to each individual point focused on, defending against the would-be attacker. Eyes should follow all defense movements.

Ten Points Essential to Form Training

1. Remember form training is a mental and physical discipline.

2. Concentration is essential.

3. Every attempt at a form requires maximum effort.

4. Perfection requires continuous practise.

5. Always remember the art form you represent.

6. In learning a new form we must:
   a. develop understanding of the overall pattern and flow of the form.
   b. master the individual motion.
   c. integrate individual movement into proper sequence.
   d. concentrate on varying speeds (slow and fast).

    e. breath control, tension and relaxation, power distribution and intent

    f. understand the mental significance and ultimate meaning of the form.

7. Never attempt a form beyond your ability or against the advice of your teacher.

8. Patience in perfecting the form

9. Develop your own psychological defense for overcoming idleness, distractions and mental blocks.

10. After practise, relax, analyse and appreciate what you have done.

As has been written before, all these points were set down by the Korean Master of Tang Soo Do, Mr. Hwang Kee. They are so thorough that it was ridiculous for the author to attempt anything more to the point. Thusly, they have been left as he wrote them with only a few minor additions.

The history of forms is long and complicated. There are hundreds, perhaps even thousands of forms. For all practical purposes, there are two schools of thought historically involved with the Tang Soo Tao art expounded here. They are hard and soft forms as characterised by the two distinct areas of China; North and South. The forms show some significant differences in their development in each of these areas due to some physiological differences of the people of the areas, the terrain, geographical location and the practical application of the forms in the area. As already stated there are many forms. The forms listed here are the ones used by the author in his own school. It is unnecessary for the purpose of this book to document any other forms than these. This is because when examined thoroughly from what has already been explained earlier and from the illustrative books, the following forms contain the entire scope of all movements common to martial arts.

The forms are a progressive development in basic movement from basic fundamentals of human coordination to highly advanced forms of esoteric significance.

Forms from the Southern Schools

Southern schools are characterised by speed, aggressiveness, dynamic action and spontaneity.

1. Kee Cho Hyong Il Bo	Basic Form 1
2. Kee Cho Hyong Ee Bo	Basic Form 2
3. Kee Cho Hyong Sam Bo	Basic Form 3
4. Pyung Ahn Cho Dan	Formal Form 1
5. Pyung Ahn Ee Dan	Formal Form 2
6. Pyung Ahn Sam Dan	Formal Form 3
7. Pyung Ahn Sah Dan	Formal Form 4
8. Pyung Ahn Oh Dan	Formal Form 5
9. Bassai Ee Cho	Cobra Snake Form
10. Bassai Te'	Coral Snake
11. Jin To	Crane
12. Woon Shu	Sparrow
13. Ro Hai	Sparrow
14. Kong Sang Goon	Eagle
15. So Rim Jang Kwon	Shaolin Palm
16. Acan Kwon	Little Palm
17. Kum Gon Kwon	Lion Monkey
18. So Ho Kwon	Tiger
19. Ta Nung Cho Yo	Praying Mantis
20. Tan Do Kwon	Knife
21. So Ho Yun	Little Tiger
22. Cum Ho Il Dan	Dancing Swan
23. Te Je Hull	Fighting In a Tunnel

Forms from the Northern School

The Northern Chinese forms were characterised by deliberateness, stability, fluid motions and slower more quiet power.

1. Tsan Tjin	Breath and Chi
2. Ssi San	Praying Mantis
3. Jin Te	Bear
4. Jion	Ram
5. Shim Pa	8 Steps of Union Man, Woman
6. Hsing Kwan II Dan	Five Elements
7. Hsing Kwan Ee Dan	Five Elements
8. Naihanji Cho Dan	Horse Form 1
9. Naihanji Ee Dan	Horse Form 2
10. Naihanjio Sam Dan	Horse Form 3
11. Jo Form 1	Stick
12. Jo Form 2	Stick
13. Jo Form 3	Stick
14. Chi Gung Kwab III Dann	Breathe and Chi
15. Lien Han	Linking 5 Elements
16. Tai Kuk Kwon 1 (Tai Chi Chuan)	Short
17. Tai Kuk Kwon 2	Medium
18 Tai Kuk Kwon 3	Long
19. Double Long Knife (proper title unknown)	Union of Heaven and Earth Grand Ultimate

English/Korean Terminology

The author uses Korean terminology due to his broad understanding of the language and also because he did much of his study in Korea.

1. Tang	Chinese Dynasty 12th Century
2. Soo	Hand
3. Tao	The Way - Chinese
4. Do	The Way - Korean, Japanese
5. Kwan	Association
6. Gup	Non Black Belt Rank
7. Dan	Black Belt Ranks
8. Cha Ri Yot	Attention
9. Joom Bay	Ready Stance
10. Kyong Yet	Bow
11. Sah Buhm	Martial Art Instructor
12. Muk Yum	Meditation
13. Pa Do	Return to Ready Stance
14. Keero Toda	Turn Around
15. Ma Kee	Defense
16. Ha Dahn	Low
17. Choong Dahn	Middle Inside
18. An Ee Ro Choong Dahn	Middle Outside
19 Sahng Dahn	High
20. Soo Do	Knife Hand Chop
21. Kon Kyoke	Front Punch Attack
22. Kwan So	Spear Hand
23. Chang Kwan	Palm Heel Attack
24. Seh (or) Say	Stance
25. Keemah Sey	Horse Stance
26. Chungle Seh	Forward Stance
27. Hugle Seh	Cat Stance
28. Bal Ro Ma Kee	Change Feet Exercise
29. Tashi	Repeat
30. Ap Chaggi	Front Stretch Kick
31. Yap Chaggie	Side Stretch Kick
32. Top Gap Chaggi	Round House Kick

Grading System

Time in grade is set at minimum standard. A student is by no means guaranteed absolute certainty of progressing so quickly. Only the finest student will be able to comply with this time standard completely. Gradings are determined upon character, ability, attendance and time in grade.

10th Gup White Belt	3 Months
9th Gup Purple Belt	3 Months
8th Gup Purple Belt	3 Months
7th Gup Green Belt	3 Months
6th Gup Green Belt	3 Months
5th Gup Blue Belt	3 Months
4th Gup Blue Belt	3 Months
3rd Gup Red Belt	3 Months
2nd Gup Red Belt	3 Months
1st Gup Red Belt	6 Months
1st Dan Black Belt	1.5 years
2nd Dan Black Belt	3 Years
3rd Dan Black Belt	3 Years
4th Dan Black Belt	4 Years
5th Dan Black Belt	Master Level

4. 6 Tang Soo Tao Pledge

I pledge to defend the virtues of Tang Soo Tao and to dedicate the efforts of my practice towards better development of my personal character and peace in the universe.

1. I will not cause suffering or harm to other living beings.

2. I will avoid lying, cheating or causing others to be deceived.

3. I will not take that which belongs to someone else or which is not freely offered.

4. I will honor my parents.

5. I will be loyal to my country.

6. I will avoid the use of intoxicants to the point that I become out of control.

7. I will uphold the morality of my own conscience, the spirit of Tang Soo Tao and endeavour to promote harmony within myself and my surroundings.

5.1 Practical Application of Defense Skills

All defense systems can be studied in two parts; defense tactics applied in pre-planned training exercises involving two partners and unplanned free-form combat. The latter is sub-divided again into two parts. Physical ability and psychological preparation.

First we deal with pre-planned exercises. Before a person can progress into effective free fighting he must first develop a strong complete knowledge of all basics contained in the art. He must be able to move to and fro with fluid co-ordination, stability and balance.

After this point, he successfully must demonstrate ability in one step and three step defense exercises and the proper understanding of forms are combined with various types of timing drills used to sharpen reflexes and to develop timing and control.

During all these preparations towards free-fighting, the power of *ki-aup*, chi development and focus must also be integrated throughout his training.

5.2 Ki-Aup

Ki-Aup is broken down into two words; Ki and Aup. *Ki* is the intrinsic energy that permeates throughout the whole body. *Aup* is the cultivation of that energy.

The martial artist must develop the ability to draw on his entire mental and physical resources and concentrate them at any time or place necessary. In defense, intrinsic energy or chi, must be focused to strike, deflect or manoeuvre an opponent to the advantage of the defendant. Chi must be properly cultivated and left to circulate throughout the body until which time it is necessary to apply this intrinsic force at a particular time and place. At the time of need, the chi, under the control of the artist, explodes into action as a powder keg ignited by a match. The chi is applied to whatever motion is utilized and immediately and unconsciously is recirculated through the body the moment the technique or action is completed. The more chi a person has the more awareness and energy he has. The cultivation of chi provides an unlimited well of resources from which a practitioner can draw infinite strength.

The use of the Ki-aup is to manifest chi in various ways to control or upset an opponent. It can also be used to render the body invulnerable to attack. In order to project the Ki-aup a student must first learn proper breathing and control of vibrational pitches. By breathing and creating specific sounds through vocal exhalation an artist can paralyse and control his opponent. The sounds range from loud blood curdling screams to high pitched vibrations which are inaudible to the human ear. The more common of these is just a loud yell which is to gather spirit and force to instill fear into the opponent. The inaudible Ki-aup is a silent attack which upsets the entire psychic nervous system and is infinitely more dangerous.

The Ki-aup can also be projected throughout the eyes to control a person's mind or to instill fear. The Ki-aup can also be used to drain the energy out of a person leaving him exhausted and totally depleted.

5.3 Progressive Levels of Free-Fighting

Once a student gains the beginning understanding of the fundamentals previously mentioned, he is then initially ready to be introduced to free-fighting. A person's first encounter with free fighting is usually a total disaster. Although he has spent hours practising various skills and combinations he finds that he is rigid, stiff, scared and rarely capable of performing more than one movement at a time. Even the one movement that he is able to make is clumsy, awkward and due to lack of control never hits the focal point. The advancement in free-fighting through the ranks is an ascending spiral of progress where a person begins the base awkward level and climbs to a high level of relaxed aware flowing movement.

As already suggested, the lower levels are characterised by erratic uncontrolled technique. The students of the same level often waste an incredible amount of energy running around the floor trying to stay away from each other. They tire themselves out easily by using a lot of energy to accomplish a small feat. Because their attacks are usually misplaced and lack focus, they are quite ineffective. Due to lack of timing and judgement their defenses are equally as bad. Thusly, students of this level don't really accomplish much when they are free-fighting. But because of these points also there is no danger of serious injury. Minor mishaps though, can and do occur quite frequently at this stage. Undeveloped kicking techniques sometimes aimed at head level often find their way in the recesses of bruised shins and cramped buttocks. At this level of training many 'off the wall' accidents, which can be extremely painful but rarely serious, often occur.

Belts of higher levels shy away from working with this grade of student because they have not yet gained any understanding of what they are doing and lack anything substantial to work with. The more compassionate seniors can only hope to get painful bruises and jammed fingers, graciously presented for their patient pointing out of the junior's errors. The level of student we are talking about is characterised by purple belt in Tang Soo Tao. The reader will remember that purple was the sign of the underworld and undeveloped explained in other parts of this book.

After this first breaking in period, students slowly gain some confidence and control. They understand the drastic need for the refinement of their basics and pay more attention to the details given by the instructor. In Tang Soo Tao, this is customary of green belt level, which is a sign of growth. At this stage, a student begins to think a little more about what he is doing. For other students in the school, he becomes slightly less of a hazard to practise with. At this point, he still has a long way to go but at least he is getting somewhere.

Next stage is blue belt. At this level of training the student feels quite comfortable in the school. He begins to exhibit an air of confidence and sometimes an over-air of confidence. He is much less afraid of free fighting and is able to use combinations of techniques with systematic effectiveness. The growth and confidence in the new found power in his techniques sometimes tempt the student at this level to exhibit his power. It is not uncommon that accidents occur at this level due to lack of control. Excessive contact or injury at this level however, should not be confused with that of the purple belt. Accidents at the higher level of training usually stem from careless control whereas in the case of the purple belt it stems from an inability to control. Nevertheless, this can be an exciting area of training for the student and the thought of red belt spurs him on.

Red belt is a break off point for the beginner student. A person's fighting ability at this stage goes through incredible changes. He is willing to try new techniques even though they jeopardise his defense position. Inner strength begins to peek through at this level of training and a student is relaxed and calm during fighting. Advanced red belts have learned to relax and make best use of their energy. They have the ability to assess the opponent with relatively good accuracy. They have reached the level where they actually enjoy the confrontation of free-fighting. The power of focus and timing is highly advanced at this stage and the person has begun to move not only from conditioned response, but from a growing inner awareness. Students at this level have the confidence and ability to fight two, three and even four people at the same time. Because part of his training includes assisting his instructors with lower belt students, the advanced red belt has begun to become aware of the science of physical movements and the psychology necessary for free fighting. He can display this knowledge through the confidence and authority of his fighting technique. He should feel at this level equally at home in light control free fighting as in a heavy full-contact environment. A red belt has experienced that there is much more to training than meets the eye. He thoroughly enjoys and pays infinitely more attention to detail and to every aspect of training. This should easily be seen in the form, art and confidence of his fighting demeanour.

Free-Fighting Points

1. Proper breath control and timing.

2. Finish what you start.

3. Once committed don't draw back.

4. Never underestimate your opponent.

5. Move with, never against.

6. Receed when attacked, move in when opponent withdraws.

7. Don't think, just act.

8. You are your own worst enemy.

9. Use no more than three or four moves at one time. (Too many moves create loss of power, concentration and driving force.)

10. Know when to rest, understand when to push yourself.

11. Never tense, always relax.

12. Be economic with movement.

13. Suit the application of power to the level of attack.

14. Don't over-react.

15. Make smooth movements.

16. What goes up must come down. (If you jump around a lot, you must stop and settle before you can execute any action).

17. Keep your one-point at all times.

18. Don't absorb another person's glance. If you can't look him in the eye, gaze at his eyebrows instead.

19. Always think big, but move small.

20. Always practise self control and never show emotion.

21. Be humble in either victory or defeat.

Black belt is the beginning of the end. A black belt needs no more colours to encourage him onwards, nor does he want any.

At this stage of training, the black belt has spent years developing ultimate sensitivity and experience and has had countless numbers of fighting situations. He has the roots of a fearless warrior. He is not afraid of any situation and can calmly move in and out of intense fighting situations involving one or more persons. A black belt is able to deliver any technique with deadly accuracy.

The most basic movement, though similar in physical motions to lower levels, contains a mindless flowing quality which can be felt rather than seen by onlookers.

Black belts have begun to develop the innate response which is the natural movements of the human being. At this point, a person cares very little for the defense aspects of fighting, for he has already become aware of a much higher goal for his training. His ego is not on the line as it was at lower levels and he uses a fight as a test of his one-point awareness and ability to respond effectively to any situation without conscious thought.

At higher levels of black belt the non-thinking detachment in the heat of full battle creates an impregnable defense which is almost mystical.

Because he is not primarily worried about defense a person's fighting ability actually becomes better. This is because he does not become involved in the action, he just does it.

Advanced levels of black belt can usually fight in slow motion and effectively defend against lower students moving at faster speeds. At advanced black belt stages, fighting with an agitated opponent is like watching the blades of an overhead fan or the spokes of a wagon wheel. Although the wheel is in actual fact moving very quickly it appears visually to be stationary.

At these levels of development, a black belt needs little actual practise in free fighting. It is more important at this level to engage in sensitivity exercises called *Sticking Hands*. These practices in time are able to develop in a practitioner the ability to defeat a student without engaging in a direct confrontation. It is possible for an advanced black belt to gain such a high level of sensitivity as to actually feel the vibration of an opponent's movement before he actually executes an attack. In Zen, this is called *leaving after the enemy but arriving before he does.*

A martial artist's goal for advanced free-fighting is best explained by the examples, *the moon over a lake* and *in water, be like a mirror.* The simile of the moon shining on the lake expresses the mental condition desired in absolute defense.

A highly advanced martial artist seeks to cultivate a mind that is all encompassing; that perceives all things and misses nothing, just as a moon's rays touch everything they come in contact with. In the simile of the water like a mirror, this describes the calmness of non-action which develops the natural sensitivity of absolute defense. If water is rough and moving, the harder we try to still it, the rougher it becomes. We can do nothing in rough water. If we leave the water alone, by it's very nature it becomes still and motionless. On a calm day, we can see our reflection in the water of a lake just like a mirror. On a stormy day, we can see nothing. A calm relaxed fighter can perceive in detail each and every flaw and weak point in his opponent. If the mind of the fighter is agitated then an opening is created for his opponent. Agitation in the mind of the martial artist destroys natural movement and creates cause for competition. An absolute free fighter has totally lost his desire to harm others.

Because this state of mind exists there is nothing substantial for his opponent to fight against. It is said that when a person's sensitivity is completely developed a fly cannot even land on that person's arm, for the arm will move under the weight and leave the fly no base to land on.

There was once a famous master in Japan during the time of the Samurai. He was known near and far alike for his expertise with a sword and for his famous school, which was called the *School of no Sword*. Many students trained under the master but none of them came close to his level of accomplishment. A well-known Samurai from elsewhere came looking for the master one day in order to challenge his skills. Upon coming to the master's home, he discovered that the master was not there, so he inquired where to find him. He was told to go to the market place and that the master could be found in one of the restaurants. Upon this advice, he soon found the master and challenged him to a fight. The master politely refused whereupon the visitor jeered and insulted the absurdity of the name of the *School of no Sword*.

Under the loud jeers, a huge crowd gathered and it seemed the situation was getting quite serious. The master would soon have to make a decision about what to do with the antagonist or suffer the loss of face. Suggesting that there were many innocent bystanders around that could be hurt, the master offered to take the challenger across the river in his boat where they could be alone and settle the dispute. The egotistical challenger, believing this to be a sign of cowardice, anxiously agreed. Both went down to the river, boarded the small boat and crossed the river. Because of the meek and mild manner of the master the challenger's confidence soared, as did the insults while they crossed the river. Reaching the other side, the master politely ushered the guest off the boat first while he steadied it. Half taunting, half laughing, the by now elated antagonist bounded from the boat drawing his sword exclaiming, 'Now we will see who fights with no sword!' As he turned around, he found only himself standing on an empty shore. There was the master calmly rowing back across the river with a mischievous grin on his face and a twinkle in his eye. Thusly, the challenger had been defeated by the master with no sword.

5.4 Psychological Factors

The act of free-fighting is a final test of just exactly what a person is and what he is not. Although a person has spent hours, months, and years training and developing techniques, basic, forms and movements of all kinds, when he comes to face the real test, it doesn't matter how well physically he is prepared because the ultimate test is mental. Every quality of character, personality and training habits developed in an entire lifetime can be tested and observed in a few moments of intense combat.

Style and perfection of technique are only the tools to develop the true qualities essential to the real situation of defense. These essential qualities are a pure spirit and the person's ability to make an honest appraisal of every detailed strength and weakness of himself and his opponent. Once committed to action a man cannot cover his mistakes, inadequacies or weaknesses.

Free fighting is an exercise in control, spirit and mental development. It requires a sound knowledge of basics and practical application.

He is naked, alone and exposed. Foolish readiness to jump headlong into a life and death situation uncontrolled in mind and body, in order to prove bravery to himself or to impress others, is deluded and not to the point.

The real tests are not petty skirmishes in class but the ability to approach death with the true qualities of a warrior. Every human being must fight the ultimate battle with death. This is every man's final test which he must face alone. There is no one to appraise his qualities but himself. Here he is confronted with what he really is and is either confident and relaxed or rigid, frightened and confused. Every man must be able to face death exactly as he faced his opponent in free-fighting. This should be with the same ease and calmness of mind with which he goes to sleep at night.

If I have a clear conscience I dare face an army of 10,000 men.

Confucius

5.5 Zen and Free-Fighting

When two opponents of equal level face each other, the purest technique will always prevail. But this purest technique is almost impossible to recognise. Why? Regardless of beauty and superb physical technique the condition of mind is more important than technique. If one man understands the totality of time he can operate the true technique. If he has attachment to self existent ego he cannot perform action with clarity of mind or deliver a pure technique. This is because the ego produces fear. Fear from the ego is produced by intellect. Intellect is not of a higher order of thought. The thought of fear produces hesitance which in turn inhibits pure movement. A pure mind can enter combat without hesitation because there is no draw back of self. However, if two practitioners were to meet, having reached this same stage there could be no conflict. This is because the pure state of mind creates total harmony. Therefore neither of them are existent for the other one to do battle with. Both have won the conflict without having fought the battle.

5.6 Time Factors in Free-Fighting

Past

When an experience is over it is finished.

To worry about it will upset the present and the future as well. When thinking in the past we cannot adequately function in any moment other than the present. Once finished, an action or movement does not exist. Often times students in fighting observe an opening after it is gone. While they are thinking about the opening that doesn't exist anymore they create one for themselves that does exist. Then they get hit.

The past is a useless mirage in defense that can only be of harm, impair growth and prevent true action.

Present

All things happening right now are present.

If we try to anticipate something that does not exist we waste time, fool ourselves and create an opening for our opponent. Worrying about what is not there, we always get hit.

It is not good to plan strategy because the circumstances may change any second, which will upset the strategy. Although we can prepare for the future we cannot depend on the future. We must be able to rely on an instantaneous mode of action at all times or we will always suffer defeat. Even one second ahead is not present. It does not exist until it happens and then as soon as it goes it is already in the past.

The time concept is not existent in nature, it is only existent in our own mind. Because what goes on in our mind is not what goes on in someone else's mind, it is not the true nature of our mind, as it only exists in our mind and no one else's. A true action that is absolute with nature must be existent all the time. If we relate to another person outside our self during a free fighting situation then we cannot perform pure technique because we are dealing with the nature of two minds. Trying to gauge your actions on the conditions of another person's actions could only create a pure technique at an absolute level if both people had the same thoughts at the same time. This is never the case, therefore we must be able to create pure action by relating only to the present moment.

Future

The future is completely out of the question. It cannot possibly exist by itself.

The only idea of future that exists depends entirely on the present. If we have a total understanding of the present then we can control the future because of its dependency on the present. This means that we can gain the ability to totally control all the actions of our opponent.

Meditation on the void, whether motionless or in movement, is the same

6.1 Personal Development

The road to Tang Soo Tao training is long, hard and covered with thorns. The number of people who begin are many, the ones who finish are few. The total commitment in time and training for years upon years of virtually every facet of physical and mental energy in order to progress; comes as a shock to many, a challenge to some, but equally demanding for all.

Anyone who begins training quickly becomes painfully aware that there is much much more to training than meets the eye. After mustering up the courage just to join the classes, a beginner student must go on to face the initial test of examining what he is and is not. From the very first lesson and for a long time to come, a beginning student's ego suffers blow after blow of humiliating defeat. Students are usually shocked to learn that they don't even know the most elementary fundamentals of life. First co-ordination exercises introduced to students clearly indicate that they don't even know their left from their right hand. Putting that together with the inability to move their feet backwards and forwards in the most basic sequence proves such embarrassment to some that it takes great courage for them even to finish their first class. Beginning students are demoralized to find that they are out of condition, they cannot listen and that their concentration span is rarely more than a few seconds. Most people having had little discipline in life, feel totally depleted. This is a painful experience which lasts for several months. However, the instructor knows this all too well and skilfully and patiently encourages the student onward to jump this most difficult hurdle. Once the student has overcome the initial stage, he has crossed a difficult path which he will never have to cross again. Although he has a long way to go and he knows this now, he has done something for himself, learned something for himself and he has achieved an understanding of what he cannot presently do, but the realization that in time he will have the ability to accomplish anything. With diligent practise under the watchful eye of a competent instructor, any and all students inevitably develop the coordination, technique and confidence they are seeking. Piece by piece the inabilities of a student gradually melt away. After some time students can look behind them and see others struggling from below where they have just come from. They can also look up and see others ahead of them, which gives them constant incentive and a goal to strive for. The lure of higher forms entice a person to increase his basics practice in order that he can learn more intricate, involved aspects of the art. Every technique and form is a new challenge with increased difficulties. New things to learn and application of techniques are infinite.

Regardless of what level a student is, he often feels as if he is back in his first day of class when he tries to unravel the difficulties of higher movement. Students of each level must work together in order to excel. After some time, a deep reliance and respect develops among fellow students. Although each person must survive on his own merits a unifying energy creates a particular type of spirit at each particular class level. Watching his peer group advance makes a person want to keep up and encourages him not to skip class. Seeing the development of others gives incentive for a person to develop himself. Watching and imitating the example of the instructor, a person constantly tries to put his best effort forward and always tries to develop himself to the maximum.

Martial art students like what they are doing. Over a period of time, they find increased energy, less sickness and more awareness. This energy is infectious and spreads outside of class as well. A change comes over the person which is notable to everyone he has contact with. Usually, a developing martial artist becomes more serious about his work and more light hearted about his problems, which in turn causes him to be more diligent in his practise. The more he practises, the more he feels this way and so it goes on.

The most important development in a student is that he gradually learns not to depend on anybody or anything except himself. Although practising and depending on one another in training develops the appreciation to interact with others, the Tang Soo Tao student realises that all obstacles depend on his practical approach to them. By his intense training he gains the intuitive insight and confidence to be able to deal with any problem that he has to face and eventually come out on top.

6.2 The Ascending Spiral

There are ten stages of development in basic training in Tang Soo Tao. Each of the ten stages are accompanied by a marked acceleration in the physical ability and the mental attitude of the student. Periods of success are in turn followed by depression and psychological plateaux, where the student sometimes loses interest in training, becomes despondent and feels as if he is getting nowhere. This stage is usually a prerequisite to new horizons and usually shows he is improving. If the student does not succumb to the temptation to quit, he will realize that what he thinks are plateaux, are really mental puzzles created by the mind. When a person gets over these stages he will find himself in an entirely new world in training, characterised by an increased awareness and an advancement of skills. He begins to move more naturally and often after going through a bad stage, a person can laugh at himself, after seeing what he brought himself through. This will last until he reaches his next plateau and the cycle will begin again.

With each new crisis in a person's training his physical and mental attributes go through an incredible purification which can be responsible for an entire change in his personality. All progress of a student is an ascending spiral towards increased sensitivity and higher development. Sometimes, a student makes the mistake of interpreting the ascending spiral to be a stagnant circle. He can genuinely feel that he is not able to progress any further. Actually, he is making incredible progress all the time, but can not always see it. It can always be observed however by outsiders and friends who are not involved in his internal conflict, but only see the great benefits of his training. Even if little physical progress is made, the ascending spiral spins continually to create firmness of conviction. With perseverance, a person's practice always produces the results desired.

6.3 Delusions

One of the biggest delusions after a certain amount of practice is in the case of a student rationalizing and feeling sorry for himself. This usually begins with periods of depression where the student feels he is not improving and so he decides to drop out. He rationalizes this with thoughts of 'It's just not for me', 'It's not what I thought it was', or 'I just don't have the time'. Then, rather than do a little for themselves, they do nothing at all. This attitude is ridiculous and never gets a person anywhere but further into their own neurosis.

When in a slump, a student always fails to see how far he has come and just how much everyone relies on him. Lower students look up to him as an example of what they are aiming at. By dropping out, he is not only hurting himself but creating an empty space in the school. A student who feels sorry for himself permits himself the excuse of believing that his feelings towards training are individually different from everyone else in the school. Students that drop out this way usually never show their face to their fellow students anymore. This is because they know they let them down. The only way for a student to get beyond this point is to try to set an example for his peer group and to help others. This will always destroy his negativity and he can find renewed strength for training. There will always be a marked improvement, thusly the student improves by training to help others rather than only to train for himself. The peer group is in some ways more important than the instructor because they are all training together and working towards the same goal.

6.4 Obstacles to Training

1. Gradings

A person can miss a grading or not have enough attendance to take a grading. At the time of the test his peer group goes up in class and he feels isolated from the energy in which he usually trains in. Sometimes, a student fails a test. The embarrassment is too much for him to handle and he sometimes throws away years of training rather than put a little more work into the next term.

2. Comparisons

No two people are alike. In Tang Soo Tao, this problem is compounded by the fact that all sexes, sizes and ages are in the same single group. Sometimes students compete with one another. They place heavier demands on themselves than what the instructor does, but for all the wrong reasons. Sometimes, one student excels faster than another which makes the other feel inferior. This is a wrong attitude, it is not conducive to growth and difficult for the instructor to expel from the mind of the student.

3. Questioning Motivations

Some people come for long periods of time and don't really understand why. They are drawn in and thrive off the energy created in a martial arts school, but are not aware of the fact that that's what's keeping them there. Sometimes, they doubt whether they should be there at all, but if they weren't they wouldn't know what else to do.

4. Injuries

Occasionally students get a few minor injuries and decide to take a break. The break gets longer and longer and they finally lose the energy that they had and find great difficulty getting back to class.

5. Ego

Some people have incredible egos. They don't want anybody to be better than them. They can't accept defeat, authority or being exposed and not being able to do anything about it. They don't want to be humble and they don't want to hear anything that threatens their life-style.

6. Physical Limitations - due to size, age, sex and physique.

People have all sorts of problems. If people cannot do everything, they feel inadequate. Such people place too much emphasis on the physical aspects of the art. They also use their limitations to cover up their slackness.

7. Parents (and Guardians)

Parents sometimes stop their children from training with excuses that it inhibits their school work. They don't understand that energy generated by training clears cobwebs out of the head, increases concentration and actually improves the intellectual capability of the student. Parents also bribe the children with 'karate lessons' as a reward for a specific deed. Often, it is difficult to instill true effort and motivation in a child because his parents threaten to stop him from training if he does not respond to their wishes. Thusly, the parent's attitudes destroy a child's respect for them and cheapens the purity of the art in the eyes of the child.

8. Friends

Jeers, snide remarks and foolish challenges from ignorant people can be disturbing to students. Friends distract students with parties, sex, dope, alcohol and all sorts of useless activities which have absolutely nothing to do with training. A person must strive to keep good company or he will fail in his training.

9. Wives

Wives usually try to make their husbands feel guilty for training, with reasons such as, working too hard, not enough time for the kids and sometimes believe the man is doing something violent. They don't understand that training relaxes the mind and creates inner peace, i.e. opposite to violence. Women also feel jealous and threatened by an activity which takes up so much time that they believe the husbands should be giving to them. A selfish wife can be responsible for destroying every achievement the man has worked for. A good wife can appreciate the significant changes in her spouse and give him encouragement to progress further.

10. Husbands

Husbands think it's 'cute' for a wife to play Kung-Fu, as long as it isn't serious. When they see a change they feel threatened at something they don't understand and are impressed only with physical signs of violence they believe characterise martial art. A wife excelling in martial art assaults and poses a threat to an immature husband's masculinity. A deeply involved martial artist sometimes suffers marital strains which inhibit training.

11. Incorrect Motivation

A person who trains only for himself, disregarding others and desires only self-improvement cannot train indefinitely. Many students fail to realize the importance of group participation in unison with individual endeavour. Sooner or later a person must desire to help people or he will get nothing out of training.

12. Senility

This means that a person is set in his ways so much that he will not accept change. He does however, accept social comments regarding his physique, his age and his maturity. These cause doubt and doubt causes problems in training.

13. Femininity

Many women are ingrained with the idea they are the weaker sex. They wrongly misinterpret weakness for inferiority. They think softness means lack of strength. In their desire to be equal they forfeit the very attribute by which they are already naturally equal, i.e. their femininity. This is their strength. Some women go through incredible identity crises figuring this out.

14. Masculinity

Men erroneously believe power is everything. They associate virility with strength. In beginning training, all men observe the incredible power behind the instructor's technique. They attempt to duplicate this power by tensing, straining and using muscle. It is very paradoxical for them to understand that the more they use strength the less power they will have and that the more they relax the stronger their technique will become.

15. Laziness

Nothing can be accomplished by being lazy. The solution is to work hard. It is very tempting to miss class and do as little as possible. None of these attitudes get a person anywhere.

16. Impatience and Boredom

Tired of the same old basics which he thinks he understands, the student becomes impatient to learn something new although he really hasn't begun to vaguely understand what he knows already.

All these obstacles to training progress can be overcome by a little practise and a lot of faith. If a person has even the most remote level of faith in himself, God, Tang Soo Tao or his instructor, he will always find what it takes to go further. Without sufficient faith nothing can ever be accomplished. According to the laws of physics, a bumble-bee cannot fly. His wings cannot support the mass weight of his body. But he doesn't know that. Subsequently, he continues on about his business.

6.5 Conclusion to Personal Development

People who begin training rarely have a true idea of what training is all about or what the instructor actually stands for. All levels of students are impressed by the status and respect exemplified by the level of black belt. They respect the instructor for his knowledge, control and manner. Motivations to start training range from personal need for self improvement, defense against rape or assault to the power and esteem of being a black belt.

Anyone who has entertained the thought of holding a black belt, soon lose much of their initial enthusiasm after their first encounters in training. They can see that there is a great deal of work to be done before they are anywhere near dreaming about high levels of accomplishment. They can however relate to the lower belt levels which are not quite so intangible. With this objective they can find a reasonable incentive to endure training. After a few minor successes and experiences at the early belt stages students have an initial glimpse of what they are in for. They can easily see the qualities a black belt possesses and it is painfully obvious that the only way they can achieve the same thing is by hard practise. Some people are just not prepared to put the kind of energy forward that it takes to achieve success. Others are willing to do anything in order to accomplish the goals that motivated them in the first place. With few occasional encouragements the stayers push on, determined not to let anything get in their way.

An instructor watches the progress of his students quietly and closely. By a persons character and training he can easily see what desires and motivations drive a student on. He uses a student's initial motivations as a primary incentive to cultivate the best possible training habits. He encourages the students often and entertains their desires for progress. Students however, never really understand what the instructor is thinking. Outwardly, he is a manifestation of the qualities they think he represents. These are actually the qualities they think they desire. By following the example of the instructor, the student can only gain the qualities for which his teacher really stands for and develop them in exactly the same way as he did. In time, the students develop self discipline, the ability to be honest with themselves and through this self confidence slowly begins to mature. Gradually and methodically, the student begins to acquire the true martial virtue.

The end result differs however from the initial goal, in that a person's feelings at advanced training levels are entirely unrelated to what they were in the first place. He can defend himself but places little or no importance on it. By the time he receives his advanced belts, it is such a natural development in his training that he holds little self-status on the position. Even the idea of self-improvement, although he is doing it all the time, has changed its meaning. Self improvement involves an awakening of sensitivity towards others rather than striving for self gain alone. Each goal a person sets out for becomes as illusive as a rainbow. Within each goal, believing each goal to be the primary objective, the student progressively sets out to reach it. Once he has attained it however, he finds that it is not what he really wanted or what he thought it was. At times, the ultimate objective appears to be right in front but when he reaches out to grasp it, it alludes him. Something however, always pushes him on.

This is the mystical energy of the martial art. Each and every achievement, no matter how small, is an epic journey which draws him nearer to something better; but he doesn't know what. Every step forward is a milestone in developing his physical abilities, innate senses and a key to understanding his most intimate feelings about himself. The more a student develops, the more he recognizes the magnitude and depth of what he has entered into. If he has the courage to go on he will gradually dismiss other hobbies and activities which have by now become useless. By channelling all his energy into one focal point, i.e. the training experience, the student enters a new dimension in his personal development. He has come to the beginning of the end. He has begun to cultivate the true virtue of a martial artist.

PART TWO
TECHNIQUE

Student Syllabus

Purple Belt

Minimum Attendance 27 Sessions

10th-9th Gup Grading Requirements

Forward Stance

Horse Stance

Low Block

High Block

Middle Inside Block

Middle Outside Block

Lunge Punch

Reverse Punch

Front Kick

Side Kick (introduction)

Roundhouse Kick (Introduction)

One Stepping Front Kick

Horse Stance Punching Position

Technique Combination 1

Three Stepping, Block-Counter - Punch

Basic Form 1

Basic Form One

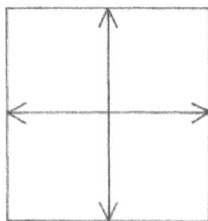

This form is the most basic fundamental form in martial art movement. It consists of twenty two movements done at regular speed in a four directional square pattern, (North, South, East and West).

The primary purpose of the form is to link the first basic motions a student learns, to co-ordinate the lower limbs with the upper. The essence of the form promotes concentration, focus and speed of technique. Besides developing co-ordination and breath control, fundamental one point movement is required. All movement is powered from the thrust of the leg and the movement from the waist, which transfers into the striking limb. Any muscle tenseness in the body, especially the arm, significantly decreases the effectiveness of the technique. The form can generally be said to be predominant in developing Yang chi.

Basic Form One

1

2

3

4

5

6

7

8

9

10

11

12

Basic Form One (Continued)

13

14

15

16

17

18

19

20

21

22

Technique Combination One

Technique Combination One is a basic co-ordination exercise taken out of the form which can be used in an actual defense situation. It can be practised with or without an opponent and gives incentive for understanding the first form.

1

2

3

4

5

6

Advanced Purple Belt

Minimum Attendance 27 Sessions

9th-8th Gup Grading Requirements

All Previous Basic Techniques

Cat Stance

Roundhouse Kick

Back Kick (Introduction only)

Crescent Kick

One Step Defense Technique

Three Step Technique

4 Point Turning Exercise

Technique Combination 1 & 2

Technique Combination 3 (Introduction only)

Basic Forms 1 & 2

Basic Form Two

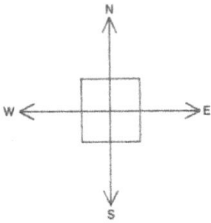

Basic Form Two follows the same structure as Basic Form One.

The only difference here rests in the three linear movements of upper blocking in the North and South directions. This is the second of the four gates, North and South, (upper and lower) which cover all points from which a person can be attacked. The upper motion is in the form of a circle while the lower abdomen must sink towards the ground. A residue of air must be held at the navel. The counter punch also is executed at face level whereas in Basic Form One it is aimed at the solar plexus level. These small but important differences in the forms begin to teach a student upper and lower motions of attack and defense while keeping the navel area at a constant height without rising.

Basic Form Two

1

2

3

4

5

6

7

8

9

10

11

12

Basic Form Two (Continued)

13

14

15

16

17

18

19

20

21

22

Technique Combination Two

This technique co-ordinates one legged balance and lower and upper body motions together in a practical application for the continuing development of Basic Form Two, as well as preparing the student for the development and understanding of the third Basic Form.

1

2

3

4

5

6

Green Belt

Minimum Training 27 Sessions

8th-7th Gup Grading Requirements

All Previous Basic Techniques

Basic Punching In All Stances

Strong Emphasis On Kicking Techniques

Back Kick

Crescent Kick

Soo Do (Knifehand Block)

1 Stepping Techniques

3 Stepping Techniques

Technique Combinations 1, 2 & 3

Emphasis on Body Shifting

Basic Forms 1, 2 & 3

Basic Form Three

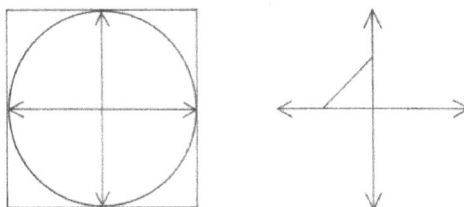

The form follows the same geometric pattern as the two previous forms. This form however, incorporates the first introduction into body shifting. The three stances used protect the body from any angle from which a person can be attacked. The form stresses perfection of the third or middle gate which is the fifth direction of centre, (in relation to North, South, East and West). The residual air in the abdomen and the balance of the one-point must begin to develop here, or the motions lose their effect. Whereas the first two forms used only the square stance, the third form incorporates a triangular stance as well as a circular stance.

The student must finish the form where he begins. In order to do this, the triangular stance (as represented by the cat stance) must be done perfectly in the four turning directions. This is also true of the forward stance (the square) and the horse stance (the circle). If a person doing the form cannot interchange smoothly and accurately between the three stances and in his turning motions, the form will look awkward and clumsy. The practitioner will fall off balance and the techniques will lack effect. This effect described is similar to a top in spinning motion. In addition to breath control and perfect balance, the upper limbs must co-ordinate perfectly with the lower.

If the leg moves separate from the arm or vice-versa, the motion will be completely limited to the unbalanced muscular potential and size of the individual. When done correctly the power of even a small person is greatly increased in a ratio unequal to the body size. Regardless of this power however, the form is still basically Yang chi development, as at this level a student is still co-ordinating external physical actions and little internal chi is used in the techniques.

Basic Form Three

1

2

3

4

5

6

7

8

9

10

11

12

Basic Form Three (Continued)

13

14

15

16

17

18

19

20

21

22

Technique Combination Three

These motions accentuate kicking technique and balance at various angles. The Combination incorporates techniques out of the three Basic Forms plus the first two Formal Forms. It is also the student's first encounter with back-kick. The kicks are not as important as the development of one-point on one leg and understanding the perfect equilibrium required to execute a back-kick. There is also a particular timing involved which cannot be shown in pictures. The timing together with the techniques used, provide an excellent ground work for good basic timing and control in free-fighting.

1

2

3

4

5

6

7

8

Advanced Green Belt

Minimum Training 27 Sessions

7th-6th Gup Grading Requirements

All Previous Basic Techniques

Low Soo Do

Middle Soo Do

High Soo Do

Kicking Off Front Leg

Free Fighting Combinations (Introduction to Backfist)

Free Fighting

Dual Set Combination

Breathing Exercises

Technique Combinations 1, 2, 3 & 4

Basic Forms 1, 2 & 3

Formal Form 1

Formal Form One

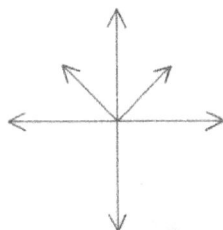

After a student is basically co-ordinated he is introduced to the Formal Forms. The first form builds off of the first Basic Form.

The geometric pattern is still basically square but by now the student has begun to solidify the one-point area and during the development of this form he can gain the rudimentary knowledge to work with a partner with relative success.

The form differs from the previous forms in that two other directions are added. These are Northeast and Northwest. (Figs 22 and 24). Another characteristic of the form is the progressive coordination of using one hand for both the defense and counter techniques. (Figs 8 and 9).

Formal Form One

1

2

3

4

5

6

7

8

Formal Form One (Continued)

9

10

11

12

13

14

15

16

Formal Form One (Continued)

17

18

19

20

21

22

23

24

25

Technique Combination Four

This Technique Combination has some similarities to the previous one. Combination Four however stresses movement in the side stance and multi directional circular punching. Following the back-kick in this Combination there is a spinning downward parry combined with a follow-up hook and uppercut punch. This is the students first introduction to a non-linear hand strike in fighting. In addition to this, these three hand motions can be used as a simultaneous block and counter with the same limb. Previous to this, the student has learned to block with one hand and strike with the other. Here, this action is accomplished with one motion.

1

2

3

4

5

6

7

8

Blue Belt

Minimum Training 27 Sessions

6th-5th Gup Grading Requirements

All Previous Basic Techniques

All Soo Do Variations

Free Fighting Technique

Basic Technique From Free Fighting Position

Dancing/Circular Movements

One-Point Exercises

Kiap Practice

Advanced Improved Basics

Advanced Warm Up Exercises

Technique Combinations 1, 2, 3, 4 & 5

Basic Forms 1, 2 & 3

Formal Forms 1 & 2

Formal Form Two

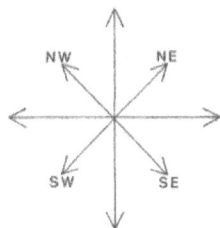

This form incorporates body shifting with circular double arm movements, used for blocking or throwing.

This is the first of the forms where both of the upper limbs are used simultaneously in defense motion. (Figs. 2 and 6). The introduction of open hand technique is also important at this stage. Also, another concept of movement is added which is both limbs going forward rather than one blocking and one pulling back. (Figs. 17 and 20). This is important as it establishes the movement from linear to circular and creates enhanced flowing movement. Other features of this form are that all the defense motions have varied applications. This is unlike the previous forms in that they incorporated a basic one block one strike defense. This form is also the first to use one legged stance and kicking, which requires significantly more balance and control. At the end of learning Formal Form Two, a beginning student has completed the fundamental coordinating pattern of incorporating the circular, square and triangular stances with the four defensive gates of the upper body, (high, low, inside, outside). Finally, the student has completed a multidirectional form which incorporates all eight compass directions inside the circle.

Formal Form Two

1

2

3

4

5

6

7

8

9

10

11

12

Formal Form Two (Continued)

13

14

15

16

17

18

19

20

21

22

23

24

Formal Form Two (Continued)

25

26

27

28

29

30

31

32

33

Technique Combination Five

These motions are taken from Formal Forms Four and Five. Here, the jump-kick is introduced and all open hand movement is used. Although a jump-kick is neither necessary or desirable in high level defense situations, the perfection of this technique greatly enhances the performer's ability to execute lower kicking techniques.

1

2

3

4

5

6

Technique Combination Five (Continued)

7

8

9

10

Advanced Blue Belt

Minimum Training 34 Sessions

5th-4th Gup Grading Requirements

All Previous Basic Techniques

All Previous Basics From Free Fighting Stance

Jump Front Kick

Jump Side Kick

Advanced Body Shifting (Free Fighting)

Advanced Dancing Movements

Eight Directional Exercise (introduction)

Improved One Step, Three Stepping Exercises

One Point Exercises

Breathing Exercises

Advanced Warm Up Exercises

Technique Combinations 1, 2, 3, 4, 5 & 6

Basic Forms 1, 2 & 3

Formal Forms 1, 2 & 3

Formal Form Three

The particular character of this form is that it utilizes various methods of body shifting.

The basic structure is familiar to that of Basic Form Three, but the clock and anticlockwise stepping motions distinguish it from the other forms. Diversified kicking as well as accentuated breathing techniques (not able to be seen), make it a difficult form for co-ordination for the advancing beginner.

Formal Form Three

1

2

3

4

5

6

7

8

9

10

11

12

Formal Form Three (Continued)

13

14

15

16

17

18

19

20

21

22

23

24

Formal Form Three (Continued)

25

26

27

28

29

30

31

32

33

Technique Combination Six

By the time a student is into this Combination his basics should flow more naturally and he should feel comfortable in his body co-ordination. This Combination develops good inside fighting technique and timing. It is also exceptionally good for body shifting and multiple attacking. If understood correctly, this Combination should enable the practitioner to follow and stick to his opponent while delivering multiple attacks. At the same time the practitioner should be able to attack his opponent from circular angles which prevent the defender from countering the assault.

1

2

3

4

5

6

Technique Combination Six (Continued)

7

8

9

10

11

12

13

Red Belt

Minimum Training 34 Sessions

4th-3rd Gup Grading Requirements

All Previous Basic Techniques

Stressed Perfection of Basics

Advanced 1 Step & 3 Step

Counter, Counter, Counter Technique Combination

8 Directional Exercise Drill

Free Fight With 2 Or More People

Jump Roundhouse Kick

Jump Back Kick

Jump Crescent Kick

Advanced Free Fighting

One-Point Exercises

Internal - Chi Gung Kwan Form

Advanced Breathing Techniques

Technique Combinations 1, 2, 3, 4, 5, 6 & 7

Basic Forms 1, 2 & 3

Formal Forms 1, 2, 3 & 4

Formal Form Four

This form is the most practical form at an intermediate stage for actual free fighting and defense. The defense applications throughout the form are numerous and it successfully combines linear and circular motions.

At this level a person has excellent control of body limbs and control of the one-point makes balance equal whether on one foot or two. Concentration and spirit are greatly enhanced by this stage, and the first formal Yin chi development is introduced in this form. (Figs. 16 and 20).

Here, a student must begin to mix slow movement with fast, both with internal breathing and external motion. Understanding the vibration in the lower belly by use of external sounds (Ki-aup), is also important at this level.

Formal Form Four

1

2

3

4

5

6

7

8

9

10

11

12

Formal Form Four (Continued)

13

14

15

16

17

18

19

20

21

22

23

24

Formal Form Four (Continued)

25

26

27

28

29

30

31

Technique Combination Seven

This is an incredibly difficult exercise in waist action. From the forward position, the practitioner must do a high back-spin-kick, without creating an opening. The two follow-up kicks move the hips in two opposite directions. Performing this Combination without losing balance is difficult by itself. By the time a person is able to use the defense motions in the Combination, he will find that it has helped him in almost every form of body shifting and offensive or defensive action that he has learned up till present. The Combination starts out from long range using leg techniques and works to the inside finishing up with hand combinations. The Combination provides challenge and diversity for the student. As has been stated before, the intricacy of kicking technique is not the end in itself but provides an excellent exercise for developing one-point and body co-ordination in defensive and offensive action of both hand and foot.

1

2

3

4

5

6

Technique Combination Seven (Continued)

7

8

9

10

11

12

13

Advanced Red Belt

Minimum Training 38 Sessions

Consistent Teaching Experience

3rd-2nd Gup Grading Requirements

All Previous Basic Techniques

Free Fighting Basics

Emphasis on Jump Kicks

Chi Gung Kwan

Advanced 1 Step - 3 Step

Dark Training

Dual Set Combination 3

Bag Work For Forms

Swan One-Point Exercises

Kiap Practice

Technique Combinations 1 - 8

Basic Forms 1 3

Formal Forms 1 5

Hsing Kwan III Dan (5 Element Form)

Advanced Warm Up Exercises

Formal Form Five

This form is developed at the advanced intermediate level.

In addition to points mentioned in other forms, the student by this level should be able to integrate linear and circular motions so effectively that one cannot discern the end of one technique and the beginning of another. Though using linear techniques the entire form is mostly circular. Various other stances are added and low and high rising and falling concentration exercises are added to the form. In addition to perfect balance and control on one or two legs, the residual air and one-point area must remain fixed whether in a low crouch or with feet entirely off the ground in mid-air (Fig. 26).

Formal Form Five

1

2

3

4

5

6

7

8

9

10

11

12

Formal Form Five (Continued)

13

14

15

16

17

18

19

20

21

22

23

24

Formal Form Five (Continued)

25

26

27

28

29

30

31

32

33

34

Hsing Kwan III Dan

This form incorporates Yang style movements with Yin chi in relation to the five elements. It is a co-ordinating form by which some of the basics become modified to control chi flow. it is modelled after the five elements, earth, fire, metal, water and wood.

It utilizes softer defense motions and a smaller geometric pattern than the previous forms.

The deeper functions of this form have been described elsewhere in this book and the more detailed explanations being the subject of the sequel to this book.

Hsing Kwan III Dan

1

2

3

4

5

6

7

8

9

10

11

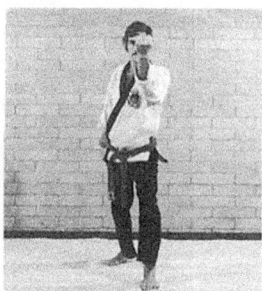

12

Hsing Kwan III Dan (Continued)

13

14

15

16

17

18

19

20

21

22

23

24

Hsing Kwan III Dan (Continued)

25

26

27

28

29

30

31

32

33

34

35

36

Hsing Kwan III Dan (Continued)

37

38

39

40

41

42

43

44

45

46

47

48

Hsing Kwan III Dan (Continued)

49

50

51

52

53

Technique Combination Eight

Up to this point, most of the Combinations involved concentration on focus and a predominant use of Yang chi. This Combination is a dramatic change from hard to soft. Taken from the soft Crane Form it stresses one continual action from beginning to end. There are no blocks, only hooking and evasive motions and all motions are done in a round, soft flow. The rise and fall techniques consisting of high jumps dropping down to low leg sweeps are difficult to master and beautiful to watch when done correctly. The beauty of the art begins to shine in this Combination. If a student has bad control and lacks flow, the Combination appears absolutely ridiculous. This Combination also contains some excerpts from the Sticking Hands practice.

1

2

3

4

5

6

Technique Combination Eight

7

8

9

10

11

12

13

14

15

16

17

18

Provisional Black Belt

Minimum Training 45 Sessions

Constant Teaching

2nd-1st Gup Grading Requirements

All Previous Techniques

Multiple One Step

Multiple Free Fighting

Advanced One-Point Exercises

Pushing Hands Exercises

Swan Exercises

Basic Forms 1 3

Formal Forms 1 5

Hsing Kwan III Dan

Bassai Ee Cho (Introduction)

Chi Gung Kwan

Bassai Ee Cho

After the Formal Forms a student leaves the first stage beginner level and enters into the second stage of advanced training.

The Bassai Form is the first form which not only gives priority to coordination but also begins a student's first experience in meditating in movement. Modelled after the observations of the Cobra snake in battle the form incorporates various levels of rising and falling and is the first real step towards Yin chi development. At this stage, regardless of how well a person can mechanically execute techniques, unless he cultivates the spirit of the form, i.e. substituting his ego in place of the snake, he will never be successful in any other advanced stages of training. The form is the first introduced to the student which utilizes Neigung exercises. A predominant Yang chi with a rising Yin chi emerges.

This basic introduction is only the first of many of a series of animal forms which follow. Each animal form possesses a particular characteristic of chi development which successfully balances the Yang and Yin chi's. At this stage of development, a student must have firm knowledge of breath control, be able to spontaneously change from slow to fast in fighting and must be able to stimulate points in his nervous system as well as his opponent by soft and loud vocal exhalations. Perfecting this form should have subtle changes on a person's character.

Bassai Ee Cho

1

2

3

4

5

6

7

8

9

10

11

12

Bassai Ee Cho (Continued)

13

14

15

16

17

18

19

20

21

22

23

24

Bassai Ee Cho (Continued)

25

26

27

28

29

30

31

32

33

34

35

36

Bassai Ee Cho (Continued)

37

38

39

40

41

42

43

44

45

46

47

48

Bassai Ee Cho (Continued)

49

50

51

52

53

54

55

56

57

58

59

60

Technique Combination Nine

Taken from the soft style Tiger Form this Combination stresses a strong Horse Stance and absolute body control while in mid-air. The jump-spin-kick requires two consecutive spin-kicks while in mid-air. Developing this technique requires agility, strength in the legs and tenacity of the sinews. The person must be light and land as lightly as a mosquito. Developing students usually throw themselves off centre and land clumsily on the floor with much noise. If the Technique is perfected correctly, besides the obvious development of co-ordination, a light agile body is assured.

1

2

3

4

5

6

7

8

9

Technique Combination Nine (Continued)

10

11

12

13

14

15

The Progression of Combinations

The basic Technique Combinations begin with the most fundamental body movements and end with techniques out of some of the highly advanced forms. They are designed to give a chronological sequence of defense motions at an equal level of the student's physical advancement in his basics, his forms and general overall understanding of the art. These Combinations contain every basic motion the student has learned in strike and defense. They also contain a systematic gradual progression from Yang to Yin chi and a natural growth from hard block/punch style tactics to soft, smooth relaxed body motion. When successfully learned and practised, these techniques provide a sound understanding of the Forms, practical application in real combat, an appreciation of the art and a general feeling of wellbeing.

Black Belt (Chodan)

Minimum Training Daily
Constant Training and Teaching

1st Gup-1st Dan Grading Requirements

All Basic Forms 1 - 3
Formal Forms 1 - 5
Bassai Ee Cho (Cobra Snake Form)
Hsing Kwan III Dan
Hsing Kwan Ee-Dan (Introduced)
Technique Combinations 1 - 10
All Kicking Techniques
All Basics From Free Fighting Position
Nihanji Cho Dan (Horse Form One)
Jo Form One (Stick Form)
Jo Free Form
1/4 Of Tae Gu Kwan (Tai Chi Chuan)
Breaking Technique (Head Butting, Side & Front Kick & Elbow Smash)
Kiap Practice
Proper Character Development
Written Essay On Two Given Topics
3 Day Black Belt Camp Introducing
1. Metaphysical Basics
2. Nei Gung Basics
3. Basic Fasting
4. Meditation Techniques

Tai Chi Chuan

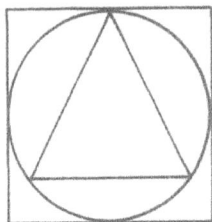

The Grand Ultimate or Tai Chi is the perfect integration of Yin Yang.

In this form the student makes the transition from total Yang to total Yin. The whole form, (which is not shown here) requires a half hour to complete. It is done in absolute slow motion and requires the utmost in concentration and control of blood flow. To successfully master the form takes between ten and twenty years. The entire form is an actual meditation, no different from sitting. All movements must be slow and flowing and there should be no break from beginning to end. The form incorporates all eight directions of the circle as well as constantly melting in and out of the square, triangle and circle. Whereas most other forms use a double weighted stance, this form requires a constant changing of weight, from left to right, but never on both. Whereas slight discrepancies in upper and lower motions do not impair technique in other forms, they are of utmost importance in this one. All movements stem from the legs. The blood flow must co-ordinate systematically with the various organs as the form is practised. All martial arts movements can be seen at some point in this form. It incorporates the Wei-gungs, Nei-gungs and Chi-gungs, all geometric patterns and the most important animal movements.

Practical application of this form, though seemingly soft, has the strongest impact. Persons working together develop defenses through sticking hands exercises. The exercises are for sensitivity and can be done at slow, moderate or fast speeds. the form and its defense exercises are practised with flowing harmony between the opponents. Internal power is increased with practise to the point that a person can be struck, thrown or moved without actual physical contact.

A sixth sense of awareness is developed in the form which enables a person to respond subconsciously with little effort. Time and space in defense also change with the practise of this form. With proper mental attitude there is no difference in defending against any mode of attack, hard, soft, fast or slow. A good practitioner can perceive another's energy similar to the way we perceive the blades of a rotating fan or wagon wheel. While gazing at the centre hub the blades appear to be moving very slowly when in actual fact they are revolving hundreds of times faster.

Tai Chi Chuan

1

2

3

4

5

6

7

8

9

10

11

12

Tai Chi Chuan (Continued)

13   14   15

16   17   18

19   20   21

22   23   24

Tai Chi Chuan (Continued)

25

26

27

28

29

30

31

32

33

34

35

36

Tai Chi Chuan (Continued)

37

38

39

40

41

42

43

44

45

46

47

48

Practical Applications

The following is a set of twelve application exercises demonstrating defense motions taken from the previously explained Forms and Technique Combinations. They are executed between two partners from a static pre-planned position and graduating to an attack from a free-fighting position unpreplanned. To avoid redundancy and tediousness, the standing ready position and pre-planned step back as demonstrated in the first exercise should be assumed in the following examples as it will not be repeated.

Exercise One

Basic blocking and co-ordinating exercise, demonstrating eye contact and basic application of Technique Combination One and Two.

1

2

3

4

Exercise One (Continued)

5

6

7

Exercise Two

Attack is linear from a square position. Defender stops the offender with a side-kick then circles behind the opponent for a strategic position and take-down.

1

2

3

4

Exercise Three

Still a basic block and counter co-ordination, this motion incorporates the use of Technique Combination Three, moving to the inside of the body for elbow strike to the rib cage.

1

2

3

Exercise Four

The defender has done basic upper block and countered with linear punch. The punch collapses into the elbow, defender's left arm then controls attacker's punch while using forward momentum to draw him down into the knee.

1

2

3

4

Exercise Five

Defender has hooked the hand of the attacker with his left hand at the same time drawing him into the right uppercut. Stance has been drawn in to defend any counter to the low level. Still drawing in with the left hand defender makes circular sweeping strikes to the neck finishing by shifti,ng the body around to the inside of the opponent, finishing with uppercut strike to the solar plexus while still controlling the attacker's arm.

1

2

3

4

Exercise Six

Lifting leg for defense against kicking is a common practice for both hard and soft styles. In Tai Chi it is called *'Golden Cock Stands on One Leg.'* Here the defender guards the groin and blocks offensive kick and at the same time covers the upper portion of his body and attacks the head. As the knee drops in Fig. 2., the left heel presses into the groin at an angle to the left leg of the attacker. This can be used either as a groin kick or a push which will buckle the knee and drop the opponent to the floor. At the same time, the left hand of the defender (left) sticks to the attacker's left hand in alert for a counter punch. Stepping back, defender uses his body shifting motion to draw opponent off balance and into his circle of defense, whereby he finishes the technique with a palm strike to an acupuncture point on the back of the neck.

1

2

3

4

Exercise Seven

Here, two opponents practise various motions of linear and circular attack trying to penetrate the other's defense. The object is to not let the opponent's hands separate once they have made contact. The winner is determined by whoever is able to touch any part of the other person's body. In this particular exercise, there is no necessity for any forceful contact. Although kicks are not included in this exercise, sensitivity should be developed enough so that if they were they would easily be deflected.

1

2

3

4

5

Exercise Eight

This is a slightly more advanced exercise used in the pushing hands practice where the attacker pushes against his opponent. The object of the exercise is to sensitize so keenly that the opponent can never get a firm touch or hold. After the attacker has exhausted the power from arm and leg motion (which the defender has absorbed), defender than leads the body off balance and uses the momentum to throw the person with the weight of his own attack.

1

2

3

4

5

6

Exercise Nine

This exercise is another exercise similar to the one previously explained. Here, by relaxing and shifting the hips the pushing attack is neutralized and the attacker's own energy used against him. In both these exercises, it is understood that any variety of strikes and or kicks can be used. At this level of training however an abrupt aggressive technique is considered inferior technique. The ability to neutralize a strong aggressive attack by a soft body shift and push is considered a much higher class of defense tactics. In a real situation, it is infinitely more demoralizing to the aggressor. This exercise produces acute sensitivity, increased blood flow and can even be practised blind folded, after learning the initial stages. The difference between Exercise Eight and Nine is in the angle of defense and projection. They constitute various ways to manipulate an opponent to one's own advantage.

1

2

3

4

5

Exercise Ten

Here, the defender sidesteps and changes the angle of the opponent's defense. Once the attack is neutralized, the defender drops his one-point to the floor, downing the attacker. This type of movement is more common to the Pa-Kua schools.

1

2

3

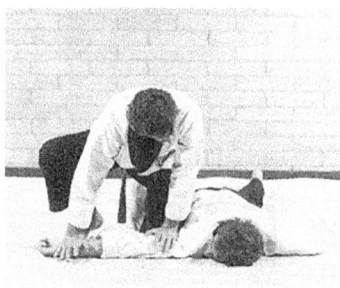

4

Exercise Eleven

This defense consists of drawing three circles in the air after receiving and neutralizing the opponent's attack. Each circle is clockwise and rotates downwards. The first circle leads an opponent out of range, the second draws him into the defender's arena for the knee counter, the third leads him completely away in a downwards circular motion to the floor.

1

2

3

4

5

6

7

Exercise Twelve

Here the defender neutralizes the punch by striking the acupuncture meridian on the inside of the arm. As a counter measure, he also strikes the rib while stepping through to the outside circle of the opponent. With no opening left for attack the assault is finished.

1

2

3

4

Exercise Thirteen

The sensitivity in this Pushing Hands practice is developed by a build up of chi generated by a continuing creation of large and small movements leading upwards, downwards, left and right. The point of the exercise, as illustrated, is to effortlessly absorb the opponent's circle into one's own and then project him away in the same type of flow with which a tornado moves. The pattern of movement follows exactly as that of the diagram on the wall in the background.

2

3

4

5

Pa-Kua

Pa-Kua is not a form which moves in any particular pattern but in a spontaneous movement of palm-changes while walking in a circle. The circle can be walked slowly or quickly. There are attacks and defenses inside as well as outside the circle. The walker must constantly be in a state of movement from the inside to the outside of the circle in his palm-changes and in his mental attitude. The diagram in the background designates this concept. Although some aspects of circle walking are introduced to students, the depth of this form is not extensively taught until after black belt level. Shown here are only a few variations of the palm-changes in the circle.

Some defense positions in the Pa-Kua

2

3

4

5

Pa-Kua (Continued)

6

7

8

9

Pa-Kua (Continued)

10

11

Practical applications of Pa-Kua defense positions

Practical applications of Pa-Kua defense positions (Continued)

'Snake Creeps Down.' A variation of the Tai Chi Form.

The Mind's Eye

The first, the last, and most important basic of all martial art technique stems from meditation and tranquillity of mind. Whether sitting or engaged in external actions, the mind's eye must remain the same.

The absolute martial art movement.

ROBERT CAPUTO

PART THREE
ROBERT CAPUTO AUTOBIOGRAPHY

Chapter 1

From as far back as I can remember, I have always been deeply interested in martial arts.

My first experience with martial arts was on an air force base in the United States where I witnessed my first Karate demonstration given by a visiting Japanese troupe. At that time I was six years old and I guess I was lucky because my father was involved in the U.S. military. Following the war, the US military bases were the first starting points of the spread of martial art to the West. Because my father was a military officer he was aware of the qualities of self defense and enrolled me in a Judo school at the age of ten. I was the smallest person there and can still remember having a difficult time with the older boys. My instructor was an American who was married to a Japanese woman and had lived for many years in Japan. He was a kind, sincere and dedicated man and to this day few instructors I have met had the type of personality he displayed at all times.

I loved every lesson that I went to and always looked forward to the evenings when my brother and I were taken to training. Although we had to move and I didn't get very far in Judo, the qualities I observed in my first martial arts instructor were unforgettable. He had successfully planted the seed of respect and discipline for martial art in my heart, which has never left me to this day.

Following my Judo experience, my father was stationed in Hawaii. Several years passed before I was again exposed to any kind of martial art. One day, while riding my bicycle home from school I heard some noise coming from a barracks near a baseball field. I went over and peeked in the window and saw a Japanese man with a black belt teaching a room full of soldiers. I stared in the window for the whole class and when it was over I waited outside the back door. I was very immature and shy in those days and I didn't know what to do but I knew I just had to ask the instructor if he would let me come to train with the soldiers. As soon as he walked out the door he saw me and smiled. I told him I had once done Judo and that I loved martial arts and asked him if he would teach me. He told me that the class was only for American military men and that it was not allowed. He also asked me how old I was and I told him fifteen. Although he told me no, he suggested I come around and look at a few classes to make sure I understood what was happening. He told me that if I still wanted to join after looking at the classes, he might let me in. Naturally, I did this and after a short time he let me begin training.

That instructor's name was Sensei Honma. He was always broke, drove a broken down car and used to teach class after working all day in his father's bakery. He rarely remembered to collect fees and never worried about anything. He was affiliated with the Wado-Ryu system of Karate.

I rarely missed training. I loved Karate and my instructor and thought I had found the most ultimate aim of my dreams. After six months, my Sensei invited me to the main gym which was down town and I began training there as well. (The base training was only three nights a week). This enabled me to train every night if I could find a ride down town. Every so often the head instructors of the school, Sensei Herano and Sensei Suchiya, would hold two and three-day live-in training clinics. I can remember how proud I was to be able to sleep over night in the same Dojo as my instructors. I can remember we all slept on the canvas floor and were woken up at 4am, in the morning to do basics, running and maki-wara training. I envied the huge knuckles of the senior black belts and the sternness of their concentration.

In those days, I was always anxious to practise sparring. Before I really understood proper etiquette, I used to ask my instructor if he would spar with me after every training session. He rarely said no and would always free-fight with me until I was tired out and had exhausted every technique I could think of. I can imagine how stupid I must have looked when I thought that sometimes I was getting in on him. He delighted in playing with me until I had nothing left to work with and would then gracefully knock me out. That was the sign to quit for the evening.

I can remember one part of my early training when he knocked me out two times a week for one month using a different technique to finish with each session. I continued in this school and was to test for my brown belt in one more week when my father was transferred to California. I was incredibly sad to leave my Sensei. I cherished every experience that I had had with the school and my allegience was so strong to the Wado System at that time that I felt I would never be able to find a school or instructor that could duplicate the qualities of that particular school.

When we arrived in California, I was friendless and had no one to talk to. I used to stay home in the day time, stretch and practise my basic forms. I had heard that one of the black belts from a down town school in Honolulu had also been stationed in California. I went to see him and met him only once, after which he was transferred to an outpost which gave no chance for him to organize classes. I spent the next eight months anxious and restless and although I didn't mind California, I'd had no luck in finding any decent school worth talking about. I visited a few Karate schools and other martial arts institutes, all of which looked sick compared to what I had been accustomed to.

At that time, I was so allegient to my old school that I felt it would be dishonourable to my instructors if I trained in a school with bad standards. I finished my high school year, travelled around the country a bit, then I came back to California and entered University. On enrolling I was told that all first year students had to do PE. There was a class there called Combatives which I joined. The teacher was so inadequate that I volunteered my services. For my first term, instead of doing PE. I was given units for being the instructor of a Combatives class. I didn't get a lot out of this but it did renew my energy for training and gave me some incentive to do something. It was also my first experience in teaching.

Not long after I had enrolled in the school, I discovered there was a black belt teaching some form of martial art at lunch time. I immediately went to the gym and waited for the lunch hour. It was there I met my first Tang Soo Do instructor of the Korean form of the art. His name was Mr. Ah Po a Hawaiian. Because of my martial art experience and our common background of living in Hawaii, we immediately struck up a good relationship.

Mr. Ah Po was an excellent teacher and had all the qualities of my previous instructors and much more. I couldn't believe how happy I was to find a man with his characteristics and development of martial technique. He was a man well disciplined, who stressed absolute perfection in basics and encouraged the utmost scrutiny to all students in the learning of forms. He was equally at home in any free fighting situation as he was doing his forms. He was incredibly innovative and could pull incredible fighting techniques almost out of mid-air from the most basic elementary motions. Mr. Ah Po never did anything fancy. Everything he did was basic, simple and direct and it always worked. In tournaments and in clinics held all over California, I watched him demonstrate his dynamic power of simple basic motion on most of the major black belts who are famous on the tournament circuit today. None of the people I saw him fight with could ever stand up to him.

He eventually stopped fighting tournaments because he'd be disqualified or knock someone out. Also I think he just got bored. Much of my fundamental principals of the external Korean art of Tang Soo Do I owe to this instructor's patient, meticulous guidance.

During the first year of training at Mr. Ah Po's school, I also was trained half of the time by his instructor, Mr. Estioko. Naturally, because Mr. Ah Po had such impeccable technique his instructor was more so. He had the most beautiful precise technique, in free fighting skills and forms of any man I had ever seen in my life up to that time. Both of the instructors ran the school and though it was the oldest one in the town, it had the least students. The training was always tough, regimented and taxed us beyond our abilities. We had mountain trips in the winter time, and often trained outside anywhere and everywhere.

Although I didn't particularly like tournaments, I went during those years because my instructors asked me to. I always did well in fighting but never won because we were not trained for tournaments. No one from the school ever won. It was painfully obvious every time we went, what would happen. The same thing happened again and again. The students from the school would go, they would be out pointed in a tag game and then go home again.

Tournaments in those days on the California circuit were absolutely ridiculous and rarely displayed true martial art ability on any level whatsoever.

The best part of training with the school in those days was that the instructors set up clinics with other black belts from other areas. The clinics were much better learning experiences than tournaments. Without trophies and winning or losing, we could just engage in training with one another in the proper spirit of the art. Our school met with the Kagu-Kenbo, Goju, Kempo and other schools as well. We used to have a good time and a big feed afterwards. Sometimes we'd even drink a few beers.

After my first year of training at the Tang Soo Do school, some very sad misunderstandings developed between the two instructors. This was a traumatic experience for them as well as for the students. All of us who had trained so hard together were forced to make a decision of which instructor to follow. Reluctantly, we had to choose one or the other. Because he was the first instructor I had met in Tang Soo Do I was morally obligated to stay with Mr. Ah Po. He founded his own school and I helped him teach and there I remained for one more year. Some of the spirit was lost for a while and the initial stages were a bit rough, but things gently picked up. At this time in my life, I had moved by myself to the country and lived on an almond orchard.

During the next year, I began the serious practice of meditation. Ideas formed ever since my Japanese instructors in Hawaii, combined with suggestions from my Tang Soo Do instructors, led me to deeply examine as much as I could, the experience of meditation. I spent a great deal of time by myself, often talking only to squirrels, cows, chipmunks and pheasants who were my neighbours. There were also a few wild donkeys who came around from time to time. I trained every morning and every evening through the winter and summer alike, for an entire year. This was in addition to the classes I attended at the Dojo.

In the winter, I used to drive to the mountains by myself and train my forms till I was exhausted, then sit in the icy river for as long as I could endure. I had read that by austere training one could sharpen concentration and develop chi. The chi was supposed to be strong enough to make a man sweat in freezing water. Although many people talked of this, up to this time I had never met anybody who could do it. At this time in life I couldn't either but I tried.

I had a friend who lived in the mountains and during the snow season I sometimes visited him. I used to strip down naked and train in the snow, then force myself to meditate after I had done my forms. I sat for long periods of time completely naked in the snow until the bottom half of my body turned blue. I had hoped that my intense desire would stimulate the psychic heat I had read so often about. But at this stage of training, it didn't. All I got was cold and pain. What I did develop however was the concentration to shut off the pain and endure it for almost as long as I desired. I knew this wasn't the intrinsic chi I was looking for, as mentioned in Buddhist texts and Kung-Fu manuals, but my concentration to endure what I set out to do was steadily improving.

I did these practices as often as possible and immersed myself in meditation and studies daily till the time I left the country. I had appreciated all that I had learned, but I knew there was something more. I believed that guts weren't everything and that basics, though very important undoubtedly, were not the end of training.

I felt something was missing from my mental and physical training and that I couldn't find it at the school I was at or anywhere in the country at that time. With only a name and phone number of a man in a far-off country that I'd vaguely heard of, in one week's time on the spur of the moment, I sold my car, bought an airplane ticket and left the country. The phone number I don't remember, the country was South Korea, the name of the man was Hwang Kee.

Chapter 2

When I landed in South Korea, I was excited and a little apprehensive. I really didn't know what to expect. This was the first time I had ever travelled outside of my own country. I knew nothing about the life in Korea and I couldn't speak the language. I had no idea where I was going, all I knew was that I wanted to train. I wanted to find the strongest most powerful training method that existed on the earth. I wanted to experience the wisdom and understanding suggested in so many books I'd read on Bushido and Zen Buddhism. I sincerely wanted to find one true master who had done everything, knew everything and was willing to teach everything to a sincere student. I knew I was a sincere student, I was hoping to find that master. With this and no other guide to help me in a foreign land, with firm conviction I got off the airplane.

The first thing I noticed was that I definitely was not in America anymore. It was a strange feeling being the only white person walking about. There were men with guns everywhere, soldiers stationed all around and large anti-aircraft guns beneath camouflaged nets. The history I had studied in high school about the Korean war had suddenly come to life all at once.

I tried my best to get some help in the airport with phoning the one number I had to rely on but to no avail. People spoke very little English and there was certainly no one named Hwang Kee on the other end of the line. So, I got in a taxi and went down town.

I was completely in a dream and slightly out of my senses. Here I was in a strange land with no one I could communicate with, heading for a place called *down town*, which for me right then meant going somewhere to meet no one. The taxi driver didn't really know where I wanted to go either so he dropped me off at the local USO, which turned out to be the best place for me to get my bearings. The USO was a military centre for American soldiers to meet, which was in the heart of the city. There were English speaking Koreans in there who translated and helped people get organized. I can remember a very kind man named Mr. Pak, who spent over an hour on the telephone arguing with all sorts of people, and almost on the verge of despair himself, ascertained enough information to help me. No one had heard of Tang Soo Do. I couldn't understand why, as it was supposed to be the national martial art. I soon found out why.

After waiting for some time in the USO, a Korean man came to find me. Mr. Pak had been able to locate someone who was a friend of Mr. Hwang Kee and he came to guide me. He spoke very little English but he was a nice man and off we went into the depths of the crowded city of Seoul. Mr. Yun (my guide) took me to an old broken down room with a tin roof, cracked walls and a partially paved, partially dirt floor. He told me I could leave my baggage there and it would be safe. It looked like the last place on earth I'd want to leave anything. I reaffirmed several times if it was absolutely safe to leave my personal belongings in such a seedy looking poor part of town. He told me again and again that it was alright and because I trusted him and had no other choice anyway, I relented. I was later ashamed to find that this was the central headquarters of the Tang Soo Do Association.

That story I will tell later.

Mr Yun took me down to the YWCA in Myong Dong. It was there that I met the man who would be my friend, guide, companion and instructor; Hwang Jin Moon. Jin Moon was the only son of Grand Master Hwang Kee. I was incredibly relieved and delighted because I knew I now had found the key to the beginning of my search.

Jin Moon was a very kind, happy person and was glad to see me. Before I had left America my instructor had written a letter explaining that I was coming but no-one in America was sure of the Korean address. Though the letter had arrived, none of the Koreans knew when I was coming. Jin Moon at that time was engaged in teaching a class for the girls at the 'Y'. I waited, observed his teaching mannerisms and then we left. He first took me downtown for dinner, collected my bags, (it was at this time that I realized that the place where my bags were was the central gym), then took me to a small hotel.

After leaving my bags in the room, we went to a small tea house and sat down for a long talk to get to know each other. Jin Moon was interested in my motivations for coming to Korea and wanted to know all about what was happening with Korean Tang Soo Do in America. I gave him a detailed history of my training in martial arts and frankly told him that I was prepared to give up anything and do anything to learn everything there was to know about martial art. Because I was so enthusiastic, he made jokes about me being a *Tosa*, which is a Korean word for a hermit, yogic master of martial arts. I never forgot the word because that's exactly what I always wanted to be.

I explained to him everything I knew about the Tang Soo Do situation in America and he listened intently. He told me about his own training experience and what martial arts meant to him. This was all in our first meeting. We talked for hours. Jin Moon was twenty-eight at the time and had become a black belt when he was eight years old. There wasn't one mean bone in his body. He had a soft face, kind eyes and there was absolutely no indication whatsoever by which a normal person would ever guess that a man so young had already trained for twenty years. The only person who could see it was me or someone who could see the pure qualities of a true martial artist. This was observed instantly in his soft movements, his calm air and his authoritive gesticulations.

After we had got to know each other, he apologized to me for the poverty in Korea. He also explained to me why the central gym had been reduced to a broken down storage shed. What he told me is a sad truth in the history of Korean martial arts which is little known to the world and of utmost significance to practitioners of the Korean forms of martial art. It is for this reason that I have chosen to elaborate in this short autobiography the story of the Korean style of Tang Soo Do. This is the story as I received it from the mouth of the master's son.

Grand Master Hwang Kee was born in the early 1900's near North Korea. He was born of a poor peasant family and lived a hard life. In his early youth he practised an art form called Soo Bak Do, which was the name of foot fighting in Korea.

His interest in martial arts took him to mainland China where he travelled around looking for one master who would teach him all the secrets of martial art. After training with many masters, he finally came across one master who excelled above the rest. This master became his chief instructor. He studied for many years with a personal master/disciple relationship.

When he had learned everything to the satisfaction of the master, Hwang Kee set off back to Korea. On the way, he had many experiences where he had to test his ability and skill. He came back to Korea and formed the Tang Soo Do Moo Duk Kwan Association and taught many students up until the Japanese occupation.

At that time, Korea was forced to stop the practise of Tang Soo Do, which lasted until 1945. Mr. Hwang Kee again established the Association and it was at this time that it began its most important developments. The Tang Soo Do organization excelled in high esteem all over Korea. It spread to the high schools, universities and became compulsory in Korean Military Academies. Tang Soo Do came to be the largest most popular martial art in the history of Korea. Due to the Korean war and the early Japanese occupation, the morale of the Korean people suffered a terrible demise. The spread of this art greatly enhanced the spirit of the people. The organization was incredibly successful and developed intensely until 1961.

At this time, there was a military revolution in Korea. During that time a high general in the army, named General Choi, desired to form his own organization. Choi was a former student of Mr. Hwang Kee but decided he wanted to be president of his own association. Using his political power, along with many acts of blackmail and intimidation, he began methodically to destroy the Tang Soo Do Association and Mr. Hwang Kee. He set up his own association and called it Tae Kwan Do. Because he was a powerful General, Choi had much influence in the military structure and influenced the appointments of defense teachers. A long bitter struggle began between the two associations. There were wars between the schools, fights, acts of sabotage and many incredible difficulties. General Choi, with his political influence and power from the recent military revolution accused Master Hwang Kee of treason to overthrow the Government. Hwang Kee was imprisoned and his family suffered greatly.

After being released from prison, there was a great struggle which began in the courts. The Tae Kwan Do Association tried to legally stop all Tang Soo Do operations in Korea. It was a conflict that lasted for many years. During that time, the bribes and intimidations of General Choi were beginning to show their effects. Some of the high members sold out their master and joined the Tae Kwan Do Federation.

In 1965, Tang Soo Do was barred from officially operating. They had lost the case. Though the case was under appeal, this gave Choi the necessary power to establish his martial arts regime.

In 1966, there was a reform to the verdict of the lower courts and Tang Soo Do was again allowed to practise. The ruling was that Tang Soo Do was a martial art and that the Tae Kwan Do Federation was part of the Korean Sports and Athletic Association. To this day, that still holds true. But although Tang Soo Do won the court case they had lost the real battle. The lack of allegience towards the master, combined with the bribes and intimidation launched by Choi succeeded in breaking the back of the Tang Soo Association. All activities were heavily monitored by the KCIA (Korean Central Intelligence Association) and any attempts to redevelop the art were crushed one way or another. General Choi had succeeded in his objective.

The purpose of this story is to show the validity of Tang Soo Do and to truthfully establish the origin of Tae Kwan Do. Many Tae Kwan Do books ensure that the art was developed centuries earlier. In actual fact, most of the Tae Kwan Do arts were off-shoots from the original Tang Soo Do Association. The author would like to state here that he has said most of the Tae Kwan Do arts, not all. Some of the Tae Kwan Do branches had been practising at the same time of the formation of the

Tang Soo Do Association, but all of them are now associated with the Korean Sport and Athletic Association. The main difference between the Tang Soo Do Association and the Tae Kwan Do Association is that the Tae Kwan Do Association specialise in fighting training which could be introduced at military levels for quick results. The standard was incredibly different and Tae Kwan Do had lost much of the finesse and spiritual aspects of Hwang Kee's Tang Soo Do.

Choi's later appointment as an Ambassador, combined with his excellent Public Relations work, made Tae Kwan Do a popular, famous, financially successful operation. Due to General Choi's enormous efforts, Korean forms of martial art became as popular as Japanese Karate, world wide. The background of the initial history of Tae Kwan Do however, combined with Choi's anxious promotion of the art, introduced an art to the world which lacked the finesse and proper spirit of true martial art in its initial stages.

There were about a dozen different associations under the name Tae Kwan Do; such as Tae Kwan Do, Moo Duk Kwan, Chang Moo Kwan, O Do Kwan and Jeet Do Kwan to mention only a few. About three or four of the Kwans were formed independently about the same time as the Tang Soo. All the rest were offshoots from the break-away school. There are dozens of intriguing stories in relation to all the To-jang wars and the formation of the various Kwans during this highly volatile time in Korean martial history. As time has progressed over the last twenty years however, much of the rough beginnings of the Kwans have ironed out and for all practical purposes, for the average person there appears to be little difference among all these various styles.

This was the end to my first introduction to the understanding of the histories of popular Korean fighting arts. After being up for 36 hours I was completely exhausted and went back to my hotel room and *died*.

The next morning, Jin Moon came to pick me up. He had told his father of our meeting and Mr. Hwang Kee was looking forward to meeting me. Needless to say, I was very anxious to meet him. Word had already got out among a few members that a foreigner had come to train. The Koreans were actually quite excited about this; I was a bit of a novelty. Although members of the American Forces had often taken up Tang Soo Do training, I was the first civilian to ever come on his own with no other ties. I was the first foreigner to come to Korea for the sole purpose of training and nothing else.

As we approached the broken down headquarters, I was very excited. We walked in the door and there was Master Hwang Kee.

My first experience with this man was truly unforgettable. He sat on a broken down bench in a filthy broken down little room in worn out but well-kept clothes. The majesty of his presence turned his clothes to silk, his chair to a throne and the room to a palace. Although he was seventy years old he looked like he was forty. He had a smile from ear to ear and I was completely happy and comfortable to be with him.

This was the first of many meetings I was to have with this great man.

He questioned me about my training and asked me about my attitudes. He was pleased and happy with everything he heard and also apologized for the situation of Tang Soo Do at that time. He briefly reiterated the story I had heard the night before and although apologizing for lack of proper facilities, promised me he would do his best to expose me to the best training conditions possible; which he did.

I stayed in Korea for the year and trained intensely. Sometimes there were classes on the military bases, sometimes in various people's houses and often right there at the central gym. Central gym comprised of one small office room and an outside flattened dirt area about twenty by thirty feet surrounded by a brick wall. For stick training, we used mop handles because no one could afford proper jo's and for maki-wara training we just punched the concrete walls.

My main instructor was Hwang Jin Moon, but I also trained with dozens of other high Dan members from all over Korea. During my first trip to Korea Jin Moon moved into a house with me which was across the street from where his family lived. I saw Hwang Kee every morning at 6am when he waved to me as I went down to practise at one of the branch gyms.

The author with the Korean Grand Master of Tang Soo Do, Master Hwang Kee, (centre), and Ee One-Jay the author's Korean-half-brother".

He was always up in the morning and although I didn't talk to him much in the first couple of months, he carefully observed my training and living habits. I travelled to every Tang Soo Do school left in Seoul and trained with every Tang Soo Do black belt that there was left to train with who had not defected to the Tae Kwan Do organization.

In order to train, I had to travel all over Seoul to different places where classes were being held. In the morning, I usually trained at a small branch gym near Hwang Kee's home. In the afternoons, I would go to the military bases and in the evenings I would again go downtown, sometimes to the YWCA and occasionally to other schools around the area.

The art form I was learning at the time taught equal development of the whole body, but I did however develop incredible refinement and expertise in kicking technique. This is definitely something unique to Korean martial art. After the first few months in Korea, I could see Master Hwang Kee almost any time I liked. I asked him many questions about philosophy, meditation and his past. He told me many interesting things over the period of time that I stayed in Korea. After a year, I had to change my visa. I used this as an excuse to live in Japan, have a break from Korean training, and to examine the Japanese culture.

The author practising the Korean Tang Soo Do's refined kicking techniques.

On leaving Korea, I had a final dinner with Mr. Hwang's family. During that year, I had become part of the household and was treated like one of their own. During that year, they had also had incredible financial difficulty and I had fortunately been able to help them out. The gratitude they showed towards my meagre generosity was embarrassing and unnecessary, I felt.

They all wished me the best and the Master gave me some pointers on how to relate to Japanese, whom he knew very well. I listened intently and what he advised me was very helpful. Before I left, he related some of the personal experiences of his travels when he was my age. They were encouraging to hear and I was surprised to find that even his son hadn't heard what he had confided in me.

With much energy and a steadily maturing spirit I set out for Japan.

Chapter 3

I arrived in Tokyo in the middle of winter. It was extremely cold. I decided to go straight to the home of Mr. Gogen Yamaguchi, the head of the Goju Karate Association. I was very familiar with Goju and also knew some high Dan members of Goju in America whom I could use as a reference. I had had an integral experience with the heart and training methods from the Master and the art of Korea, now I was deeply interested to analyze the difference between Korean martial art and culture, with that of the Japanese. I also was very interested in what I had read about Aikido and decided if possible I would give both a try.

Japan was very different from Korea. It was modern, rich, well-organized and clean. The cleanliness was a refreshing break from the Korean scene but the automated way the country ran boggled my mind as soon as I got off the airplane. I easily found Mr. Yamaguchi's home, as everyone in Japan knows who he is and many know where he lives.

I arrived in a taxi to a huge building surrounded by a lovely garden in the middle of Tokyo. I opened the gate, went inside and came to the first floor of a three storeyed building. Inside a sliding glass door, I could see a well-established Karate Dojo with a picture of Mr. Yamaguchi on one side and his instructor Master Miyagi on the other. I knew this was the place, so went inside, and knocked at the door. Mrs. Yamaguchi came to the door and I told her why I was there. She smiled and nodded and I thought everything was alright. A few moments later, I realized that that was traditional Japanese custom to smile and nod at everything and that really she hadn't understood a word I'd said. I didn't speak Japanese and she didn't speak English.

She took me upstairs and introduced me to a high school boy who was living there. He spoke English, so there was communication. I explained myself again and she immediately ushered me into the house and introduced me to Mr. Yamaguchi; just like that. He took me into his study den, where we sat down.

My first impression of Mr. Yamaguchi was entirely different to that of Mr. Hwang Kee. I felt as though I was in front of a dauntless warrior, which I was. His eyes were sharp, his motions precise, his attitude curt, friendly, but noncommittal. He glowed all over and the energy that surrounded him filled the room energizing everything including myself. He laughed easily, smiled often and nodded his head a lot (a gesture I soon became familiar with when dealing with Japanese people). I explained in brief my personal history and my motivation for being there. He appeared very happy to meet me, and graciously offered me a room in his own home- I was very surprised and naturally I accepted.

The building in which he lived had three large floors. The bottom was the Dojo, the middle was the meeting hall on one half, his personal living quarters on the other. The top floor was a Shinto Temple (Shinto is the national religion of the Japanese).

I began training there almost immediately.

The central gym did not have many students at that particular time and most of the classes were run by 1st and 2nd degree black belts whom I was senior to. This didn't bother me, however. I happily stored away my black belt and put on a white one. I was already familiar with basic Goju. I was more interested to study the attitudes of the people than the basics of their preliminary training. I found these people to be incredibly rigid, both in attitude and training technique. They did however, have incredible pride and spirit in their art and tremendous respect and dedication for their master; a trait which I honoured highly. I had an opportunity to study the attitudes of the students thoroughly, but I didn't particularly learn anything which added to my physical ability. I found most of the people in the school mildly aloof but not unfriendly. During my entire stay, I had only a few misunderstandings with some of the black belts.

After a class one day, one of the students was doing some stick work. There were a few others around and as I walked by he made a few threatening gestures at me. It was one of those situations that you feel uncomfortable in. He was half joking and half showing off to his friends. Also, he saw that I was only a white belt foreigner and half heartedly tried to exercise some of his seniority. I mildly deflected a mock strike which he gave me half-heartedly. When I did, he again gave another one with a bit more intent. I smiled and tried to shrug it off and walked towards the door hoping I wouldn't have to get into something sticky. But it didn't work.

Still laughing and glancing at his friends, he continued a semi-real fight with me. Finally, with a smile on my face, so it wouldn't seem too serious, I tried to end the joke. I easily deflected the stick and pushed the man to the floor. This made him extremely angry however, and I think he suffered a loss of face. Because he was wearing a black belt and I was wearing a white belt, this may have caused some agitation in his heart. He jumped up and really attacked this time and I had no other recourse. I completely disarmed him and smashed him into a wall and threw the stick on the floor on the other side of the gym. This won me no popularity in that gym and created a bit of tension seeing as how I was living upstairs.

On another occasion, we'd finished some basics and were swapping sparring partners. One instructor was commenting on the sparring method I was using with one particular green belt. As is usual custom, he was going to demonstrate the proper way on me. I wanted to honour his seniority but at the same time I wasn't going to let him smash my stomach in when I knew my technique was not wrong, only different. He tried to demonstrate his technique on me, which didn't work. He got angry at this because he was instructing the class and this turned into an all out free fight, which ended with me just short of knocking him out.

After that however, I lost a bit of energy to train downstairs. I felt alienated from the people, didn't particularly like the Japanese way of life and wasn't really committed to Goju, but I certainly didn't want to do or say anything that was disrespectful. I tried my best to fit in with their program but something didn't quite fit naturally for me. I felt very bad because I didn't want to insult my host whom I respected very much. This is all I can say about Goju training in the gym. The training in the gym was not the primary reason I was there but the essence of Goju was. That rested in one and only one man, Mr. Yamaguchi.

Mr. Yamaguchi was unfettered by anything that happened downstairs. He extended every opportunity to me to help me with my training and questions. He was very interested in my progress in Aikido which I had started at the same time I had moved in there.

He was also extremely pleased that I was mostly interested in yoga and spiritual training. He invited me up to join him in his prayers in his Shinto Shrine each morning. He said he would be happy to explain to me and teach me anything I wanted to know about Shinto and Zen but first I would have to learn Japanese because he wasn't about to learn English. I sat and meditated in the morning, while he and his wife did their ritual chanting. I didn't understand everything he did at that time, but I do now.

Once a week on Wednesday night, Mr. Yamaguchi would do yoga with myself and one other boy who was slightly retarded. This is one of my most precious experiences with the man. I can remember the strange feeling, listening to the loud yells, grunting, groaning and smashing of maki-wara boards downstairs, while I sat with the Grand Master upstairs doing meditation, stretching and relaxing. I never figured out why I was so fortunate to be there with that young retarded boy. That boy had nothing to do with Goju. For all practical purposes, I had nothing to do with Goju. This kindled a thought in me, that maybe, Mr. Yamaguchi no longer had anything to do with Goju either.

Before continuing, I would like to clarify the views expressed here lest any sincere Goju practitioner misinterprets the intentions of the author. Firstly, the stories in the book are related as the author experienced them. The book is written in respect to chronological sequence in the growth of a martial artist. Throughout the narration, I have tried to capture my personal feelings and experiences at the time they happened. They don't always necessarily reflect what I feel now.

Wisdom, maturity and experience are virtues I certainly lacked at the beginning of my travels. Natural biases and prejudices are liable to any person once he becomes involved with a style or practice. My driving force at the time was not to imitate a different style in martial art but rather to capture the ideal inherent in it. My reference to Mr. Yamaguchi not being involved with Goju certainly does not mean the man had nothing to do with Goju, but rather that his method, as any method, martial, religious, yogic or otherwise, was only a means to an end. Once the man has reached the other side of the river in a boat, he no longer needs the boat. I believe that this mans's art was his stepping stone, as are all methods.

As stated earlier, a good instructor gives the student what he needs and is able to demonstrate his art and apply his art to any situation Mr. Yamaguchi certainly demonstrated this to me. The spirit he extended to me upstairs in the Temple was far greater than any physical action he could have showed me downstairs in the Dojo.

Mr. Yamaguchi had related to me that only late in life had he become deeply involved with yoga and that he really wished he had started earlier. I respected his frankness and advice and from that time on until now I have made yoga an integral part of basic training for beginner students as well as myself. Although he had started late in life, it was obvious that Mr. Yamaguchi was indeed well on the path to becoming a great yogi.

During this time as mentioned earlier, I had also enrolled at the Aikido Honbu.

Coincidently enough, one of the first people I met was Mr. Yamaguchi's yoga teacher, Pierre Winter. He was a young Canadian man in his late 30's who had lived and studied yoga in India for eleven years. Because I was living in the Dojo, he was very happy to speak at length with me on the various aspects of yoga. Talking with him helped clarify the difficulties I had with translations while training with Mr. Yamaguchi. As most of the classes were in the morning, they conflicted with no other parts of my schedule. I trained Aikido everyday of the week including Sunday. Because I'd had a lot to do with spirit and meditation by this time, I understood the essence of what the Aikido instructors were trying to do. From all my previous training, it was easy for me to pick up the fundamentals of basic movement. I enjoyed Aikido greatly because it did not rely on relative strength and because there was not an egotistical confrontation between the two players.

I soon found that there were many different varieties of Aikido which varied from instructor to instructor. Different emphasis was also placed at different levels of training, depending on the instructor. I often went to double classes in the morning and sometimes even three. The morning class was always taught by the son of the founder, Mr. Ueshiba. The second and third classes in the morning were taught by different instructors daily.

During this time the chief instructor of the school, Tohei Sensei, not only taught Aikido at the Honbu but also had classes in his own private Dojo. Three times a week, besides the morning classes, I also attended afternoon classes led by this man. Although he sometimes taught Aikido, he spent a great deal of time teaching only the spiritual aspect of the art which developed chi through chi exercises and meditation. These particular classes were different from the Honbu in firstly, the Honbu never directly taught anything to do with

Tohei Sensei,
Aikido Master of Japan.

chi. They taught that it could only be developed by practising the art. Secondly, anyone could come to Tohei's class even if they didn't do Aikido. I found Tohei Sensei to be a highly intelligent man who was far advanced in his ability to teach the spirit of his art to all; much more so than any other instructor I had met in this art.

During my stay, a great disagreement arose between the instructors at the main Honbu and the Chief Instructor, Tohei, regarding training, teaching and philosophy. Things got so bad that Tohei finally had to leave the central Aikido Association altogether. This was very sad and reminded me of experiences I'd had in the past in other arts. It was disconcerting to see rivalry among high level teachers in a school based on harmony. Nonetheless, I did my best to extract the essence of the art from all the instructors. I watched all of them closely and daily after training; other students and myself would relax with various teachers in the coffee shop. I would listen to many stories and advice on daily practise. The instructors talked often of the founder, Morei Ueshiba, as if he were a God. Many believed he was enlightened. Stories of this particular man were enthralling but it was difficult to find anyone near his level of accomplishment.

I thoroughly enjoyed training Aikido and I loved its beauty but there was still a completeness within myself that the art or the instructors were not able to satisfy.

All during these training experiences throughout that year I was constantly reading every bit of translated material on Zen and martial art, and any form of related Buddhism. I visited numerous monasteries and temples. I took periodic breaks from my training and visited the monasteries of Kamakura and Kyoto. I talked to any and all types of people. I trained in country Dojos for both Karate and Aikido. I discussed with instructors about the meditational aspects in relation to what they understood about their arts. I found monks who believed in Buddha but had not become a Buddha. I found martial artists who revered a spiritual quality of past instructors, but had not yet achieved these levels themselves.

I had learned a great deal in Japan, but I felt it was time to move on. For my personal needs something was still missing.

I began to long for the more relaxed attitude of the Korean people compared to the hustle and bustle and autonomy of Japanese lifestyle. Feeling much wiser and more relaxed I paid my last respects to Mr. Yamaguchi, thanking him for his help and returned back to *the land of the morning calm.*

Chapter 4

It was just like returning home when I got off the plane. Unlike the first time, I was comfortable, relaxed and knew where I was going. Mr. Hwang Kee and Jin Moon were very happy to see me and anxious to know what I had learned in Japan. I told Mr. Hwang Kee all about Mr. Yamaguchi, Mr. Tohei and all about my experiences at the monasteries. He was happy that I got everything that I went after and that I had learned something.

By this time, they had moved the central gym and had a place a bit bigger than the last one. Sometimes I slept there, sometimes I slept at a Korean friend's house. I began training right away in the small gym with various black belts who came in from time to time.

During my second visit to Korea, Hwang Kee began to tell me stories of how Korea was before the war and of his travels to China. He told me he had once been famous for flying while he worked in China. He told me he really couldn't fly but that he had the ability to jump very high while using a rope and grappling hook. He could run full speed at a high building or wall and in one leap scale the wall very quickly by throwing the hook while jumping. He told me that as a boy, he could observe tigers in the mountains and he watched their living habits.

One night, he invited me to dinner and as we sat cross legged on the floor he asked me if I could jump over the table without uncrossing my legs. I said no; he told me after the proper training I should be able to.

Another time, he told me about when he travelled to Northern Mongolia near the Russian border. He stopped in a restaurant and a big fight started over some woman in the restaurant. I don't know how the fight started because I couldn't understand Korean that well. Anyway, he was attacked by twenty-five men and within five minutes had killed all of them. He told me he tried to revive everyone as much as possible but that they were too dead. Then he asked me how he did it. I guessed as many answers as I possibly could.

I asked him if he got tired; he said, 'No'.

I asked him if he did it with internal yogic exercises and again he shook his head.

He asked me again, 'Where does the power come from to be able to defeat twenty-five men and not be tired?' I had no more answers and he told me to wait. I waited many years for that one, but now I know.

During that six months period, I travelled all around Seoul and sometimes to the country where I began training in a Shi Palge school. My first Shi Palge instructor was a man named Mr. Kim.

My luck with instructors amazed me. Mr. Kim was a humble dedicated man who immediately liked me from the start. He had only two students who were as devoted to the art as he was. I became the third. I was referred to Mr. Kim by one very good Korean friend. When I was introduced to him I described in brief my history and he asked me to demonstrate everything I had learned. He was impressed with much of my technique but criticized some of it as well. His criticism was always in terms of chi, concentration and fluidity. My Shi Palge instruction at this time was my first real understanding of power through softness and grace.

The Shi Palge movements roughly translated mean eighteen ways of escape. It is difficult to describe the training, in this book, because it was so involved. Generally, it had some round movements that were in some ways similar to Aikido. It did have round deflecting actions that could be called blocks I suppose and it gave great importance to the cultivation of the internal energy through certain exercises called Nei Gung and Wei Gung.

Besides certain meditations, the Shi Palge taught ways of moving about the room *hypnotically*. According to my instructor, when fighting, the best man can disappear from his opponents sight while standing right in front of him. I practised very hard and I didn't quite get to that level but I gained a keen sense of awareness to the movement of anything around me. There were also many types of meditations involved in the many kinds of forms we had to do. I trained this art form early every morning and then went to the Tang Soo Do school for training in the later hours of the morning.

One morning, during my second training session, I was concentrating deeply on all types of movements. My instructor asked me to free fight with him. We sparred for about three or four minutes and then as he attacked a strange feeling came over me. I moved in and touched him in a certain way and he lost all control. I felt as if I fell through a large hole and it seemed as if l was looking at him through a long tube. There was nothing he could do anymore and there was some kind of strange energy in the room, so we both stopped. He realized that something had happened that day, and it had. I tried to explain to some people around me what I was experiencing but nobody understood. I felt that I had found a hole in time and space. That day was an epic experience in my life as a key to understanding power through total passivity.

I redoubled my training efforts in my forms training and exercises. After morning training at the Shi Palge school I would come to the Tang Soo gym and always find Mr. Hwang Kee just cleaning up after training himself. No one was ever there in the morning and I just usually trained there by myself. But almost daily I'd see a crack in the door and I'd know that Mr. Hwang Kee was observing my training habits carefully.

One day, Jin Moon told me that he had to leave Korea. His father had decided it was time to try to strengthen Tang Soo Do outside of the country. Due to the corruption within there was no reason for Jin Moon to waste his talents staying in Korea. In a short time, he left the country. I, as a last gesture, bought him his ticket and said goodbye at the airport. He flew off to Greece and never returned.

I moved into a house by myself and lived alone. Through my training, I had heard of another man in the Shi Palge art named Mr. Chang, I went to visit his school to compare what I was learning with what he was doing. Chang's school did a great deal of yoga and specialized in points. Because I had afternoons free and now that Jin Moon was gone, I trained at two different schools. Mr. Kim's in the morning and Mr. Chang's in the afternoon. During the break I trained myself, had lunch and taught a few English classes for

Winter time at the Korean monasteries.

extra money. Mr. Chang had inherited certain so-called secrets from his father who had learned them from one of the monks in a country monastery. They included certain internal exercises and strange forms of moving meditations that were similar to acting drunk. I trained diligently at both schools for the next six months. It was also during that time I was taken to several various country temples to do some training in seclusion.

The place I lived in, in Seoul, was in a bad section of town. There were often many fights and disruptions in the area. In Korea, there is a curfew and all people must be off the streets at night by midnight. People found out after midnight are taken to jail and sometimes even beaten up. Foreigners are not supposed to be out but are not usually bothered as much as the Koreans are.

One night, I had had some dinner and a few drinks with some friends downtown. I lived far away from where we were and because it was late and could only get a taxi part of the way home, I then had to walk the rest of the way. I wasn't far from home when I turned down an alley way only a few blocks from where I lived. I heard a strange noise and turned towards that direction. A man dressed in dark clothes leapt out from a building and came towards me. He spoke half English and half Korean and it was obvious he was trying to rob me. I backed up slowly and was going back to the main street when from behind another man grabbed me. I spun around and automatically punched straight at his temple. As I did, the other man attacked simultaneously from behind. Still spinning, I struck the other man the same way. I elbowed the man behind me while against striking the first assailant who had by then dropped to his knees. Everything happened so fast I really don't know what was going on. My mind was blank and frightened. One moment I was whistling cheerfully down the street, the next, as I checked, two men lay dead at my feet. My torn shirt was still in the hand of the man who'd gone down first and there was blood everywhere.

After curfew, police frequently patrolled the streets. Because there were no witnesses and because martial law was in effect, I was really worried what might happen to me. I remembered taking off my torn shirt, stuffing it in the nearest garbage can and running as fast as I could down dark alleyways, hiding in dark shadows in case someone should see me. It seemed like it took ages to get home, and when I finally arrived it was a great relief. Though it was near winter, I threw all my clothes away and jumped into a bath of cold water to wash off the mess. I stayed in my room for days after that and I didn't eat anything.

I went over and over again in my mind what had happened a few nights earlier. I thought and thought about my training and wondered if I had done the right thing. I wasn't happy. I wasn't sad. I wasn't anything. I just had a strange feeling about the whole thing and I wondered if there wasn't some other way I could have handled the situation.

After a few days, I slowly got over my feelings and deemed it was safe to come out again. I resumed my normal activities and didn't tell anyone what had happened. Within a few weeks, it would be time to change my visa again and I knew shortly I would be leaving Korea. I had been there now almost two years and was ready for a change. I had decided to go to India and on the way to stop in at Taiwan, Hong Kong and visit martial art schools there.

One night, just before I was about to leave, some friends asked me to go to a party. We drank a lot of Korean wine and got incredibly drunk. We all left from down town at the same time and my old problem of making it half way home came up again. Rather than walk the rest of the way home, I stopped in a cheap hotel. In that part of town, women went with the room for an extra charge and being merrily drunk, I didn't fight the custom.

The night's festivities were almost over and I was just about to drop off to sleep. The last thing I could remember was the dim red glow of the night light above the bed. Then from nowhere came a loud commotion and there was much screaming and yelling just outside the door. Half asleep, I shouted in Korean for everyone to shut up. So ended a peaceful night. I heard somebody trying to tamper with the thin rice paper door and I was half on my feet to check what was going on when a deranged man flew through the entire door. The room was extremely dark and all anyone could see were shadows. I felt a body up against me and punched straight forward instinctively. By this time, the girl in the room had turned on the normal light, and I grabbed the man I had just punched and threw him out the window.

After the commotion had finished, I realised I had a paring knife lodged in my chest. I pulled this out and by now was fully awake and as you can imagine I wasn't happy about the situation. I was bleeding profusely and definitely regretted my choice of overnight accommodation. I stuffed a towel inside my shirt to stop the bleeding, got dressed and walked for a mile to a local hospital where I spent the night. I hadn't lost too much blood and the wound wasn't too serious, so the next day, I was allowed to go home.

I had trouble walking and breathing for the first couple of weeks and during that time I decided not to train in case my instructors found out.

A couple of days later, however, I had to stop at the central gym to deliver a package. One of the guys I trained with started playing with me and I accidentally got bumped in the chest. I almost fell over and the blood showed through. My secret was out.

At the same time, Mr. Hwang Kee just happened to be walking past. He saw something was wrong and immediately approached me and wanted to know what was happening. I knew I was in trouble. I explained as little as possible about the situation without lying and he got the picture really quickly. He checked me over and after he was sure I was alright he asked me if I learned anything. I said yes, and he smiled. All he said was to be more careful next time and there was never another word said about it.

That was only one week before I had to leave Korea.

My experiences taught me three valuable things. Firstly, if you put yourself in the wrong place you're asking for trouble. Secondly, never use an intoxicant to the point where it dulls your senses. Thirdly, never get caught with your pants down!

Chapter 5

I arrived in Hong Kong soon after and was amazed at the change. Everything was much more crowded, people were smaller and nobody paid much attention to anybody else. I didn't know anyone in Hong Kong and I had no addresses. I walked around a lot and looked in the phone books for some sort of guide to martial art schools. I found many acupuncture schools and all sorts of restaurants but no fighting arts.

I finally stumbled across a Karate school which was mediocre but they gave me some suggestions on where to go. Most of the schools I found were small, little rooms in apartment complexes. I generally found the Chinese rather reclusive and they didn't seem to be very interested in outsiders. I think just about everyone has experienced the same sort of things about the ways of the Chinese and so I won't say much here. I didn't see a great deal of discipline and generally people were not interested in talking about meditation.

The standard of the schools I did see were not up to par with anything I had ever seen before and there seemed to be some sort of energy lacking. I generally found most of the Chinese people I talked to very aloof and non-committal. I also got the impression that if you were not Chinese you didn't have the spirit to really delve into the recesses of martial arts. They all talked of Nei Gung and Chinese alchemy but I couldn't find anyone who was really accomplished in these sorts of things. I am not saying there wasn't anything there, only that I was not able to find it. I also found that anywhere I asked questions, they always wanted me to demonstrate what I knew. I knew their game, but wasn't in any position to say no.

I watched mostly in Hong Kong. I watched the lifestyle of the people. I watched the quality of the average Kung Fu centres and I watched the Tai Chi in the mornings with the old people. Of everything I saw, the elders took the cake. Some of the Tai Chi that I saw was excellent. I had seen all I wanted to of Hong Kong and even if I found something worth staying for, it would have had to be really great. It was a nice place to visit but not to train and live. After a short time, I was satisfied with what I came for and decided to move on.

My next stop was Thailand. I had decided from all things I had seen that I would go straight to the most Buddhist of countries that I could find and see if I could find the vital link that I was looking for in my training. I found the Thai people to be very friendly and loving. The only sport they knew anything about was kick boxing. I hadn't come to Thailand for that particular reason but as long as I was there I decided to have a look. I watched the kick boxers and found them to be very spiritual and dedicated. They train as hard for their arts as anywhere I have seen. But all I could see was mediocre boxing technique mixed with bad kicking form. It is purely an external activity which cannot be practised by anyone but the youngest and fittest. I got on a bus and headed out of town after a week of looking around Bangkok. My purpose was to find as many temples as I could and closely examine the methods of meditation that the Thais practised and to see if it had anything to do with my training.

I stayed a short time at every temple I came across out in the country. One particular abbot of one monastery, wanted me to become a monk. I said no, but that I would like to stay there for awhile and study the way of life in that monastery. Because I was a foreigner the monks liked to hear me talk so that they could practise their English. One night, there was a large assembly of monks from all the local monasteries. The Abbot asked me to give a speech about myself and my experiences. I told the history of martial arts to all the monks. They listened intently as I explained how Bodhidharma came from India and established the Dharma through the martial way. I then did a demonstration for all the monks which delighted them as they had never seen anything like it before. They however, didn't know anything about what I was talking about and failed to see any true significance with the Dharma and martial art. I felt really strange throughout the speech and demonstration. Here I was, a Western man, 2,500 years after the time of the Buddha and 1,000 years after Bodhidharma, giving a discourse and demonstration to a huge assembly of monks. Instead of making my ceremonial bow to the flag, I was bowing to a huge statue of the Buddha; instead of bowing to students or instructors I was bowing to this assembly of monks.

Life in the monastery was comfortable and nice but I found that generally the monks didn't really meditate much. They also didn't study a great deal either. They were kind gentle people but had given up the thought of enlightenment in one lifetime and hoped to collect merits by being good people. They were very much like the average Christians who believe that when you die you go to heaven if you are good and if you're bad you go to hell. The kindness of the monks was fantastic but none of them practised hard. I found them all to lead rather leisurely lives and take it easy.

This wasn't for me, so I decided to go to India. I went back to Bangkok, then travelled over land through Malaysia and found some Penjak Silat practitioners and some more Tai-Chi people on the way.

As I travelled throughout the country of Malaysia, I noticed there was a great contrast to life in the cities with that of the jungles. In the cities, modern ways of the West had taken over the life styles of the people. In the jungles however, the people lived much the same as they always did in the past with very little change. I decided to go into the forests and see if I could get a little closer to the real Malaysian people.

I arranged transport into the country and went to a local lodge frequented mainly by strangers. A lodge was not a hotel. It was a grass house about twelve square with a family living inside. A visitor could stay on a grass woven cot for ten cents. As soon as any stranger arrived the news would be all over the village in a flash. Boys and girls would come around and stare and the villagers would examine the clothes I was wearing and the things I travelled with. If a person stayed more than a day in any of these places he always met the village elder. Once I had eaten or visited with the head of the village I was accepted more by the people and though they were suspicious still, they were not so afraid. I didn't know much Malay at the time, but I could utter a few words and some of the boys in the villages knew a few words of English. Together with that I was able to communicate somewhat.

Everyone knew the words *Penjak* and whenever I mentioned the word they always smiled. All the villagers had stories of the best fighters in the area. The young boys sometimes kicked around with each other and showed some basic knowledge of a form of free fighting that was a few steps up from brawling. I was determined to find out where they picked it up from. I began by playing with some of the younger boys and then demonstrated some basic forms. Their smiles faded and the other villagers gathered around to watch. People came for a closer look and their faces were more serious than before. It was a strange energy in the forest. I was the only white man for miles around and probably the only foreign man anyone had ever seen doing the kinds of things I was doing. The jungle was hot and extremely humid. Bugs crawled out of nowhere but the people were taking an interest and I thought I was getting somewhere which I was.

Some of the older men approached me and started doing some sort of forms which were very round and low to the ground. They demonstrated on each other the practical applications of the moves and we had a small exchange of ideas. This type of experience accompanied me in many of the villages I went to. I found out through my travels that there was no firmly established way to learn the fighting arts but that there were certain men in each district that kept the important knowledge and taught sporadically from time to time.

There was also a certain amount of mystique attached to the Penjak people. They sometimes went without food for days and entered into strange trances. They had reputations for being able to make special potions to stop themselves from bleeding or being cut. This made sense to me because all the local people carried long machetes which was a common necessity for life in the jungle. Besides building and chopping wood, the knives were used for farming and fighting.

The Penjak people had a long history of knife work and so they had also devised methods of keeping themselves from being injured by knives. As I also found out they did a lot of free form work when practising with knives and took dangerous chances with their form work. If they drank their special potions before fighting or practising they reduced the possibility of injuries.

One night, I stayed in a village where I was approached by a man and his wife. He told me of one of his uncles who knew a great deal about the fighting arts of the jungle. He divulged to me that there were ways that they could insert certain rods of various substances into the arms and legs which made a person invulnerable. He also told me that the person who underwent this had to make a special pledge of secrecy and allegiance to the master who inserted the rods and explained to him how to use the powers they would afford him. I learned that there were ways to prolong a person's life indefinitely by using certain potions secretly made up by these particular masters. To qualify for these things a person had to undergo a series of initiations and tests given by the master. If he passed this, he would then have to go into the jungle alone with the teacher and go through all kinds of rituals in order to purify himself before receiving the final teachings which accompanied the insertion of secret rods.

I was told that the elder who performed these rites had gone to a neighbouring village and would return in about a month. If I wished, I could stay around and wait and this man would introduce me to the elder.

This was all incredible information but I had no desire to stay in the mosquito jungles waiting for what appeared to be a village witchdoctor. From all my past studies and experiences, I had learned not to doubt anything I heard without serious consideration. Although I was interested in the secret ways of the Penjak people, I was reticent about becoming involved with what could possibly be forms of *black magic*. I had seen people go into trances and I had seen people possessed with strange energies; but I worried if by entering these states a person wasn't giving up the control of his own mind. I decided to move on.

I left the jungles of Malaysia and travelled to the modern city of Singapore. I met and talked to so many Chinese men that it would be too much to put down on paper. Generally, I found that everybody had a few bits and pieces of Nei Gung cultivation.

Every school and person I talked to had different varieties of meditations and internal energies. There were all sorts of stories of powers that could be achieved and I witnessed every kind of training technique from hypnotism to magic potions.

One thing stuck out more than anything. The more secrets and rituals involved in the art, the less virtue I saw in men. I saw rivalry between instructors and schools and among village leaders. I met many people who trained for power but none that trained for wisdom. I watched, listened and learned and even exposed myself to incredibly embarrassing situations in order to get involved with people who practised the arts.

From Singapore I went to Indonesia. I travelled on a river boat throughout all the islands of Sumatra and Java to Bali.

My first meeting in Indonesia was with more Penjak people. The boat I was on had stopped at a small island and I had to wait for a few days for the connecting ferry. There was a teenage boy who spoke English who came out of nowhere and started talking to me as soon as I got off the boat. He invited me to his house and I decided to go along. Along the way, he asked me why I had come to that small island. I explained I was travelling the world studying and comparing the lives and habits of martial artists and that I had come to Indonesia to see the Indonesian style of Penjak Silat.

As fate had it, the boy practised this art and immediately sent for a few of his friends. He gave me a small demonstration first and then asked me to show them something. I showed them a few forms and they asked me if I would teach a small class in the evening. Three young men and myself gathered that night in a grass hut lit up by kerosene lamps. I trained with all of them and though they were not highly advanced I was able to examine the style in which they moved. There was some difference in their art and the Malaysian one.

I made some good friends in that village and they all came down to say goodbye as I left when the boat arrived.

I travelled through Sumatra until I came to a village called Padang. There was one very nice hotel there. The river boat captain, whom I had travelled with for days, bought my bus ticket and instructed the driver to take me to the best place there was. I wound up in a very old and beautiful hotel. The Dutch had inhabited Indonesia years before and had left some influence there. Padang was a nice town, with horse and cart for transportation which were also used as local taxis. I stayed there to rest for a few days and did some shopping. Because my pants were being washed and I had no others to wear I put on my uniform trousers for the afternoon. I went to a local restaurant and a boy observed that I was wearing training pants. He walked straight up to me and asked me if I did Karate. I said yes and he told me his uncle was the Silat teacher of the town. This was a pleasant surprise and I made arrangements to meet his uncle that evening.

When I went to the house the man whom I met was very muscular, middle aged and had a hard face. He asked me why I was there. The attitude and energy surrounding the meeting made me feel as if I was a visiting gun fighter in some western town. I explained to him that I was just passing through and was interested in the local art. He asked me to demonstrate something which I did. He did a few moves and then sat down.

I asked him if he was willing to exchange a few ideas, but he said no one could learn Silat unless they were prepared to stay for many years. I explained that I didn't want to learn his entire art; I was only interested in a cultural exchange. His attitude was incredibly defensive and then he began talking about the importance of spiritual attitude necessary for training. I decided the guy was having me on a bit and I was getting a little uncomfortable and felt I wanted to leave. Whatever the man's intentions were they certainly weren't straight forward. He mentioned a few things in his talk about spiritualism, that resembled some of the things I'd heard in the Malaysian jungle. I wanted nothing to do with it and excused myself. Nothing more significant happened in Sumatra and I travelled the rest of the way as a normal tourist until I hit Bali.

In Bali, I took a nice rest and ate good food as I was beginning to get very travel weary from all my journeying. Since I had left Korea, I hadn't been in any one place for a particularly long time. Food and diet varied anywhere from a piece of fruit, a few mouthfuls of rice, to half fried chicken wings of emaciated chickens.

Bali was a relaxing refuge for me. While I was there I noticed a magical attitude in the people. The Muslim influence in Java and Sumatra seemed to instill an entirely different attitude in those people, than the Balinese. It was interesting that Bali was the only island with heavy Buddhist influence, rather than Muslim. The people were very spiritual and also very superstitious. They danced the Ramayana dance which reflected the stories that traced back to Indian culture and Hindu philosophy. The Balinese dancing reflected an incredible similarity of Kung Fu arts that I studied. Because there was such an amazing similarity and because of the story behind the dance, I saw a very strong link between the story of Ramayana and Kung Fu.

While there I met some people with a boat who were sailing among the islands. I thought it would be nice to see the other islands, so I went along for the ride. The next island was Lombok.

Our boat sailed into the harbour and we were met by throngs of people in small boats. They were excited over our visit and were very friendly. We bought provisions and stayed for a couple of days.

During that time, I saw one of the children playing with a stick one day. I grabbed a boat oar and did a stick form for the children who were playing in the area. They loved it and in no time at all I was surrounded by crowds. I got a bit embarrassed and stopped and went back to the boat.

Because we had been sailing for a week, I felt a bit out of shape and went out to a rice paddy to do some forms and stretching. I went to a rice paddy where I thought there was no one around and when I had finished

I did a small meditation and got up to leave. As I started walking I noticed there were hundreds of people hiding all over the palace, in trees and ditches and coming out of everywhere. They were smiling and laughing and my secluded training had turned into a public entertainment. I was a bit embarrassed and went towards the town where the boat was.

On the way, some of the local policemen came up to me and told me they had learned some Karate. They asked me to go to the Police Station. There they had piles of bricks everywhere and they wanted to have a competition. This was completely ridiculous for me, but then that's what was happening right there and then and so I decided, *When in Rome, do as Romans do.*

So the competition started.

All the men broke two bricks with chopping and punching in different ways. I smashed up all the bricks they had and finished off by breaking a few with my elbows and broke the last few with my head. This was all done in good fun and I felt very light hearted about it. The people however, loved me for it and threw a little party in the village for me. The policemen brought me a few bottles of Bintang beer which was the local brew and demonstrated their true sincerity. (On their wages, this beer was an incredible luxury and very expensive). We all had a good time and even more than the bricks, they were impressed with how much beer I could drink. We left Lombok with good memories and sailed off into the blue.

The captain of the boat was a terrible navigator and didn't know anything about sailing. We got blown off course and got caught in a terrible storm. We lost sight of all land and were completely lost for days. Finally, with a cracked mast and a crippled ship we drifted towards a small island with no idea where we were. From the shores, we saw dozens upon dozens of dug-out canoes coming towards us. We had no idea what was happening. As the boats neared, we saw they were filled with natives half-naked, bare-footed and clad only in their loin cloths and batiks; it was exactly like a scene out of Jules Vernes.

The Captain spoke Indonesian and we soon found that we were the first white men to visit the island since 1946. It came as much of a shock to us as it did to the natives. They helped us tow our useless boat further into the harbour where we dropped anchor and went ashore.

The people there lived in a small village of grass houses on the shores of the beach. They fished and raised chickens and pigs for a living. Their houses were native grass, elevated on stilts and contained absolutely nothing in them. The people were very poor but happy.

We were brought to the hut of the village elder and I can remember it was a very proud day for him. His first gesture in extending friendship was to offer to fix our teeth! The prize object in the entire village was in his house and this was an ancient drilling tool which was foot operated, made in 1910, and came all the way from Holland. They demonstrated for us how it worked and we were all worried. How we were going to get out of this one without insulting their hospitality. Because we didn't know where we were and there were hundreds of villagers outside proud to demonstrate the modern advancements of their town, we wondered about our etiquette. It took about twenty minutes to wiggle our way out of the situation. But we did so successfully by letting everyone examine the beautiful silver fillings in our teeth. They were all impressed and left us alone; but I'd had one more problem to deal with.

The people shaved raw pieces of bark with their knives and then rolled huge cigars of raw tobacco, tied by a string. If we didn't get our teeth fixed, we at least had to smoke with them. They refused to take no for an answer.

The other people in the boat smoked before but I was not used to it. We sat down and it was lucky we did, because as we passed around the cigars, my head started to spin, my joints turned to rubber and I had to lean against the wall of the hut for support. If I'd had anything to eat previously, I would have vomited. I immediately got an incredible headache which lasted for days and the experience was mildly traumatic. Whatever those people were smoking, certainly was powerful stuff, but I definitely didn't want to make it a part of my lifestyle.

At this time, I didn't quite know what to do. The people who were sailing were totally incompetent, the boat was a wreck and we were stranded on a south sea island without any idea of location. One thing I didn't want to do was get back on that boat after the experience we had had in the storm. We found out from the natives that there was another town on the other side of the island where supply boats sailed to. It was a day's journey by donkey and chicken truck. I set off in the back of a filthy truck, filled with blood, chicken shit, scores of people and piles of chickens. I was cramped in a corner unable to move for hours; engulfed in stench with very little air. It was an incredible journey and by the time we reached the small fishing village, twelve hours later, I was entirely wiped-out.

I pried myself off the truck and went to a small restaurant to get myself something to eat. The small town was relatively modern compared to the last one and the first place I walked into I met two men from South Africa. They owned a boat and were sailing to Australia. They had room on the boat and invited me along.

Rather than India, I was now on my way to Australia.

Getting off the island was not as easy as I had hoped for. The two men were the only two English speaking people on the island and they had brought an Indonesian sailing boat, of which the style and rigging had not changed in the last thousand years. The sails were hand-woven and the rigging hand carved and roughly hewn. The two South Africans didn't know anything about sailing, nor did they speak Indonesian. They paid four Indonesian men $50 each to sail the boat to Australia.

With a sack of rice, a dozen cans of condensed milk and a few fish, we prepared to set sail. The sailors were all local boys who had never sailed further than nearby islands. There was only a small hand compass for navigation and a pocket atlas which showed the Indonesian islands with the continent of Australia. There was also one chart, old and tattered, of Bathurst Island. These were all we had, it seemed insane to travel this way but there was no other choice.

Before we left, the sailors, who were very religious and superstitious waited for an elder to come to the boat and do a particular ritual. The ritual lasted for hours and the men had to give a quarter of all their money to the elder. He invoked a God on the ship which entered into him as he went into a trance. He danced and rolled all over the ship like a madman. He pulled out a dagger and stabbed himself many times. He slashed with the blade at all parts of his body, completely immersed in a frenzy. It was an incredible spectacle and the energy in the air was charged with tenseness. It turned out the man was one of the Peniak people. He came out of the trance unscathed without any cuts in his flesh. There was no sign of blood and he was totally unharmed. Obviously, the stories were true about these men, but from the state I'd seen this man enter into I was happy on my decision not to become involved with this art form, which appeared more and more like sorcery, all the time.

At last, we set off for Australia.

We had no idea what was in store for us. The first few days went well while we sailed among the last of the islands. We visited Flores and Timor, stopping into get a few provisions on the way, then we set out for the last leg of the journey.

For the first few days, things ran rather well. The men caught a few fish, the winds were favourable and things seemed okay. After a few days, however, the wind completely stopped. By now, we were totally out of sight of any land and had just sailed south. The logic of the South African men was that we didn't have to worry about hitting Australia, because it was too big to miss! Neither I nor they realised that because of the isolation of Northern Australia, if we missed our mark and landed anywhere else except Darwin, we would have an extremely difficult time finding civilization.

With no wind, the boat bobbed up and down like a cork for days. It was hot and uncomfortable with seven of us crowded on a small boat. There was only fire wood aboard, and besides matches, there were no other modern conveniences on board. To cook the rice, which was our only staple besides the fish we could catch, we had to make an open fire on deck in a small fire place. This was done by lighting a small stick, holding it to a larger piece of wood and blowing through a bamboo tube.

Also the boat constantly leaked and we all took turns around the clock driving the bilge pump which consisted of a bamboo tube that went into the hold and worked like a butter churn. We were without wind for seven days. It seemed like an eternity. Everybody was depressed and demoralized, but there was nothing we could do.

One evening, just as the sun went down, we saw a black cloud off in the distance. We felt a slight breeze and immediately put up the sails and everyone was overjoyed. The boat began to move along and I laughed like a madman. The joy was short-lived.

The wind became stronger, the night became blacker, white caps appeared and soon we realized that we were on the brink of a raging storm. Huge waves engulfed the boat while incredible winds tore at the sails and cracked the mast.

Someone had left a kerosene lamp on inside and it had spilled into the fire wood supply. Outside the boat, the men were struggling from being thrown into the sea and trying to steer the rudder to stop the boat from being capsized. Inside, I was fighting a raging fire and I think I was more scared than I'd ever been in my whole life. Two other men and myself succeeded in putting out the fire while being flung uncontrollably around the inside of the boat. The storm raged for hours and with incredible luck we managed to keep the boat afloat.

By morning, we were all totally exhausted, but still alive.

The boat sailed on that day as the men made repairs to the damage. In the middle of the next night, we ran aground on a reef. Barefooted all of us had to get out and try to force the boat off the reef. My feet were cut in the process, but I didn't notice till later.

We got the boat off the reef and dropped anchor till morning when we could see where we were going. We had sailed into a bizarre obstacle course of reefs which had to be navigated through carefully, lest we ran aground again. With one man at the top of the mast and our winds holding up we managed to get through the hazardous reef.

The next day, we had good winds and fine weather. We sailed on for a week, not knowing where we were going. The terrible storm from earlier had completely disorientated everybody. The cuts from the reef had turned into coral poisoning and my legs swelled up like balloons. I had difficulty walking and daily I had to cut an X in my legs, and press to squeeze out the pus. To do this, I had only an old diving knife that left greats scars in my legs, which are still there today.

The men were not able to catch any fish and our food ran out. The wind stopped again for some time and things got worse. I lost all conception of time and had become quite skinny except for my huge swollen legs that were still badly infected. As another week passed my mind began to wander aimlessly. My thoughts turned to death and I thought of all the stories of shipwrecked sailors and people who had been blown off course and lost at sea. They were all incredibly true and I was now threatened with the same fate. I reflected on my experiences and my goals in this life and thought about the masters I had trained under. I felt disgusted that I had ever travelled by sea and that I hadn't finished finding out all the answers while I was alive, when death looked so imminent.

By bits and pieces, winds came and went and with a little pocket compass, no one could do anything except continue sailing South. We saw no signs of life anywhere and with the food supply completely exhausted, the huge cockroaches, who were in great numbers on the boat, crawled all over our bodies as we tried to sleep. This experience was endless and everyone almost gave up trying.

One day, we heard an aircraft. It was unmistakable. We got a little excited, watched it fly by and that was all. The wind picked up for a few days, then one evening we saw a flashing light far off in the distance. With no other objective to sail for, we sailed for the light. We sailed for three more days, seeing the light in the evenings and sailing towards its direction in the daytime. When we arrived at the light, we found another light off in the distance. We knew we were on to something. We sailed for a few more days and when we found that light, we saw off in the distance what appeared to be a reef. As we neared closer, we thought we could see a building but we weren't sure. The winds stopped again and we remained there for two days.

Desperate, myself and one other man paddled a dug out canoe, half a day towards the reef, in case it might be land. We finally arrived to a sandy shore. We saw trees and went completely mad. We didn't know where we were but we knew it was land. I jumped around for joy and then we both went off to explore. We found a road and saw a tower, which was the first sign of civilization we had seen for over a month. We came to a paved road and not long after, a car came down the road. We both stopped the car and asked the person where we were. He looked at us quite strangely and told us we were in Australia. We screamed and jumped and asked him to take us to the nearest town.

We had miraculously hit Darwin! We arranged for another boat to bring in our boat and after clearing immigration we all went our separate ways.

Chapter 6

I moved into a small room in a boarding house and relaxed while deciding my next move. It was an incredible culture shock to be back in the West again. Years had gone by since I had first left my home back in America. I'd been through many experiences and had changed greatly. After my first visit to the hospital, it took an additional two weeks for my infected legs to return to normal. Darwin was a nice peaceful town. It was quiet and the people were very friendly. Because of the quiet easy way of life, it was the perfect place for me to stop and organize all the things that had happened to me since I'd first left home.

I found a small training hall and trained there every morning. I soon learned that there were various martial arts conducted there in the evenings. While I was training there one evening, some students approached me and asked me to teach them. One of the students was very keen and although only a green belt he ran a Karate school there. Darwin at the time had very few black belts and those who had come, rarely stayed long. I agreed to teach a few students and the numbers gradually multiplied.

I approached the YMCA in an attempt to find a better suited

The author's first demonstration in Australia and the beginning of the Darwin Tang Soo Tao Assoication.

place to train. The manager there, after seeing one of my demonstrations, was so impressed that he organized a hall for me. Following that, I was given a television series which lasted three months. In a very short amount of time, there was a firm foundation for the Darwin Tang Soo Tao Association.

This all happened so naturally I didn't have time to think about it. I had no intentions of opening a school, yet all of a sudden I was a chief instructor of a to-jang. I made enough money to pay my $14 a week rent at the boarding house, buy plenty of food and that was enough. During the next year, I analysed each and every aspect of my martial experience. I examined all my strong points and I checked for any weak ones. I reflected on words and personalities of the Chinese, Korean and Japanese instructors who had taught me. I loved my training and my art but though I trained hard and continuously, I felt there was still something missing.

I analysed my Korean Tang Soo Do training and all my instructors. Everyone was kind and taught the importance of developing spirit in the martial arts. Though they always mentioned Buddhist roots, they never showed the direct link. Master Hwang Kee was indeed a great man who researched the internal and external systems of almost all existent martial arts.

The black belts I trained with however, even up to the rank of 7th Dan, had no teaching in the training he expounded. Many were good technicians, but they did not meditate. Many had fantastic kicking technique of the Soo Bak Do, but did not develop hand motions. Although Hwang Kee understood internal arts and had recorded them in his book, not one instructor I had ever met in Korean Tang Soo Do had any knowledge about what was contained in those pages. It appeared plain to me that Master Hwang Kee, although he himself knew these arts, rarely, if ever, passed on the entire art to anyone. To me Master Hwang Kee was the embodiment of Tang Soo Do. All other people were bits and pieces of what they thought it was about. I was in no position to doubt his judgement on how he taught to whom and for what reason, I only knew that the Tang Soo Do secret remained bottled up in one man. I had never met one Korean in my life who could even do the master Tae Kuk Kwan form, other than Mr. Hwang. Some of these people had trained under him for up to forty years. This didn't make much sense to me.

Shi Palge was a beautiful and intricate art, but once again, although the instructors were good, I didn't see their qualities in the students. I gained a lot from training with my instructors only because of my many years of previous training experiences. Though we did many internal exercises and meditations, there was a particular energy that I was looking for that seemed to be absent. I could definitely feel I was being taken somewhere in Shi Palge but I didn't have the confidence as to where. In Japan, I found that although Karate people boasted of the fine integration of hard and soft, basically Karate was always more hard than soft. I felt this kind of chi development was not well rounded and also that the excessive pride of many of the artists made it difficult for them to accept other martial arts. To me this inhibited their ability to learn with an open mind. I found most Japanese (though not all) to be so nationalistic that though they taught Western students, they did so with a condescending nature. I had a feeling that the Budo arts that I learned in Japan expressed love and nature through Japanology, rather than love of nature through universality.

In the Goju school, I examined Mr. Yamaguchi's Shinto, Zen and yogic philosophies. I had even met one of his teachers. The philosophies he expounded were well rounded and made sense. There were however, two points about which I knew to be true. The first was that he had not yet finished his own objective, although he was well along the way. The second was that outside of Mr. Yamaguchi, no one did the art as he did. He, like Mr. Hwang Kee, was the only one. Mr. Yamaguchi was Goju. The other practitioners were doing bits and pieces of what they thought he represented.

In Aikido training, I observed a flowing graceful art similar to fast moving Tai Chi. The good points I enjoyed in Aikido were the non-stop flow, the lack of competition and the emphasis on universal harmony. The faith that most Aikido people had was also refreshing. Aikido taught a spiritual philosophy through a physical culture. The art was based on the realizations of the said enlightened master, Morei Ueshiba.

One of the drawbacks I felt in the art was that it lacked practical application in the defense aspect during the initial periods of training. I could see that the only reason I could osmose any part of the art was due to my many years of previous experience. Most of the high instructors in the Honbu had also held other high grades in martial arts before entering Aikido. Some of them even suggested that a person be at least black belt level before beginning the art. I could easily see the reason for this but at the same time felt there was a loop-hole in progressive development of the defense aspects of the art.

The great master himself was highly involved with many other arts before developing his present system. This suggested to me that perhaps the art was not complete in itself, but must be developed along with some other variable. Another aspect of the art was that it was based on the realization of an enlightened master. The problem for me was that I had not met him, he was already dead, and no one else as far as I could see, was either enlightened or anywhere near the level of his ability they talked about. The schism I had seen among the highest instructors of the so-called spiritual way of harmony, made me question if the master's teachings had really been received correctly.

For my age and experience in the art, I was in no space to question anyone. I didn't have the level of wisdom to understand the rightness and wrongness of any of the master instructors; so I didn't. But what I did question was the energy I was receiving, and if it was producing what I was looking for. As an art form, Aikido was tremendous. As a defense art and a spiritual philosophy it was stimulating, but I felt there were many places lacking in practicality. I didn't know if it was the art, myself, the instructors, or a little bit of each; so I pondered.

The Chinese I had encountered up till then had been very reserved. It seemed they harboured secrets and covered them in a veil of mystery. They always kept one guessing how much of the secret they were hiding or if they were just trying to hide what they didn't know. Again, I found ethnic bias in the ways they taught. The Tai Chi Chuan had similarities to Aikido, in that it was perfect in every way, esoterically. It covered all the angles and was developed from the wisdom of enlightened masters. But completely by itself, it lacked a progressive practical application at lower levels of training. There was no middle way to reach the Tai Chi Chuan. Because of this, few people entered into and completed the path. Even in this most gracious art, I'd found conflicting personalities.

In the lowest parts of Asia, I'd found a mediocre quality of martial art movement combined with a certain type of spirituality. But what was the spirituality? To me it was a personal desire for power and self gain. To achieve this, men tampered with sorcery and black magic, which were things I didn't even want to know about. Although the great masters of Japan and Korea and a few of the Chinese men I met were pure and virtuous, I found very few men in martial arts whose virtue coincided with their expertise in training or vice versa.

Some men I met were indeed masters, but many questions and thoughts surged in my head.

- If martial art was founded on Buddhism, what was the direct relation?
- What was Buddhism?
- What was the primary goal of martial arts training?
- If martial arts training was to develop perfect and pure spirit of harmony, as taught by the masters, then how did one develop the progressive way to develop this spirit?
- If martial art was a way to truth, why weren't more practitioners like the masters?
- What was truth? What was life? What was death?
- What made the masters, the masters?
- Some masters themselves had told me they had not achieved the ultimate goal.
- What was the ultimate goal?
- If martial arts contained truth it should work for everybody who practises it.
- Why were there so few masters?
- Why didn't everybody that practised martial art have the wisdom of the masters?

- If one stayed at low level technique he became stagnant and could not progress further.
- There was high level technique and there was low level technique; if one didn't progress through low level technique, he could not advance to high.
- If one began at high level technique it would be like giving car keys to a baby. He would lack the understanding of the low level which contained the secret for understanding the high.
- Martial arts primary aim as taught by all masters, was to develop spirit.
- The medium used must help defense technique.
- If one loses the defense aspect of the art it is useless to use the defense art. We should cultivate an alternative method, i.e. yoga, religion etc.
- Buddhism taught to live for all sentient beings.
- Martial arts should try to help as many people as possible, should be non-exclusive and without bias.
- Too few people had reached a high goal.
- The best way would be a practical method that progressively moves from low level to high level movement.
- Each and every level should have a practical application for the student at that level.
- While working towards the absolute it should utilize the relative and not depend on the absolute, until which time that absolute is achieved.
- Each progressive level should contain a parallel with the spiritual objective, equally proportionate to the physical technique.

After closely examining all the arts that I had trained in, I found that up till now no particular art or instructor had successfully answered these points for me. I had found some masters who had attained high levels, but they had left no progressive way for a student to follow. I also found discrepancies in the ways the arts were handed down from disciples to seniors. I respected and loved every person, high or low level, that had helped me this far but I knew there was something more I had to discover if martial art was to prove its true worth in the present day as it did in the time of Daruma.

Chapter 7

I trained hard daily. I woke up at 5am every morning and did forms for two hours. I read, studied and trained constantly.

Time after time, I wrote notes to myself on my progressive ways of thinking. I analysed again and again attitudes of my instructors, my personal feelings, my ego and every movement that I had ever learned. I studied intently the basic attitudes and qualities of the people who joined my school. I watched baby animals and adult animals. I studied babies' movements and adult movements. I analysed the initial mistakes common to most people and the effects of modern society on natural movement. I personally guided every person who came to me giving as much experience as I was able concerning the spiritual and physical movement in martial art.

During the three months television series I conducted, I was contacted by some Aboriginal people. I knew nothing of Aboriginals. They asked me to go to a settlement and teach in a small community. At another time, I taught a school entirely of Aboriginals. I learnt a great deal about myself and the art in relation to the black people. Where as the white people were attracted to the power from my initial demonstrations, the Aboriginals intuitively related to the beauty of the forms. Because their own tribal dances and way of life were based on harmony with nature, they easily understood the qualities inside forms such as the eagle, sparrow, tiger and snake etc. I found that though they were a primitive people their natural instincts automatically attracted them to martial arts. I found also that because of their unnatural instincts the white man's inadequacies attracted him to martial arts. This in no way means that one race was superior to the other but it clearly showed me the damaging effects of uncontrolled modern civilization.

The spontaneity and naturalness of the Aboriginals has always impressed me and it still does.

I trained daily for almost a year, analysing all the points I have outlined earlier, going through every technique and meditation. I had decided that I would have to return to Asia and this time to India. I heard many stories about India, some good and some bad; but I decided to try to find an answer to my questions in a channel of yoga, non-associated to martial arts. I sent a ticket to a black belt friend of mine to help run the school in my absence and made all the arrangements to go. While waiting for this instructor to arrive, for the first time in my life, I took up a small hobby not associated with martial arts.

That was sky diving.

In the building where I ran my school, there was a parachuting organization. I had a secret desire to experiment with my one-point concentration when I didn't have the normal forces of nature to rely on. The idea I had toyed with came to fruition when a parachute instructor made an unusual arrangement with me. He said he would give me one parachute jump if I would give him one martial art lesson. So I agreed.

One Saturday afternoon, I practised a few jumps off a box and the next week I was in an airplane flying through the air. I only wanted to experiment concerning a few one-point exercises while skydiving. I had no desire to be a skydiver. I also had a question in my head whether a person with perfect control and reflex could survive a fall if his parachute didn't work. It was interesting to think about but certainly no one would want to test it.

I took up skydiving after Saturday afternoon training for a couple of months. Besides the fun of the sport, I was surprised at what I didn't know about my one-point. One Saturday afternoon, after jumping all day, we were all about to leave the jump site. The sun was going down and it was beautiful out in the Australian bush. I had finished jumping for the day and was packing up to go home. Because the plane needed one more jumper, they asked me to share the load. I didn't really want to but a few people insisted, so I went along. It was a 6,500 foot jump which is a thirty to fifty second freefall. We were all going to do a link up in mid air and every one was supposed to come down together. We all leapt out of the airplane and had a beautiful time. The time of the day and the beauty of the fall was just like an incredible dream. Everything went perfectly until I went to pull the rip-cord.

My harness had moved and my main line had shifted behind my shoulder. As I reached up to correct this I lost my stability and tumbled through the air out of control. Before I regained myself, I was way too low for safety. Instead of taking any chances, I pulled my reserve chute. Nothing happened. I had no time to be shocked I just couldn't believe it. I yanked the pack apart with my bare hands and threw up what there was of the parachute. It had been packed incorrectly and there was nothing but large handkerchiefs full of holes flapping in the air. I knew I was done for and there was absolutely nothing I could do. I pummelled through the air and watched the ground rush up at me. I decided to put my feet together, try to relax and roll the second I felt anything. That thought was much shorter than the time it takes to read about it. I no sooner thought it, when I smashed down into the earth. Everyone thought I was dead, and so did I. I was knocked out for a short amount of time and when I regained consciousness the entire world moved around slowly and I wasn't sure what had happened. As I regained consciousness slowly, no one could believe it, but I'd lived. Some of the teeth in my mouth were broken and I'd badly broken my foot, but the rest of me was all there. Bruised and sore, but all there. That was the end of my jumping experience and also the end of my training for quite a while. It also changed all my plans for India.

I was out of commission for several months and had only my few senior students to help keep the school going while I coached from the side lines. My foot was injured so badly from the accident that I still have a great deal of trouble with it even now. When I got out of the plaster I expected to start teaching again right away. My expectations were quickly ended. It would be a long time before I would train properly again. The week after I had started to walk without the plaster a terrible cyclone hit Darwin like an atom bomb. It entirely destroyed the whole town and there was nothing left of anything. Too injured to travel to India, and with no town left existing in which to live, I decided to return, after so many years, to America.

On the way back to California where my parents lived, the airplane stopped over in Hawaii. I still knew some people there, so I got off for a few days. The friend I was staying with lent me a car and I drove to all the old places I used to know. Hawaii had gotten more crowded but other than that it hadn't changed much. I went to my old school of Wado-Ryu which I had trained at eleven years earlier. It was in the same area, but the old dojo wasn't there anymore. In its place was a large modern one. The old instructor wasn't there at the time and I felt like I was in a time warp. Standing there, I reminisced about the times I spent in the old dojo. The park where we used to run was still across the street and other than the old school being gone I still felt somewhat of a familiar energy. I didn't know anyone there so that was about all for the visit. It would have been strange to train there again if I was able. (My foot was still badly damaged). I visited, with my friend, a few Karate schools, but at the time since I had been to Japan for a long period and I couldn't train anyhow, I didn't get much out of it. After a few days, I took off for California to visit my parents and to recuperate the busted foot.

On the way home, the plane stopped off first in Southern California. I got out to visit a friend and fellow Tang Soo Do man, Fred Kenyon. Fred was a twenty-year veteran of martial arts. He was older than me and was my senior. He had a similar injury as I had and was very sympathetic to my situation. He helped to get me back on my feet again, literally. Fred was a Tang Soo Do man of the Korean martial art. He had had many political problems with the Association. From him, I learned all about the goings on of the American martial arts scene. It hadn't changed much since I left and if anything, had gotten worse.

I explained to Fred all the experiences I had had up until that time and he told me of his also. There was a lot in common. Not only were there missing links in the martial arts world but there was so much politics involved that it wasn't even funny. I wanted nothing to do with it and neither did he. We trained and compared notes together for quite sometime then I invited him to visit with me after I got settled down in North California.

The author with Fred Kenyon in his Californian gym in San Diego.

I left for Northern California and went home to find that my parents had moved. I went to visit one of my old instructors. He had a large family and was struggling more than ever to keep things going. He seemed to be having a very difficult time running his dojo, but that was nothing new; he always had. Competition in a large city and difficulty in keeping students create a strain on many instructors trying to make a living from the arts. He was also heavily involved in the incredible political situation which had sprung out of the Korean organization. I had seen too much of this in the past and I didn't want to stay around long enough to become involved. I gave him as much advice as I could, then went to the country to live. I was still deeply involved with disseminating the essence of the art and I certainly wasn't worried at this time about organizations. I lived a quiet life for the next eight months, trained by myself, making periodic visits to Southern California and examining a few yoga centres. Also I met a lot of nice people, but I felt like a misplaced person. I was trying full speed to get my foot back together.

One day, I got a letter with an airplane ticket from my students back in Australia. The city of Darwin was basically salvaged and they needed their instructor back. I didn't have any other choice and so it was back to Australia.

Rob Caputo and Fred Kenyon at mountain training camp.

On the way, I visited with my Korean instructor, Hwang Jin Moon and his Mother. It had been a long time since we met but he hadn't changed much. The last time I had seen him he had gone to Greece but due to the political situation, was forced to leave. Finally, he ended up in the Eastern United States. I visited with him for a week. I talked at length with him about my experiences and my objectives and I remember that he told me he wished there were more people like me around. His school was successful but he worked very hard. He had inherited one huge incredible headache, created by trying to organize fifteen years of extended complications of no proper leadership on the American Tang Soo Do scene. There were arguments, standards problems, misconceptions and so many things I couldn't relate them here. All he wanted to do was teach and practise the art. All I wanted to do was teach and practise the art also. His inheritance separated us. My lack of finishing what I started out to do sent me to the other side of the world. I reassured him that one day I would still be that *Toso* he talked about when we had first met. We both still smiled, but now it had a different meaning.

Mr. Kenyon showing perfect execution of
one of the most difficult techniques - the flying side-kick.

My ticket had a free stop over in England, so I decided to have a look at British martial arts before I returned to Australia. I travelled about London and the outskirts for three weeks. It was miserably cold which affected my foot so bad I could hardly walk. I went to a few martial art schools and the standard was very poor. The students there paid by the lesson, instead of by the month. This created for the instructors the problem of inconsistency in the students. Most of the schools I visited had very rough physical technique and none had anything to do with meditation. Most of the English people I met however, did seem interested in the spiritual aspect of martial art but just hadn't the exposure from their instructors. Also, the weather was very cold and not a good time to assess training at its best.

Chapter 8

It was good to get back to Australia again.

Everyone was still living in make shift houses since the cyclone, but the easy going attitude was still there. Because of its isolation, Darwin remained unfettered from the problems of the rest of the world. The life was plain and simple and people didn't want to know anything past their own noses. I hadn't had the final answer to all my questions by this time, but I knew what a martial artist should and should not be. I vowed to myself to train my students with full energy and work to achieve inner peace and harmony through diligent practise. Through that first year I formulated the most comprehensive study of movements and technique combinations that covered every martial art movement I had ever seen. I even developed forms which added to things I found lacking in my own. I changed nothing of any art I had ever learned, because I knew this would taint tradition and heritage, but I did add to all of them.

I searched for the practical way to introduce a gradual movement from hard movement into soft, All experiences showed me that hard stayed hard and soft stayed soft. Even the Tai Chi form, which is a perfect union of the Yin Yang at the absolute level, contained too much Yin in the primary stages. This created difficulty for the students to balance. I tried to work out the best system, which combined and added to all the systems I had seen and practised. The level and quality of the students was continually increasing and I was happy with the results the school was producing. I knew that the nucleus of my school must contain the essence of all that I had learned. If I couldn't pass it on, then it would be as ill fated as other systems I had seen and experienced. I wanted to gradually and methodically progress as many students as possible towards a stronger realization of martial spirit.

During that year I visited several schools in the large cities of Australia. In one particular school, I met a man named Mr. Rainer who had spent as much time in Asia as I had. Many of his experiences were very different to mine and much of his philosophy of life also very different. Nonetheless, there were some very obvious experiences that we had both undergone. He explained to me yogas and methods of his internal art system, Tong Soo Do. (Note spelling - Chinese art not to be confused with Korean). Some of the things were similar to what I had learned already and some were interesting additions.

Mr. Rainer was a much more practical man than I was in some ways. My mind was more in the spirit and his had an explanation for everything. His knowledge of Chinese medicine surpassed mine and he spent most of his study in Taoist alchemy, some of which coincided with my study of Buddhist alchemy and some of which was different, at the time. Regardless of the obvious difference in our lifestyles, it was an inspiration for me to find another martial artist who was working with some of the same things I was. He had changed around most of his teaching techniques in order to find a better way to help his students. He tried to maintain a good standard, he didn't sell his art, he was completely fed up with oriental politics as I was and he had made a comprehensive study of Taoist yoga which he used as the basis of his art and techniques. Up until this time, I had never met another foreigner as myself, who had studied as extensively.

During the same trip, I went to a course given by a Tibetan Lama who was visiting Australia. I had read much on Tibetan Buddhism and was especially interested from a Zen point of view in the art of dying, which was made so famous by the *Tibetan Book of the Dead*. Because of the isolation of Tibet, which lasted a thousand years, I was deeply interested in what this man had to say. His sincerity and wisdom moved me deeply. He taught basic fundamentals of Buddhist philosophy.

A lot of it seemed a bit religious at first and I wasn't too impressed at all. But I left my mind open as much as possible because I felt he had a lot of knowledge behind what he was saying.

He didn't say a lot about dying but he talked a great deal about the origin of man. He also made references to a man god named Dalai Lama, whom I had read about a few times before. The Dalai Lama was this man's guru and the head of his religion. Not only that, but he was the king of a mystical land called Tibet, which has now been overrun by the Chinese.

The speaker placed the validity of this art on the King of Tibet, the Dalai Lama. It was said that this man was a reincarnation of a Buddha. The Tibetan name for this Buddha was called *Chenrezig*. This Enlightened Wisdom Being was said to have reincarnated fourteen successful times since the 12th Century.

The lineage of Buddhism was preserved by the Dalai Lama and other high Lamas in the isolated country of Tibet after the religion suffered total extinction in its native land, India. The Buddha and his Enlightened disciples were said to have never died. Through the yogic techniques which the Buddha had taught, successful yogis and meditators could transfer their mind into other bodies as easily as changing cars.

The present speaker's name was Lama Yeshe. He talked a great deal about the psychology of mind and the philosophy of human existence. There was much logic in what he had to say. The thought of a living man who had reincarnated fourteen times in a row was fascinating. This fact by itself was only sensational and I didn't go in for sensation, but the simple logic, the truth and the energy with which the mere disciple of the Dalai Lama spoke, was some definite evidence that there could be something deep in what he was saying.

After this man's brief teachings were over, I met a western man who had become a monk. He could speak Tibetan fluently and had met this God King of Tibet. He explained to me that not only one, but three identical gods had reincarnated into a branch of Tibetan Buddhism called the Gelupa Sect. I talked at length with this young man and was surprised how much he understood about Yin Yang philosophy. Because there was depth in what he said, I hinted in the conversation of the secrets of alchemy. He stayed with me all the way. I knew he had learned something and he had nothing to do with martial arts.

He was going back to India within the year and I decided that I must check this thing out further. Several times already I had decided to explore the depths of India and this was the best excuse to plan for this. I made arrangements to see him at a later date then went back to Darwin.

In Darwin, I had already made plans to make one further trip to Asia. I trained my students so that they could handle things well in my absence. I knew I would be travelling a lot in the next year or two and I needed a strong nucleus if my school was to survive without suffering standard or leadership problems. I then went out into the bush alone for almost two weeks. I lived in absolute solitude, training and meditating eighteen hours a day. I slept sitting up most of the time and lived on a rock next to a waterfall. I ate no food and drank only water.

During that time, I gained an inner experience as to what to do with the rest of my life and on how to run my school. When I finished, I returned to the city, gathered several of my senior students and took them also to the bush for an additional eight days fasting, meditating and training. After this, I returned home and prepared for my next trip.

Chapter 9

I went back to Singapore and trained with some martial artists there. I visited Kung-Fu schools, Karate schools and Korean schools. I went to the Chinese Aikido Association and talked to the instructor there, as well. I had some students there with me at the time and I made a few demonstrations around Singapore. I listened to what every martial artist had to say about the philosophy and technique of martial art.

Things were more thorough now than they had been on my previous trip. I had had much experience with Chinese. I'd also had firm conviction from my experience running my school and was also representing myself with my students. From there I went to examine martial arts in the Philippines.

The author after a training session with the friendly people of the Singapore Tai Chi Chuan Society.

I would like to mention here, that the main purpose of this trip was to visit Taiwan and to stay once again, in Korea. I spent two to three weeks at each place along the way to basically observe things I may have missed in previous years.

When I arrived in the Philippines, I went straight downtown. Within an hour I was asking and searching all over town for any information I could find. I went to tourist boards, talked to taxi men and all of them sent me to the most popular school in the area. Upon visiting this school, I had an interview with the instructor who said he had a date with his girl friend, then quickly dismissed himself. I made an appointment the next day to come back. When I came in the next day the instructor wasn't there but the students had gathered the biggest most muscle bound Filipino I had ever seen in my life and they wanted me to fight him. I tried to remember if I'd ever fought anyone so big before and I wasn't sure that I had. I fought American Negros that were taller but they were not so grizzly. It wasn't exactly what I had come there for but I couldn't back down now, so I put on my uniform and got ready for the showdown.

It was a very small room, about twelve foot square. I circled around my opponent slowly and made a few feints to check his responses. He made a few vain attempts to punch, which failed. If he didn't grab me I was confident I'd be all right. After checking him out, I launched an attack. I punched him in the solar plexus once and he reeled backwards and doubled up, peddling backwards. I hit him with a well controlled backfist to the face and he held his mouth with a look of shock. I punched twice more at the body and that was it. No big deal. I was actually disappointed, but so it goes. They all thought this was great and wanted us to come to the main park to show off our skills to everyone, which I didn't want to do.

My students and I visited a few more gyms in the area from addresses we'd been given and found them all trying to give us a quick sign-up routine. We hassled everyone we could to examine what Manila had to offer and we didn't come up with much. We were told that all martial arts clubs met in a large park on Sundays, and so we went there.

There were Chinese people doing very high quality Tai Chi arts and it was good to watch. In other parts of the park, we found all varieties of Karate, Kung-Fu and Tae Kwan Do. Almost everything we saw was not worth talking about. Trying to be a good sport about things, I did a small demonstration in the park with a few other martial artists that were there. We gathered a big crowd and a good time was had by all, but nothing formidable took place. We moved on to Taiwan.

In Taiwan, we visited the Master of the Taiwan Kung-Fu Association. He talked at great length about Chinese medicine and esoteric spirituality. Then he pulled out a pack of cigarettes and offered us one, along with a bottle of Coca-a-Cola. We politely refused, keeping as straight a face as possible. He then took us to one of his branch schools. They mostly trained in Pa-Kua. It was mediocre quality with some very good yoga exercises and after the class they practised some acupuncture. The students came up after the class, extended a polite courtesy and asked if we were interested in Chinese Kung-Fu. We politely answered yes, and they proceeded to tell us in earnest about the unfathomable martial art spirit. This lasted till midnight when our host took us home.

The next morning, we met my friend from Sydney, who had brought his students to a tournament in Taiwan. We had not planned to come to Taiwan for a tournament, it was coincidental that it was happening during our trip through. I had received word before I left Australia that if we could time our visits it would be nice to meet there. This conveniently happened and so there we were.

My friend asked if my students would fight in the tournament. We didn't see that it could hurt, so we said yes. It was a full contact affair, which is against my general beliefs and I told my students so. I gave them a choice and they decided to give it a go, just for the experience. The difference in quality in the students was almost embarrassing. We found the Chinese to be very angry and unsportsman like. The unquestionable slaughter of their students, by mine, brought up the old idea of 'face' again. I knew only too well the ill feelings that arise from tournaments when things don't go as planned.

Visiting the temples of Korea.

We were sincerely visiting as martial artists and cared nothing for face or sport, but only in the virtue of martial art which appeared absent at this particular time. We skipped all the ending formalities and went on to Korea.

The students had a nice holiday, I showed them around a bit, then they went back to Australia. I went back to my old University to begin the study of Korean language. At the same time, I looked up old Tang Soo Do friends and explained exactly what I was after. I located the student of a monk who had been one of Hwang Kee's closest friends, thirty years earlier. At this time, Hwang Kee was no longer in Korea, but in America with his son.

I was taken to a very small temple that took a day and a half by bus and a half a day's wait to reach. The abbot of the temple was a Chinese man from Peking who had come to Korea forty years earlier. He was absent but his student of twelve years was there. I compared form work, did some stick work and discussed various meditation techniques with the monk.

The main practice of this temple was the Amitabha sect. All the monks arose at 2am and walked in circles for hours. They then chanted Sutra and, just before dawn, the martial art practitioners would break the ice and sit naked in the icy river, practising heat yoga meditation. After this, they would all gather in the main hall and eat breakfast together. The head monk was incredibly strong and robust. He pointed out to me some weaknesses in my practises and helped me as much as he could. I practised meditation at the temple and after my training returned to Seoul.

In Seoul, I visited several Sorim schools and trained at random with each. I finally got on to one man who was a Pa-Kua instructor and I studied with him till I left Korea. His name was Mr. Chang. He was a young man, as I was, but had studied Pa-Kua for twenty years. Though he was Korean, his instructor was from China, and had come to Korea in the early 1900's. His form to date is the most excellent I've seen in the Pa-Kua school. He was extremely honest and insisted on a two-hour session each morning. At least one third to one half of the entire session was yoga and internal breathing exercises.

The man was a virtual master at Hatha Yoga, and his Pa-Kua was flawless. He trained personally with me every morning, walking the Pa-Kua circle. I found that Pa-Kua had no new techniques to add to the master form of Tai Chi, but the hypnotic trance and the incredible concentration gained from walking the circle was magnificent.

During the time of training with this man, I solved the last few parts in a complicated puzzle of the science of physical movement I was trying to develop in martial art. During the times I wasn't training, I meditated on invisible opponents so strongly that I could almost see them. I trained every morning for two hours and in the evenings contemplated for great periods of time on movements in time and space.

At this time, I had also found an excellent man to teach me more detail about Chinese medicine. After morning training in the Pa-Kua school, I stayed all morning and sometimes late into the afternoon at the private home of my acupuncture teacher, who was the President of the Korean Acupuncture Association. He had agreed to teach me personally because I was a good friend of his brother, who was a 6th Dan in the Korean Tang Soo Do Association. Through him I learned more details of special points on the body, bleeding and revival techniques, as well as Chinese Massage. In the late afternoon, when I left his house, I went straight to the University, where I continued my studies of Korean Language.

I could never speak Korean very well and I still don't, but I could always communicate and read well. I had one very good friend named Mr. Lee, who was a post graduate in the English department of Yonsei

University. He needed help in writing his Masters thesis and in writing a dictionary. In turn he aided me in translating texts and often when he had time, accompanied me to my teacher's house. Together, we finished everything my instructors wanted to teach me and I decided to direct my energies towards going home. On the way, I once again stopped in Taiwan.

This trip was very different to the first. I checked into an old hotel and through the manager immediately located a man who was a Kung-Fu master living upstairs. His name was Mr. Wang. I immediately approached Mr. Wang, gave him a brief history of myself and asked him to teach me. He told me that he had never taught anyone before. Mr. Wang was sixty five years old and had been practising Chinese Kung-Fu, specializing in Tai Chi Chuan, for the past fifty years.

He had inherited the art from his grandfather. He owned a whole building in downtown Taipei, was a millionaire, but lived like a pauper. He was unmarried and lived by himself. Interestingly enough, he had a young twenty-five year old girlfriend. This didn't seem unusual as he barely looked over thirty five himself.

Mr. Wang asked me to do a demonstration of everything I had learned, which I did. After that, he told me he wanted to see me demonstrate my skills at a nearby Kung-Fu school. He took me to a man named Mr. Chen. Mr. Chen had trained for eighteen years in an internal system I never had heard of before. Without any ceremonies, uniforms or formalities I confronted the man in an upstairs office building. We competed for about ten minutes.

At the end, Chen was completely exhausted, I was still full of energy and Mr. Wang was impressed. He said he'd accept me as his student but only if I made the traditional request. This entailed inviting all the Chinese in the area to the family shrine. Prostrating to the master and to the family relics, making offerings of fruit and money and pledging to uphold truths and values of the art. All this I did in good faith and thus was formally accepted as his student.

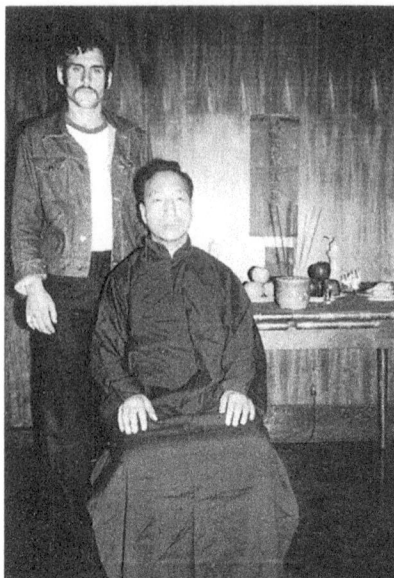

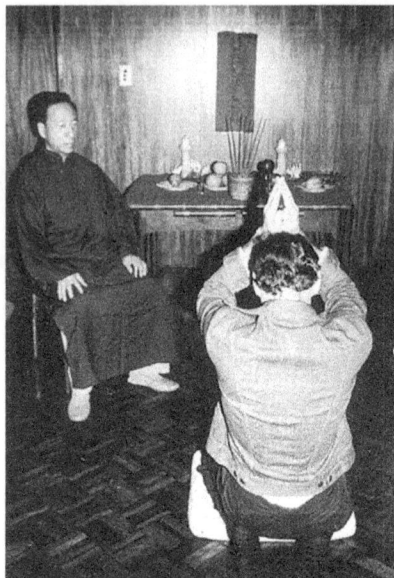

Initiation day with Chinese instructor of Tai Chi, Master Wang

Through Mr. Wang I met many Chinese people. Unlike before, everyone was incredibly friendly and remarkably open. Because Mr. Wang had accepted me it seemed that everyone had accepted me. Everyone I came into contact with was more than willing to help me.

Mr. Wang was young at heart, flexible and energetic. He immediately established a training schedule of six to eight hours a day, with him and myself. We trained for two hours in the morning, two hours in the afternoon and two hours in the evening. Seventy per cent of everything I learned was meditation and Taoist yoga. The rest was the physical application of the defense art. Mr. Wang explained to me the importance of hearing with the palms and feeling antagonistic thoughts before they actually became physical.

He demonstrated to me the differences in the meditational and yogic practices of all the various Kung-Fu schools. He woke me at twelve o'clock midnight, put me on the back of his motorcycle and took me out to the country where we slept for several hours. He woke me at 4am in the morning and taught me internal practices for concentration and sperm sublimation.

One morning, while it was still dark he took me to a dark place in the forest. All I could hear was yelling, moaning and howling, coming from the darkness.

In pitch black, Mr. Wang ran up the mountain with me following him. When we reached the top we heard voices and saw shadows moving about. Everyone greeted us as if we were expected. On top of this mountain were all the Kung-Fu practitioners practising various methods of purification and using special sounds. Everyone trained and meditated until sunrise at which time all activities finished and everyone returned home.

I trained with Mr. Wang until one day, he received word that his son was very ill and that he must leave for some time. This coincided with my visa which had run out and I knew it was time for me to return to Australia.

Chapter 10

I returned back to Australia, again stopping at Hong Kong and Singapore, doing more of the same things I have mentioned so often already.

When I returned to Australia, I made the final adjustments to the art that I am presently teaching. I developed a new series of movements which could be introduced at regular speed, which incorporated Tai Chi and Pa-Kua movements. This was only at black belt level.

This could be done by adjusting certain stances and changing the breathing of the lower basics. It was a progressive natural transition which did not alter fundamental traditional movements of lower basics. I did not want to create a new art form; there are too many already. I had developed a practical art form which met all the physical requirements of all the things I have already outlined in this book. It is complete, practical at all levels and clearly traces the fundamental moves of basic level training to high level martial art. As far as the art went, physically I was finished. There was more training to be done, but no longer any new things to be introduced. Physically, one could not have more in an art form. Spiritually, I still had some questions to be answered. In a few months time, myself and the young monk would be off to India, for what I hoped would be some link to the ultimate objective for why I was training.

The time passed very quickly and I, with one of my senior black belts and one Canadian Buddhist monk headed for North India. I didn't care about Buddhism anymore. I didn't care about martial art anymore. My primary objective was to meet one man who could successfully link together years and years of bits and pieces of all the studies I had made. I was on my way to meet a legendary God King and his teacher.

The God King was the Dalai Lama, his teacher was named Ling Rinpoche. I had no idea what to expect and thousands of thoughts went through my head. The trip was a long one.

We travelled for thirty or forty hours non-stop to get to New Delhi, India. From there, it was an all night train ride to a small town called Pathankot. After which was an additional three hour jeep ride to the base of the Himalayan mountains.

Finally, we went by foot another four miles up the mountain. We were six thousand feet up in the Himalayas by this time and we had left the hustle and bustle and the heat of the lower plains of India far behind. There were few Indians where we were. We had come to a refugee camp of the exiled Tibetans. Everywhere we went there were robed monks, praying, chanting and reciting mantras. Even the local people all carried rosary beads and turned prayer wheels. The entire population of this small village in the mountains was one entity of moving, praying people. It was a strange energy and something I'd never seen before. The sound of loud trumpets and horns filled the air and clashes of large cymbols rang in our ears. It was pouring rain as we walked up the mountain the first day. We came to the village centre which consisted of a street only a few hundred metres

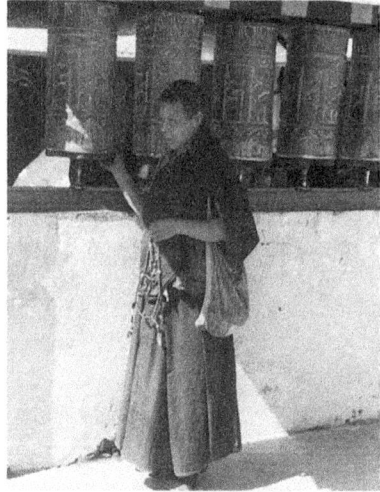

Tibetan nun turning the prayer wheels at the Dalai Lama's temple in Dharamshala.

Tibetan dancers performing traditional sword dance.

long. The town was comprised of a series of broken down, one room shops, selling trinkets and Tibetan artifacts. It was filled with all kinds of hippies and wayward travellers. The Tibetans themselves looked and dressed much like the American Indians. They had impressive Mongolian

The refugee camp of MacLeod Gange

Tibetan woman selling goods
in the local market.

features of high cheekbones and dark complexion. Everyone we met was smiling and praying. We all bedded down in a small room for the night and I prepared for my first meeting with the high Lamas of Tibet.

The next day, we had first secured an appointment with the throne holder of the entire Gelugpa sect. He was the Senior Tutor to His Holiness the Dalai Lama.

His name was Ling Rinpoche.

Ling Rinpoche was nearing eighty years of age. He was regarded by the Tibetan people as the Buddha himself. According to legend he was the cousin of Lord Shakyamuni Buddha and had maintained his reincarnations from 2,500 years ago to the present time. He was considered to be the emanation of a deity and he had proved successfully with each rebirth that he was indeed the same man as from the lifetime before.

The lamas had ways of testing the authenticity of such a being. There were certain signs and physical characteristics that appeared at birth. Rainbows appeared in the sky. Celestial sounds were heard by people in the area and bright stars appeared in the heavens. Sometimes the lamas would even predict the mother and the place where they would reincarnate. The methods and ways were numerous.

His Holiness, Ling Rinpoche.

We walked up the hill with our young western monk, with no idea what manner of being I was going to meet. After a brief wait in a small room we were led into a reception room and given a seat. There sitting on a high couch was the highest Lama in Tibet.

He had blue eyes; something very strange for a Tibetan. His gaze filled the entire room. The walls of the room disappeared, the people with me disappeared and the chair I sat on disappeared. The man looked huge and he seemed as large as a house. My body tingled and from the first moment he set eyes on me my entire consciousness was absorbed in an indescribable experience. There are absolutely no words that could relate to a reader what happened in that room. He spoke his first words which were low in a deep voice and, although he spoke softly, the sound came out like thunder. I was not nervous nor was I afraid. There was a peace that emanated from the man that made me feel like a small child and there was a power along with it that was the most awesome thing I could ever imagine. Whatever manner of creature was in front of me, I knew it was not ordinary and that no man had ever existed in my experience as what sat in front of me.

We went through the usual formalities of introducing ourselves, where we came from and about our travels. He made a few friendly comments to make us feel at home and then asked us the main purpose of our visit. It was only a formality, for it was obvious he knew why I was there. Everything was a formality, because as I stared at the man I had the direct realization that he knew I was coming, before I even got on the plane in Australia. I have been told that this Lama never saw any foreigners except on Wednesdays, but he had accepted to see us and it was not Wednesday.

I gave him a brief history of myself, explained something of my travels and how I wound up sitting in front of him. He listened intently to everything I said.

I point blankly asked him to teach me the essence of what he stood for. He politely refused and said his manager was sick. We finished off our meeting after a cup of tea and left. I was in a complete dream. I knew from the moment I laid eyes on this person that he contained the key to every question I had ever had in my life. I knew this from looking in his eyes in the first twenty seconds of our meeting. He had known me a million years.

When the meeting was over, we went outside and had a brief word with the servants. I enquired as to what was wrong with the manager and he told me his problems. As I practised Chinese medicine, I offered my services, which he accepted. I was to see him daily for the next week. We went back to our rooms and went over and over again the experience of the meeting,

The next day, we had another meeting with the second of the highest Lamas. His name was Trijang Rinpoche. I had known one of his students, who was a Lama who had visited Australia.

Trijang Rinpoche was another emanation of a Tibetan God. He was the Junior Tutor to the Dalai Lama and a reincarnation of the charioteer of Lord Shakyamuni Buddha and had assisted him after he had left his princely Kingdom 2,500 years earlier. He was the second of the three Buddhas of Tibet.

We walked in and sat down as before. The Lama smiled and again we felt like babies. There was an incredible peace in the air, but the energy was different.

His Holiness, Trijang Rinpoche and the author after receiving teachings.

His voice was softer than the other and he was a very thin man. He asked all about us and we went through the formalities again. He was interested in the Lama I had known in Australia and asked after him. While he spoke to us he held his eyes closed and it seemed as if he was not there at times. I had the feeling he was appearing and disappearing in front of my eyes and the feeling that the room was disappearing came back. During our conversation, I explained that I would like to receive a particular teaching from him that he was famous for. As he was leaving shortly, he referred me to his senior pupil and apologized for not being able to teach us. We had a warm relaxed meeting then we left.

From left, the Canadian monk Jhampa Zangpo, Manager of the Dalai Lama, Doboom Tulku, and the author

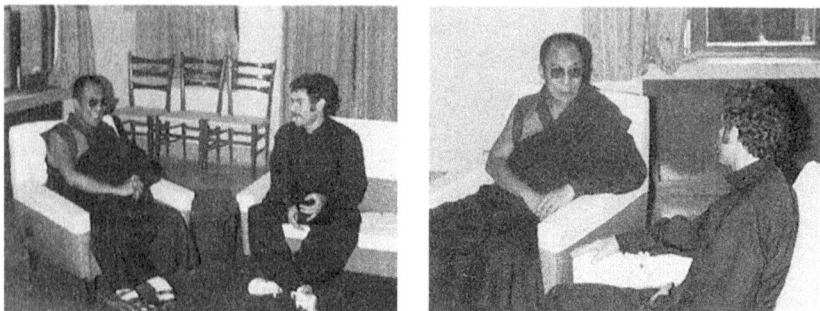

The author in his first interview with His Holiness, the Dalai Lama

We went home and I lay down to rest. The incredible peace and love I had encountered with both Lamas ran through my head. There was a distinct difference in both of their energies but a common force of love and wisdom that seemed to come from both also.

The next day, I was to meet the third of the three Buddhas, His Holiness the Dalai Lama.

We walked to the palace and were stopped by the gate guards for a routine search and submitted our passports. From there we walked up a steep hill to the entrance of the palace.

We walked up the steps and were ushered inside by the Manager of His Holiness. We were led inside, told to sit down and were interviewed by the Manager. The Manager was an incredibly powerful man who by his very presence commanded order and conduct. He spoke English perfectly and was very fluent in his movement. I gave him a brief history of why I was there. I had prepared to discuss with the Dalai Lama as much as time permitted of the essential ideas of spiritual practise and martial art. I had also worn my uniform with my student and was prepared to give a demonstration as well, as part of the discussion.

A visiting Lama walked through the door and left the room. We were the next to go into the main room. My heart pounded, my energy vibrated through my body. I felt as if I had touched a live wire. We walked down the hallway and into the main palace room of His Holiness the Dalai Lama.

He turned around with a huge smile and almost ran over to shake my hand. He spoke perfect English and he had a low deep voice which penetrated every atom of space. He had us sit down comfortably on a nice couch, then sat next to me. His entire body was radiant and the entire room was brightened by his presence. The vibration of his voice shook through my body as he spoke. I was comfortable and happy and totally in a trance. His Holiness was younger by forty years than his Lamas and because he spoke English perfectly, we needed no translator. As he sat in front of me I felt my body expand and contract. His body grew huge and the floor disappeared underneath my feet. I explained the purpose of my visit and he was extremely interested. I began my history and related every experience I could remember of significance in my life as a martial artist. He listened intently with total perception. I explained of my teachers, of other Buddhist monasteries, Zen and internal yoga. I described all my experiences, accomplishments and setbacks.

My student and I moved all the furniture in the room aside and we gave a demonstration. I explained the history of Bodhidharma and the spread of Buddhism through the Shaolin monasteries. I explained everything. Suiting the words to actions, my student and myself took turns demonstrating the entire forms that I had learned. When I was finished I sat down and he was impressed.

My mind was a complete blank. I had never experienced anything in my forms as I did as I stood in front of him. I had no preconceived ideas before I went into that room. As I did my forms, my entire being entered a space that was completely empty of my own self. Only when I finished did I realize what had happened. I finished my explanation and His Holiness continued to listen. There was no rush and he waited till I was completely finished and then he spoke.

He looked straight into my eyes and there was absolutely no one talking to me. He was completely inside myself and it seemed as if a voice spoke from within me. He explained there was no martial art in Tibet, that there had never been. He explained that he had never even seen martial art before and knew nothing of it. He explained that the art by itself, had nothing to do with Buddhism.

What he did explain was that there are two fundamental practices in Buddhism. One was called Kye-rim and the other Dzog-rim. He explained all the internal yogas as fundamental exercises for purification of internal body energies. He said that there were many kinds and that it didn't matter which ones were practised that they all fit in the same category.

He described Samadhi and Shunyata meditation, which were the one-point concentrations and the all-pervasive emptiness of Zen.

He explained the basic fundamentals of purification of body, speech and mind through daily life, morality and meditational practices.

He also explained that Bodhidharma and other Chinese as well as Japanese and Korean, all had made various adaptations to fit the time and the need of the people.

He said as long as a person develops himself for the benefit of others, there was a link to Buddhism. As long as there was a form of Dzog-rim it could be linked with Buddhism.

He explained that the most important aspect of any practice, be it meditation or physical yogas, must contain a direct lineage to Lord Buddha or it would be difficult to sanction its validity. The key to the lineage was that it must be passed from one man to the other before death. The person passing it should have received it directly as a transmission from his teacher. The person transmitting any lineage should have the realization of the energy he is transmitting. He explained that any adaptations, as long as they were in direct lineage and did not go against the moral codes of the ethics of the Buddha Dharma, were valid.

He complimented me highly for my training and said I was developing good understanding. He also warned me not to place too much emphasis on the physical and with my practise to always include conditions of time and space away from the earthly realm.

We stayed for a long time. When we were thoroughly finished, he asked me if there was anymore. I had explained everything and he had answered all. He grabbed my hand and held it tightly. We walked hand in hand to the door and my monk friend took a picture of us both.

I thanked him for his time and as I was leaving he took hold of my head and brought it against the crown of his and drew our heads together until they touched. I didn't know what this meant at the time but later it was explained. My body was completely light and filled with a blissful energy which I will never forget. We walked out of the palace, down the road back to our room. In an hour and a half I had learned the final key to every question I had ever had concerning martial art, myself or anything. The answers that I have briefly stated here can in

Elation at the long end of a search.

no way convey the energy and force that was transmitted directly to me from our meeting. The Dalia Lama had understood every movement and word that I had said and organized it perfectly for me to understand. I was completely whole inside and went home to dwell over what the Dalai Lama had conveyed.

The power of the energy which the Dalai Lama had given me changed from day to day. Every word he had said, every feeling that I had, changed the meaning of all my experiences everyday for the first week. Even now at this writing, the new reflection of his words create an energy which consistently brings me to a deeper understanding of every movement and action I've ever made since the day I was born. I was completely awestruck as was my student, for many days.

Shortly after the demonstration, I received word that Doboom Tulku, the Manager of the Dalai Lama, wanted to see me. I happily went back to the palace. Doboom was incredibly friendly and said that His Holiness along with himself enjoyed our demonstration very much.

He was very interested in exercise because he had a terrible weight problem and also he was so busy taking care of the affairs of His Holiness that he had little time for anything else. He also frequently caught colds and had some trouble with his sinuses. To my surprise, he asked me if I could come and teach him some exercises to keep his weight down and to aid his health. I was only too happy to do so.

Three times a week I walked down the mountain from where I stayed in order to meet him in the evenings after his official duties were ended. He was ready and waiting with complete training outfit and all. Because Dharmasala was small and because of his position, it would be embarrassing if anyone was to see him acting any way other than the stately *manager* of the Dalai Lama. Because of this he shut all the windows, locked all the doors and reserved a private room which we could use to do all the exercises. He was industrious, perceptive and learned really fast. He huffed and puffed and tried very hard. I explained to him the difference between normal exercises and special internal exercises for health.

The reader must remember here that the Tibetans entire life style is based on meditation and prayer. Many people confuse yoga with health exercises. This is not yoga. The Tibetans had the pure lineage of yoga from the Buddha. The Buddha was in fact who Doboom Tulku worked for. But this did not mean he knew anything about exercise. Tibetans are hopelessly uncoordinated and have no feeling for anything whatsoever that has to do with physical culture. Their minds are undoubtedly there but their bodies do not follow along easily. Doboom Tulku and I got to be great friends. Though I didn't observe much weight loss, nonetheless his sinus problems improved and he felt much better all around. I thoroughly enjoyed teaching him and because of his purity, I myself gained more energy each time I taught him.

Life in the little town of Dharmasala was simple. There were only a few shops and restaurants. That was all. The village thrived solely on the fact that the Dalai Lama and his two tutors lived there. We ate meagre food which was rather tasteless and I began working on the Manager of Ling Rinpoche. He was an extremely happy man in spite of his failing health. He had been with his Master for over twenty-five years and travelled with him on their escape from Tibet. His family had been killed by the Chinese and his entire existence rested in serving Ling Rinpoche. He had firm belief in Chinese medicine, which in some ways had some resemblances to Tibetan medicine.

Kungo the Manager of
H.H. Ling Rinpoche

The first time I acupunctured him was a unique experience. His skin was soft and pliable but I couldn't get the needles in. First, I thought I might have missed the acupuncture point which alone puzzled me because I had done it so many thousands of times before. The needles were small and sharp and his skin was extremely soft so there was no reason why they would not go in. Completely baffled, I forced the needles until they bent. I had the translator tell Kungo (the Manager) that something was wrong. I was confused and really embarrassed because I'd never experienced anything like this before. Slapping his head and exclaiming something in Tibetan he sat up and laughed. He knew what was wrong. Around his neck was a thick necklace of human bone, given to him by the Lama. He had worn it ever since Lhasa and it contained the power to stop any object from piercing his skin. It was amazing to hear but already I'd seen the proof. He said he had had the same problem once before, when he forgot to take it off at an operation in a western hospital. I could imagine the confused western doctors blunting their scalpels on baby skin. Anyway, he took off the necklace and the needles glided in as smooth as silk. Faintly, in the back of my mind, I reminisced my experiences in the Malaysian jungle but this energy and the situation was totally different.

I grew to be good friends with Kungo and he told me that he would help me to get teachings from the Lama. I had been able to help him some, but he also went for an annual check up at the same time to a nearby city. When he returned from the visit he began to brighten up daily. Staying true to his word he approached Ling Rinpoche and explained that I was very sincere in my desire to learn from him. I was given another audience with the Lama. He expressed his gratitude that I had been able to help his manager and said he would consider giving me teachings in the future. He was testing my patience actually. Weeks rolled by and I frequented the household of the Lama often but received no word as to anything definite.

Chapter 11

During this time I had gone to visit a Lama called Ratto Rinpoche.

He was the senior disciple of Lama Trijang Rinpoche. When I met him I found his energy exactly the same as his Lama. He was not only the chief disciple, but was actually a duplicate of Trijang Rinpoche. I remembered the Lama's last words when he excused himself from teaching me and referred me to Ratto Rinpoche. He said that if I received teachings from Ratto Rinpoche it was exactly the same as from him. They were both one. Here indeed was still yet another Buddha. The Lama was badly ill when I visited him. He could hardly stand and even his voice was weak and feeble. I begged for some teachings which I wanted to receive. He told me that the energy to teach me was too great for him and that he did not have the strength.

Many Lamas suffered greatly in India because of the drastic change of living conditions from their native Tibet. He was one of them. I told him that I was a master of special exercises that were extraordinary and that I possessed a special power to heal sick people with my knowledge. He was surprised a little and said that that was very good, but they wouldn't be able to help him because his illness was too set in and besides he was too old. I had come a long way to India and everything I believed might rest in any one of these Lamas. I knew from my experiences that the Lamas had the key and the power to what I was seeking and I was determined to get it.

I moved a small tea table that was between him and me, grabbed his arm and hoisted him off the couch where he was sitting. He was shocked and surprised as was his household. They had never seen anyone act this way towards their Lama before.

Lama Ratto Rinpoche in his garden in Dharamshala.

It was unseen of, unheard of and just not done. I felt this, but because we were using a translator I played dumb as to customs and manners. I hoisted the Lama over my back and gave him a big shake. He began laughing and was awestruck, as was everyone else. I vowed to him on all my honor that I had the ability to cure even the most serious disease and that it was his duty to let me try and to give me the benefit of the doubt. He was impressed by my energy and sincerity, so conceded. I worked on the Lama for an hour that day and every day for the next month. He quickly began to improve and everyone was amazed at the incredible results.

Daily as I worked on him I began to explain the details of the arts that I had studied and learned and their foundations. I told him of my meeting with the Dalai Lama and Ling Rinpoche and the demonstration. He began to understand me thoroughly and we became very close.

After he was well on the road to recovery I again asked him to teach me. He told me the seriousness of what I asked and that although what I had studied up to now was associated with it and had brought me this far, that the essence of the Tantra of Tibet was so secret and involved that once entered into there could be no return or going back. It was a path so deep with commitment that once a person undertook this way, failure would result in certain death. I was absolutely ready to do this at all costs. I understood well what he was talking about and I had already

Ritual preparations.

The special day of teachings

decided that failure to accomplish what I had come for was as good as death to me anyway. I persisted for the teachings until he gave me serious consideration. One day, he talked and meditated with me for over an hour and a half at the end of which time he cast the Tibetan form of the I Ching. It was an oracle about me. He was not satisfied with the results, but did it over and over again. The results of the oracle indicated that he should give me the teachings I asked for.

That same evening, he made all the necessary preparations and we were to start the next day. I could hardly sleep that night. Finally, when I did go to sleep my mind entered a strange state I had never known before. I was aware that the Lama had already begun to teach me. The next day, I hurried down to the Lama's house.

High teachings involve a direct empowerment of energy from teacher to disciple. It involved a long initiation ceremony which lasted two full days in which time I received empowerments and instructions on how to use them.

During that time, I was given many kinds of meditation techniques and various yoga disciplines. I was required to take many kinds of vows which must be kept in the strictest sense. All the teachings given were from the direct lineage of the Buddha, carefully preserved in Tibet for 1,000 years.

During the teachings, the Lama changed from the man I had been treating. His voice was deeper and the way he did things suggested an unseen power that was not usually exposed.

In the evening, when I retired I noticed that something in me was beginning to change. To say that it was uncanny is a gross understatement. When the teachings were finished I felt as if a great burden was lifted from me. I found myself completely exhausted as was the Lama. He was older than me so that made sense, but I was young and extremely fit and to be laid back for days was very unusual. All had gone well with no interferences and I had received the first of a lineage of many teachings I was destined for that would change my life. I was told afterwards that I was the only foreigner to have received these teachings, and that since leaving Tibet, Ratto Rinpoche had taught them rarely to anyone, even other Tibetans. All these things were strange to me and I didn't understand everything.

All I knew was that I was supposed to be there.

After my initial set of teachings, I stayed in a small hut on the mountain doing a short retreat along with the foreign monk who lived next door in another small hut. He was the only friend I had there and besides doing all the translating, he took all the teachings with me. His name was Jhampa. He was the same age as myself and had been a monk for ten years. He was an unusual fellow who had become a monk just out of high school when most other people in the western world begin their adult social

The monk Jampa Zangpo with R. Caputo.

lives. He cared little for anything else except retreating in his small hut and was known and loved by all the Tibetans in the area. He had also become part of the household of Ling Rinpoche and because his father was dead, Ling Rinpoche adopted him as his own. We talked often and I taught him how to take care of his health which was failing like so many other people who lived in India's degenerate conditions. Because of his relationship with the household, and because he was my guide and translator, while I was there, I had the opportunity to visit Ling Rinpoche very often and I became close to him and all the household.

The small retreat hut in which the author lived for six months.

News of Ratto Rinpoche's improved health spread fast and often I was visited by mountain lamas who had been in yogic retreat for years. They always came to Jhampa's house first, then he would come down to translate for them. I met men who should have been dead with the kinds of things they had wrong with them. The yogis had completely disregarded their bodies during years of austerities and meditations.

The Tibetan culture, although it provided the most pure and perfect meditations and forms of esoteric training, cared little for such mundane things as the body. The only reason that any of the yogis ventured down at all was that they thought I might have a quick way to ease certain discomforts which ailed them, so that they could prolong the length of their meditations. I told them I could do much to help anyone but this I couldn't do. The only way to prolong their meditations was to take better care of their health. This must be done by consistent practise of basic body culture. Many of the lamas didn't want to have anything to do with this because they were set in their ways, so I did what I could considering the circumstances and they would be off to the other side of the mountains again.

All the Lamas I met were happy and peaceful. It was obvious that their physical ailments didn't bother their mind, only their bodies. Watching the yogis and lamas however, I became aware that there might be something missing in their art as well. This was the middle way of body culture. From my experience, too many martial artists lacked love and compassion, while placing much faith in martial skills.

Here I noticed the most moral, virtuous people imaginable, suffering from even the most easily curable ailments due to lack of exercise and knowledge of physical culture. I knew wisdom and compassion were more important, but I also knew that there were definite benefits of having both. I remembered the life story of the Buddha who after six years of austerities shocked the yogis of the times by returning to a semi-leisure life style which was more conducive to meditation.

During the time after my first teachings, while I practised the yogic instructions I had received, I made consistent reports of my progress to Ling Rinpoche. He was pleased at the news of Ratto Rinpoche and also that I had received one of the most important empowerments necessary to practise Tibetan yoga.

One day when I visited him, he kept me for a long time and offered me tea. He asked me a lot of questions and then at the end of the meeting he told me that he had decided to give me all the teachings I had requested. I was overjoyed and didn't know what to say or how to act. They brought in a calendar and began deciding when the stars would be right. All the teachings of this sort were usually given at particular times according to astrology which played a heavy significance in anything to do with important teachings. This was a particular time that was very auspicious. The planets were lining up in some kind of pattern that happened only once every five hundred years. This was to take place that very week and so the date to begin was set. All the preparations were made for the main initiation and afterwards there would be a long training period which would go on for nine days. To begin with, I was extremely excited and the tension built up as the day of the initiation drew near.

The teachings began as scheduled. The power and knowledge of the Lama were unbelievable. For nine long days I was immersed in the utmost concentration and study which taxed every ounce of energy I possessed. I learned the truth of the first beginning of man. I was instructed in ways of death and how to utilize it as a path of meditation. I was told the exact step by step method of transferring my consciousness to other realms and beings.

The beginning of teachings.

My Lama gave me detailed instruction on how to go back in time to the very beginning of existence: how to discover and examine the nature of my own mind before it inhabited it's present body. He instructed me on how to guide my astral body safely through the realms of demons and the underworld. I learned how to utilize an invisible protective force shield which could guard against harm and evil influences. By the transference of his own energy into mine he planted in me the seed of empowerment to discover the very cause of the energy which was not only responsible for my own existence, but was the absolute cause for the existence of the universe.

The experience spoke for itself. It could not be doubted. During the teachings there were times when my entire being seemed to be falling into bits and pieces like great boulders tumbling from a mountain in an earthquake. I disbelieved how my eyes and senses could have lied to me about the truth of what really exists in our world of false illusions. I marvelled at what manner of creature or being this was in front of me day after day expounding so effortlessly the secrets which controlled the entire universe. All these things amazed me. Each night, after returning to my hut I pondered and queried the essence of my soul late into the night until tired and exhausted I fell asleep.

Part of the initiation and teachings of the Lama, required me to have the understanding of ancient rituals and ceremonies. This was necessary in order to have the medium in which to work when dealing with esoteric forces. The names of the various ceremonies were called pujas. Pujas involve various breathing exercises, understanding the use of mantras, which is the study of virbrational pitches which control matter. They sometimes involve many kinds of meditations which utilise various geometric shapes and patterns to be done in unison with the vibrational pitches. Externally, I had to learn special hand movements called mudras. These directed the inner energies of the nervous system, by opening up the energies of the psychic forces in the body. By practising and perfecting the techniques in each puja, all forms of energy and life force could be controlled internally and externally. The powers generated from the practises ranged anywhere from simple matters of controlling the weather, gaining clairvoyance, to changing the energies of the entire physical and mental body.

My Lama taught that the human race at its present stage was in the age of degeneracy. Through delusion and negative action mankind had lost psychic powers and awareness that they once possessed. I had experienced this even when teaching people Tang Soo Tao. People's natural ability as I've talked about in other parts of this book, was all but lost. So, I understood these teachings well. Gaining powers used in elevated states of consciousness, required man to lift the veil of ignorance which he himself created by negative action. Negative actions were in turn caused by selfishness and egoism. The energy generated by the practice which he taught me created a purification and a lifting, piece by piece, step by step, of negativity, which deluded and blocked man from wisdom and Enlightenment.

Listening, watching and learning from Ling Rinpoche, I discovered the absolute origin of martial art movement. He did everything from a sitting position. The geometric meditations (mandalas) directly corresponded to the forms and patterns of advanced training I had learned in martial arts. His hand movements were identical to Tai Chi form. The internal yogas were similar in many aspects to the ones I had learned, with a few minor exceptions. The one-point concentration, aimed towards emptiness, had the same objective. There were far too many things observable in everything I learned to be called coincidental.

H.H. Ling Rinpoche in ceremonial dress.

I had now become clear of Bodhidarma's improvements introduced when he went to China. It was clear and obvious. As days went on things fell more and more into place. The history of martial arts and all the training I had done up until now, all took perfect shape. By the time the teachings were ended, I was clear, satisfied and aware of all the things I had ever trained for.

Following the teachings, I entered into a retreat to practise and meditate deeper into the understanding of the essential nature of all existence. I arose in the early morning long before the sun and meditated for hours. I began a schedule of training twice a day, followed by long sessions of yoga. I ate only once, meditated, then again trained and so on. I varied little from this schedule and the energy that I generated was intense. Though I had little room to train, I shortened all my movements and did the best I could. Every movement became an intricate part of the meditations I had learned from the Lamas. Every meditation I practised from the Lama became a movement in one of my forms. They had become absolutely inseparable. The meditations and the training caused an energy to flow through my arms and legs and throughout my entire body. The total integration of all these things created a link to the most infinite power I had ever experienced.

After a short time, I began to have some difficulty sleeping. Sometimes I'd have beautiful dreams of the Lamas, sometimes of Jesus Christ and sometimes just beautiful women. Other times, I'd be plagued by terrifying nightmares.

One night, I woke up screaming in a very loud voice. The monk next door ran over to find out what was wrong. I explained something had tried to grab me. By now I was awake. We dismissed it as a nightmare and both went back to bed. The same thing happened for four nights in a row.

The next evening, I fell asleep as usual and my astral body floated about the room. A huge grey round figure entered the room, that was as large as the whole room. It came at my dream body which had re-entered my human form with a jolt. The creature had engulfed my entire body and was trying to suffocate me. I was entirely conscious but in a cataleptic state and unable to move. I was terrified. I tried to scream but was unable to make a sound. The time went on endlessly. Suddenly, I was awakened by a large pounding and screaming at the door and Jhampa, the monk next door, was again at my rescue. I had finally released a loud yell which had woken Jhampa up. We discussed this problem the next day and were beginning to wonder if there might be something happening, more than we could understand.

The next night, I woke up, sat up in my bed and the demon remained in the room. The energy was evil and terrifying. I commanded at the top of my voice for it to leave. It refused to go and came towards me. Now totally awake, I yelled for the monk next door who had already intuitively woken up and was coming anyway. This time he saw the demon himself. As he came out of his house he watched it shrink away into the forest.

The next day, we went to see Ling Rinpoche. I explained my problem as I thought it was serious. He smiled, gave a small chuckle and advised me that when a man is poor he has nothing to fear because he has nothing for anyone to steal. As a man becomes more wealthy, more people take notice and he must guard his possessions. Such was the way with the spiritual path. He wrote down the name of an exorcist puja and charged me to have one particular Lama, who lived in the area, to help me. I immediately contacted a poor old yogi, who lived in a small mud room, with no space even to stand up. It was dark and damp in the room. There was barely room to lie down and I believe this man rarely did. I gave him the note from my Lama and he told me he would need a day to prepare.

The next day, at dusk, the exorcism began. He bought with him three small ritual cakes, in various shapes and colours. I was told to remove some of my hair, cut off a piece of clothing I was wearing and eat a piece of food, but to leave a portion.

The ritual began, lasting only about an hour. By now, it was totally dark outside, and all the things were taken outside and away from the house. I was instructed in a special position to sleep and that I must turn everything in my room to the opposite direction. I was then given some further instructions regarding some particular meditations and the Lama returned to his house up the hill where he sat vigil for the night.

I had no idea how I was possibly going to sleep, as the energy of this whole episode was not the best aide to sleeping. I laid down on the bed, totally awake and the next thing I knew the sun was coming up. There had been no space in between when the Lama left my house till now. I happily got up and went to fetch some water. I met the Lama shortly thereafter, his door was open in his room and he was rocking back and forth chanting. He saw me and smiled and asked if I was all right. The big smile on my face told him yes and I had no more disturbances of that nature for the rest of the retreat. Although I did encounter some visitors from time to time, they were never of the type that I have mentioned here.

There are hundreds of stories concerning strange events which happened on that mountain. Spirits of all sorts seemed to inhabit the enchanted little village. Throughout the day and far into the night the sound of bells and drums echoed through the mountain. Burning ritual cakes were often seen thrown somewhere into the wood. Often they were after pujas similar to what had been done for me. On one particular occasion, a girl was cautioned not to go near a certain sacrificial cake. Being nonchalant, disrespectful and all too blasé', she picked up the ritual cake and ate it. She immediately went mad and acted like a savage dog, causing a great deal of trouble to everyone she came in contact with. People who knew her couldn't understand what was wrong until someone came across the fact that she had eaten the ritual cakes. The girl was taken to one of the lamas, who muttered a few mantras, slapped the girl and she immediately returned to her normal self. She was completely exhausted and had been in a frenzy for nearly a week. Within seconds the spirit that possessed her was gone.

Another time, I had just completed a particular yogic practise which called for a ceremonial 'fire puja'. The puja entailed making a large bonfire and gathering all sorts of grains and offering substances. Also I needed several lamas to aid with the ceremony, which took a couple of hours.

As the day of the ceremony drew near, there was much excitement and preparation. On the actual day of the event, large gloomy clouds filled the sky. It began to rain. After so much preparation I felt everything would be a failure. With the rain pouring down I visited my Lama and asked him what I should do. As this was the middle of the rainy season I didn't feel there was much hope of anything clearing. The Lama just laughed and said not to worry about it. He told me to go back down to where the monks had prepared everything and the puja would be a success.

I went back to the ceremonial site. Only minutes before the puja was to begin the sky above the house cleared and the rain stopped. I sat down and began. For near two hours the fire raged and the puja was a complete success. Within minutes after the rite was completed, rain poured down, and so continued for the rest of that day and into the night. I remarked how strange it was to all the monks helping but they only smiled and acted quite nonchalant about the whole affair.

These are only a few of the many strange incidents that occurred on the mountain.

Top left, Tantric monks conducting traditional ceremonies. Top right, traditional Fire Puja. Tantric monks conducting Fire ceremony.

All went fine till the end of my time in Dharamshala. As Ling Rinpoche prepared to go south for the winter, Jhampa and myself planned to accompany him. Before I left, I again visited the Dalai Lama. I was now clear and resolved and understood much more in the brief time I had been on this mountain, than when I came.

During my retreat, I had written an entire book of notes on my experiences, my feelings, my understandings of Tantra and my realizations through my martial arts experiences. I explained all these in full to him and asked him if I had made any mistakes in my judgement. He told me I had done very well; that what I had understood so far was very reasonable and valid. He found a few weak points in some areas and pointed them out clearly. His knowledge, wisdom and clarity, were even more remarkable than the first time I'd met him. I stayed a good part of the afternoon and clarified every detail of my meditational experiences.

By the time the meeting was finished, I knew I had accomplished what I'd come for. As I walked out of the palace I knew I'd done what no other martial artist had ever done. I knew I had rediscovered the perfect link of Buddhism with the martial way. In my heart, I was happy for myself, but more so that

A funeral procession on the way to the Burning Gats.

I had opened the way for anyone who would have the insight to listen and believe the story of my experience. I returned to my hut and meditated the rest of the day.

Before I was to leave, the Dalai Lama once again invited me to his palace. I had asked him for a teaching, which he had no time to give, but in its place he had granted me another one instead. The teachings was given on the day I left Dharamshala. Next to me sat Doboom Tulku. In front of me sat one of the high Sakya Lamas and his son. The teaching was on the loving compassion of Bodhicitta and the emptiness of Shunyata. More perfect teachings could never be given as a final gift to solidify the link I had established.

We were on our way to Bodhgaya when we stopped in new Delhi for a few days. I went to a place called the Burning Ghats. In India, the usual custom of the Hindus is to cremate bodies at death. Along the Ganges there were several main places used for these purposes. Families carried the dead bodies, wrapped in cloth, through the streets to the Gats. They immersed the entire body in the holy river, chanting prayers to the family deities. The immersed bodies were then placed on a pile of logs and burned. It takes many hours for a body to burn, during which time the brains boil, the sweet smelling flesh peels off and the internal organs spit and hiss. I spent hours watching these scenes over and over again. Dozens of bodies come in each day to the crematorium. I watched the reactions of people towards death and I reflected on the teachings of impermanence, referred to time and time again by my Lama.

Any person who has ever watched a body burn can never forget the experience. We logically understand the fate of all of us but the ego will only permit the mind to go so far and then it will not accept that its fate will be like all the rest. The Lamas taught of the delusion of self-existence and here people suffered and mourned about one of the most normal natural things that exists in our life, and that is death.

Boatman on the Ganges in Benares

We travelled through many places of India, visiting the yogic ashrams and making pilgrimages to holy places. I stopped for a brief visit to

Bodhgaya, where Buddha practised six years of austerities.

Benares, Jhampa and I took a boat ride down the Ganges; dead cats, dogs and people floated on the water, clogging the oars for the boatmen. People swam, drank, washed and defecated along with the dead bodies. On one side of the river there was a ghat and the other side of the river was an empty beach; empty of living, but not dead. Children, people who had died of smallpox and lepers, were not allowed to be burned at the ghats. Their bodies were left to rot on the other side of the river, to be eaten by the vultures.

We made our way finally to Bodhgaya; the famous place where Lord Buddha sat under the Bodhitree. All the oriental countries had each made a temple in the area. When we arrived, there was a room in a monastery awaiting us. Ling Rinpoche's Manager met us at the temple gates. Because we had done a little sight seeing on the way they had arrived before us. We stayed in a small room with two wooden beds. Daily we woke at 4am, practised meditation and trained till 7am. After the sun came up, we had breakfast. Daily, His Holiness Ling Rinpoche circumambulated the large Stupa (Shrine), in the heart of the town.

I walked behind him everyday.

Monks in Tantric ritual in main temple.

Temple at Bodhgaya.

During my time in Bodhgaya, I taught Tang Soo Tao to the household of my Lama. By now, everyone was enthralled in the art. There was a small temple adjacent to the main temple. It made a perfect training hall. Rather than bowing to a flag, we had a huge altar of Buddhas. Here I was again, a western man, a thousand years later, bringing martial art back to the Buddhist temple from where it had originally come.

Everyday for a month, I visited the Lama's house. My room was right next door to His Holiness Ling Rinpoche and at this time, everyone in the house had some minor ills of some sort or another. I more or less became the family doctor. Four mornings a week I stayed with Ling Rinpoche and acupunctured his knees for rheumatism. I was able to cure his knee problem and during the time I worked on him he told me many stories about old Tibet.

I learned of the large palaces, the mystical yogis and the invasion of the Chinese. He told me how he had personally taught the Dalai Lama for twenty-five years. He also related to me when the Dalai Lama himself and Trijang Rinpoche had all been invited to Peking by Mao Tse Tung, only a few years before the Chinese invasion. He related to me how he had fled on horseback with the Dalai Lama over the mountains as the Chinese bombed and machined gunned the holy city of Lhasa. I was told of the merciless slaughter of men, women, children and high lamas. His stories were gruesome of how the Communists armed with modern weapons stormed the passive buddhist country and burned, raped and tortured the defenseless Tibetans. I had heard similar stories from other lamas, who had arrived in India with bullet holes in their robes but no marks on their skin. Still others who had crossed infested communist borders virtually unseen, through hails of bullets and shrapnel. These miraculous escapes were attributed to spiritual protectors who guided many of the fleeing refugees to safety.

All the stories were interesting and incredible. I got to know my guru well, as both guru and father. The most mundane actions and discourse from the Lama emulated wisdom and compassion. Daily he advised me about my spiritual practice and gave me encouragement. While I was there, he also gave more special teachings which after he had finished, his Manager confided that he had given only twice in twenty-five years.

Shortly before I left, the Junior Tutor to the Dalai Lama, Trijang Rinpoche also came to stay at the monastery. Because we lived next door to him and because of my now close association with my Lamas' household, I saw him daily. I gave some medical advice and worked on curing his Manager's ill health.

In Bodhgaya I was able to receive the teachings from Trijang Rinpoche that I had requested in Dharmasala, before he had left. I had learned everything and much more than I'd ever dreamed or hoped for and my time in India was coming to an end. I advised my Lama that it was time for me to go and he had a huge feast prepared for me.

When I went in to say my last goodbyes, the Lama gave me his final blessings and wished me a safe journey home. During the six months I had been with him, he had taught me everything that was the essence of life and the heart of the Dharma. He had accepted to be the spiritual head of my Tang Soo Tao Organization and to aid me to keep the direct lineage of the Buddha alive in the practice of martial virtue. He would accept to teach any students of mine whom I recommended. He had given me the entire universe and I was happy beyond words. As a final gesture, before I turned to go, he handed me one of the oldest thangkas brought from Tibet. It was his own personal painting of his special deity, which had been a special gift to him from the abbot of a monastery in Lhasa. I had never received anything in my life so precious until then and I felt I never would again. With the final blessing of the living Buddha, I made my way back to Australia.

I arrived home a different person, exuberant and anxious to share my new experiences with my students. Before that was to happen however, a few things remained to be sorted out at the home school. Although energy and standard were satisfactory, in my absence several misunderstandings and misinterpretations had cropped up among some of the black belts. A small amount of rivalry combined with inexperience had created an uncomfortable climate among the seniors, which could have become serious had it not been tactfully disposed of. It took several months to sort out many small details but in time all was back to normal. But this experience demonstrated to me the incredible expectations I myself had demanded out of other schools and instructors where I had been. If I could encounter such difficulties with running only one school, how much more difficult was it to maintain correct interpretation of standard, spirit and motivation in many schools. I could see the difficulty the masters faced after having cultivated the nucleus of their art in trying to preserve and pass on this essence untainted to others.

Regardless of the level of the teacher, nothing could be transmitted to the student until the student was ready. This was not necessarily in accordance with a student's age, time in training or even his seniority. I had long known this but I now reflected on it with a much deeper understanding.

The art through the lineage I had found, took on an entirely new meaning. My energy for teaching and training had completely changed. Every aspect towards running the school was accented with a heightened awareness. The various practices I had learned seemed to cultivate into one smooth energy.

Before leaving India, I had set a date with my Lamas to return with my most senior students so that they could develop along the same path as myself. There was only eight short months to prepare my most devoted students for the most important experiences of their lives. There was not much time and there was much to do.

The students were taught and trained like never before. The energy from the Buddha exuded out of everything I did. The blessings of the Lama generated the school and all the students. They felt the energy and although they didn't know what it was everyone knew something good was happening. During the next eight months, I formulated my last objectives for teaching a martial art, which could develop pure spirit in man. I had found the weak points and I had discovered the strong points of my martial arts experience.

In my years of training, many instructors talked of facing death but they themselves didn't know the experience of death. I had been taught the way to discover this. Many instructors had taught me internal sciences of yogic alchemy, thinking that this was the cultivation of chi. This was not the cultivation of chi. The cultivation of chi lies in the spirit of man. The basic spirit of man is in the heart and the heart energy is cultivated by morality. Only after developing perfect spirit and morality can anyone gain the benefits of the internal yogas. The yogas can be done with steady growth of morality, but are self destructing solely as a means for power with no other motivation.

Some instructors I had talked with spoke of harmony. But they had not the clear experience themselves, or a direct lineage of training method from a master with that experience. Although I had found a few truly genuine martial artists, I had found in my entire travels around the world that in general, in these particular times, compassion, love and wisdom were missing in many martial arts. When I had found genuine traces of loving compassion, I saw that masters had great difficulty passing their virtues on to others. Without these virtues there was no happiness to be gained from the martial art experience. With these virtues man had the essential ingredient to cultivate perfect chi. There is no cultivation of chi without virtue.

I trained and meditated non-stop till the time I was ready to go again. I felt the connection so strong with my teachers that there was actually no difference in being in Australia or living next door to them. In my dreams, I saw my teachers and in my waking state I felt their energy. The sensitivity in my training increased incalculably. There was a depth in training that I couldn't explain to anyone. It was so fantastic that by myself I sometimes went into fits of laughter. Everything went perfectly in the months that followed and I prepared for what was to be my last trip to India for a long time.

Chapter 12

I set off for my second trip to India with three of eleven students. We were to go first, then be followed three weeks after by the rest. The time had passed so quickly and I'd come to know my gurus so well, that although I did not like India, returning to my Tibetan teachers was the same as going home.

Since I had been there, a comfortable hotel had been built on the mountain. Books and news coverage had popularized the Dalai Lama and the Indian Government had put up a tourist hotel. I couldn't say I minded. It was a nice change from the hovel I'd lived in the year before. I immediately visited my root guru Ling Rinpoche and my other two Lamas. We brought mountains of presents for the households and they were overjoyed. My new students met the Lama and we organized a date for when the others would arrive.

After Ling Rinpoche, we visited my other Lama, Trijang Rinpoche and were able to receive teachings for two weeks just before he made an annual trip to the southern monasteries. This year everything was set and organized and everyone was bending over backwards to help us.

Finally, I went to visit Ratto Rinpoche. One of the longest, most complicated teachings was scheduled with him. Unhappily, I found him in a very sorry state. He had known I was coming and did not look forward to the meeting. He knew that I expected a very special teaching which he was not able to give. He was sick and weak and could not even read his prayer book. This did not stop the torrents of love and compassion that fell down on me when we entered the room. He was very happy to see me again, as I was him. Barely before I asked concerning receiving teachings for myself and my students, he explained that even talking for more than a few minutes, caused him great problems. I didn't worry about it at all and told him that I would start all over again and surely fix him. He said that all the doctors he had seen had told him he must do nothing or he may die at any moment. He told me things were not the same as last year and that I was powerless. But I not only had my knowledge now of all my years of training, I was young and I had all the energy which all the Lamas

Health and happiness.

had instilled in my spirit. I insisted to start immediately on curing him. Not only did I assure him that I could fix his problems once and for all, but I told him to give me one month. He was too feeble to say no and as before I started then and there.

I went down daily. Every day, I explained in great detail exactly how the physical human body worked. Because he was too weak, I used acupuncture and Chinese massage with herbal remedies for the first week. After that time, he was able to exercise himself. I taught a series of exercises that linked all his vital energies together and within two weeks he was 100% improved. By the end of one month, he was spry and healthy, took long walks daily and was healthier at this time, then he ever had been in his entire life. At the same time, my students who accompanied me taught Tang Soo Tao to his household. Everyone was amazed at the quick results and especially at the new vitality of their Lama.

The news spread far and wide. Soon, people from all over were coming to our hotel after hearing of the wonderful results of my Lama. We did demonstrations throughout the town and the people became very interested. We were able to help Lamas with partially paralysed arms and legs, rejuvenate their limbs.

Tang Soo Tao practitioners demonstrating Chi gung for the high Lamas of Tibet.

By the time the rest of the students arrived, the town was saturated with the spirit of young healthy people. All my students and myself did a demonstration for Ratto Rinpoche and Ling Rinpoche at Ling Rinpoche's house. Ling Rinpoche was very happy for the other Lama's good health. Trijang Rinpoche, instructed his disciple to carefully note, document and practise the arts I was able to teach. I was incredibly happy that I could give something back for the valuable knowledge that these divine beings extended to me and my students. All my students received the essence of the Tibetan lineages and were beside themselves with amazement with what they had learned. I knew their elation, for I had felt the same way myself a year before. This year the energy was so great, it was almost uncontrollable. The students took turns massaging, teaching and instructing sick Lamas and meditators back to health. In a small way I felt as if I was Daruma returning form the West back to the East.

I had seen the perfect spirituality preserved in Tibet. I had also learned the perfect way to health and longevity through martial arts. I never doubted what I learned of spirituality from my Lamas, but I wondered how man could achieve his goal on this earth without his health. Indeed, too much emphasis on an impermanent thing like a body leads nowhere, but neglect of the body deprived the person of the tool he needed to work with. The middle way of the Buddha was certainly true.

One high Lama expressed to me that because of the age of degeneracy, enlightened masters were becoming fewer and fewer. It was getting more and more difficult to accomplish our important goals with traditional methods. A blind man could not see and a man with broken legs could not walk. So the blind man with the good legs carried the crippled man with the good eyes, on his back. Together, they slowly made their way down the road.

Our visit was short, our objective was finished. As the year before, I went to pay my last respects to my root guru Ling Rinpoche. He was very happy for all that I had been able to accomplish in the few months that I had been there. He explained to me that few Tibetans were able to receive as much as I had been able to. I knew this to be true. He gave me some last words of advice concerning my life and direction. I was ready to leave when he pulled out two small boxes. I didn't know what to expect. Out of one he handed to me a Buddha from the Dalai Lama. Out of the other, he handed me his own ritual instruments that he had personally taught me with and that he had used for the past eighteen years. I couldn't believe it or understand it and all I could do was accept them with shaking hands. There was nothing more that could be said, the pact was sealed for ever with my Lama and myself. I floated out the door in total disbelief.

I went to say goodbye to Ratto Rinpoche whose house was last on the way out. To say good bye to Ratto Rinpoche is ridiculous to try to describe in a book. He also gave me his own ritual instruments, which were different and complimented the ones I had received from my other Lama. There was nothing I could say and nothing I could do. My students, stunned as myself, watched on as he passed down to me the implement that symbolised the lineage he had already given me. This was the final blessing of the Buddha. I had come as a martial artist, my Lama had given me the supreme virtue, the virtue and the art had finally become one.

The majesty of the Guru.

Conclusion

The martial way emerged out of ancient Buddhist culture. A martial artist does not have to be a Buddhist and all Buddhists are certainly not martial artists. But anyone who is exposed to martial arts comes face to face with various methods which are related to this ancient culture. By its nature in history, martial arts training utilizes numerous methods of mind and body control. Just as a wise man never dives into strange waters, it is up to each individual who begins this path to go slowly and carefully, testing every part of the way.

The uniqueness of martial art is that it incorporates the essence of high esoteric principals in a simple, practical art of self defense. It appeals to the most fundamental instinct in man; the will to survive. It provides a tangible way with which people from all walks of life can progressively develop themselves to the highest physical and mental potential. It makes a man think. It is difficult to find any other method that works so simply and effectively.

The martial way cultivates the pristine awareness necessary to discover the heart of true morality. This is not a morality based on what others tell us, but on our own personal experiences of what we really want out of life. The way of martial virtue instills in all men a sense of true direction based on experience gained from their own labour.

You can learn nothing from this book. Its purpose is to make a person aware of what exists and to understand what he has experienced after it happens. Reading this book does not give you the wisdom or experience of practise. It is merely a guide and hopefully an incentive to find your own experiences.

Many people come into a training hall and watch students practise.

They depend only on their eyes, which cannot see the spirit of martial art, and depend on their inadequate experiences which cannot enable them to evaluate what has really happened. These people flatter themselves that they have seen and fully understood martial art. You should never confuse intellect with knowledge. Intellect is only the tool used to build the foundation for right understanding. Watching a black belt does not make you a black belt. Reading this book does not give you the experience of the author who wrote it. Knowledge of a teacher is like a rainbow; although it can be seen it cannot be grasped. No amount of words can explain to a blind man the beauty of its colours. To experience true knowledge we must become a rainbow ourselves.

If you are satisfied with the quality of training and understanding you have, then this book will be of little help. If you are not, then you must ask yourself, why? Each person must examine his own training method and motivation.

If there is something written in these pages that you have not personally experienced, then don't criticise it until you've tried it.

If there is something that inspires you in this book, don't blindly accept what is written, but contemplate a way to experience these things for yourself. This may not mean to buy a ticket to the orient in search of mystical lamas and oriental masters. What works for one person does not necessarily work for another. Just examine what you read, evaluate what you need, think about it, then go slowly.

The author's personal quest was to find the essence of Bodhidharma's teachings and how he linked Buddhism with martial arts. He not only discovered the method, but found the essence and realized that Bodhidharma had done a very good job.

'Happiness in martial virtue.'

Instructors of the Tang Soo Tao School after receiving teachings in India.

ROBERT CAPUTO

Contact

Australian Tang Soo Tao Federation

Phone: +61 0427994573

Address: 26 Tectonic Cresent,

Kunda Park, Queensland

Australia 4556

Website: www.tangsootao.com.au

Contact page: www.tangsootao.com.au/contact-us/contact-federation

www.ingramcontent.com/pod-product-compliance
Lightning Source LLC
Chambersburg PA
CBHW030421100426
42812CB00028B/3053/J